A Voyage Round the World, Vol. 1
1827 - 1832

by

James Holman

The Echo Library 2007

Published by

The Echo Library

Echo Library
131 High St.
Teddington
Middlesex TW11 8HH

www.echo-library.com

Please report serious faults in the text to complaints@echo-library.com

ISBN 1-40681-550-0

"Man loves knowledge: and the beams of truth
More welcome touch his understanding's eye,
Than all the blandishments of sounds his ear,
Than all of taste his tongue."

—Akenside.

4

[Note: The beginning of this dedication was missing from the text.]

...that your Majesty may long be spared to a nation that is so sensible of the influence of your Majesty's exalted character.
With the most profound feelings of gratitude and devotion,
I have the honor to subscribe myself,

Your Majesty's Most faithful Servant,
JAMES HOLMAN.

CONTENTS OF VOL. I.

Corps—Vaccination of Natives—Medical Opinion—Departure from
Sierra Leone

CHAP. V.
Cape St. Ann—Dangerous Shoals—Old Sailors—Liberia—Origin
and History of the Colony—Failure at Sherbro Island—Experiment
at Liberia—Difficulties Encountered by the Settlers—Differences
with the Natives—Final Adjustment—Improving State of the
Colony—Laws and Morals—Remarks on Colonization

CHAP. VI.
The Kroo Country—Religion of the Kroo and Fish Men—
Emigration of the Natives—Sketch of their habits and customs—
Purchase of Wives—The Krooman's *ne plus ultra*—Migratory
propensities—Rogueries exposed—Adoption of English Names—
Cape Palmas—Dexterity of the Fishmen—Fish towns—The Fetish—
Arrival at Cape Coast—Land with the Governor—Captain
Hutchison—Cape Coast mode of taking an airing—Ashantee
Chiefs—Diurnal occupations—School for Native Girls—
Domestication of Females—Colonel Lumley—Captain Ricketts—
Neglect of Portuguese Fortresses—A native Doctor

CHAP. VII.
Recollections of the Ashantee War—Battle of Essamacow—
Accession of Osay Aquatoo to the Throne—Battle of Affatoo—
Investment of Cape Coast—Flight of the Ashantees—Martial Law
proclaimed—Battle of Dodowah—Ashantee Mode of Fighting—
Death of Captain Hutchison

CHAP. VIII.
Embarkation—Departure for Accra—Land Route—Accra Roads—
Visit to Danish Accra—Dilapidations of the Fortresses at Dutch and
English Accra—Captive Queen—Mr. Thomas Park—Cause of his
Death unknown—Departure for Fernando Po—First view of the
Island—Anchor in Maidstone Bay—Early History of the
Settlement—Capt. Owen's Expedition—Visited by the Inhabitants—
Site for the Settlement determined—Author's Mission to the King of
Baracouta—Visit of the King—Native Costume—Ecstacy of the
Natives—Distribution of Presents—Second Visit to the King—His
Majesty's evasive Conduct—Renewed Interviews—A Native Thief—
Intended Punishment—Cut-throat, a Native Chief—Visit to King-
Cove—Purchase of Land

CHAP. IX.

CHAP. X.

CHAP. XI.

CHAP. XII.

CHAP. XIII.

CHAP. XIV.

9

(new style)—Melange, Devotion and *Gourmanderie*—Curious Flying-
fish—Weather—Whales—Cape Pigeons—Anchor off Rio Janeiro—
Distant Scenery—Custom-house Duties—Hotel du Nord—Rua
Direito—Confusion thrice confounded—Fruit Girls, not fair, but
coquettish—Music unmusical, or Porterage, with an Obligato
Accompaniment—Landing-place—An Evening Walk—A bad
Cold—Job's Comforter—Shoals of Visitors—Captain Lyon's Visit,
and Invitation to the Author—Naval Friends—Packet for England—
English Tailors—Departure for Congo Soco—The Party—Thoughts
on Self-Denial—Uncomfortable Quarters—Changes of
Atmosphere—Freedom by Halves; or *left*-handed Charity—Serra
Santa Anna—Valley of Botaes—The Ferreirinho, or little
Blacksmith—Dangerous Ascent of the Alto de Serra—Pest, an
Universal Disease—An English Settler—Rio Paraheiba—Valencia—
Curiosity of the People—Unceremonious Inquisitors—Comforts of a
Beard—Castor-Oil for burning—Rio Prëta—Passports—Entrance to
the Mine Country—Examination of Baggage—Attention without
Politeness—The Green-eyed Monster, "An old Man would be
wooing"

CHAP. XV.

Advantages of Early Travelling—Funelle—"A Traveller stopped at a
Widow's Gate"—Bright Eyes and Breakfast—Smiles and Sighs—The
Fish River—Cold Lodgings—Fowl Massacre—Bad Ways—Gigantic
Ant-hills—The Campos—Insect Warriors—Insinuating Visitors
(Tick)—The Simpleton—Bertioga—A Drunkard—Cold Shoulders—
Mud Church—Feasting and Fasting; or, the Fate of Tantalus—
Method in a Slow March—Gentlemen Hungry and Angry—No
"Accommodation for Man or Horse"—A Practical Bull—Curtomi—
Hospitable Treatment at Grandie—Horse Dealer—A "Chance"
Purchase—Bivouac—Mule Kneeling—Sagacious Animal—Quilos—
A Mist—Gold-washing—Ora Branca—Hazardous Ascent of the
Serra D'Ora Branca—Topaz District—A Colonel the Host—
Capoa—Jigger-hunters—Mineralogical Specimens—Mortality of
Animals—Pasturage—Account of Ora Preta—Gold Essayed—
Halt—Journey resumed—Arrival at Congo Soco

CHAP. I.

Passion for Travelling—Author's peculiar situation—Motives for going Abroad—Resources for the Blind—Embark in the Eden, Capt. Owen, for Sierra Leone—Lord High Admiral at Plymouth—Cape Finisteire—Arrival at Madeira—Town of Funchal—Wines of Madeira—Cultiwition of the Grape—Table of Exports—Seizure of Gin—Fruits and Vegetables— Climate—Coffee, Tea, and Sugar Cultivation—Palanquin Travelling— Departure from Madeira

The passion for travelling is, I believe, instinctive in some natures. We have seen men persevere in their enterprises against the most formidable obstacles; and, without means or friends, and even ignorant of the languages of the various countries through which they passed, pursue their perilous journeys into remote places, until, like the knight in the Arabian tale, they succeeded in snatching a memorial from every shrine they visited. For my own part, I have been conscious from my earliest youth of the existence of this desire to explore distant regions, to trace the varieties exhibited by mankind under the different influences of different climates, customs, and laws, and to investigate with unwearied solicitude the moral and physical distinctions that separate and diversify the various nations of the earth.

I am bound to believe that this direction of my faculties and energies has been ordained by a wise and benevolent Providence, as a source of consolation under an affliction which closes upon me all the delights and charms of the visible world. The constant occupation of the mind, and the continual excitement of mental and bodily action, contribute to diminish, if not to overcome, the sense of deprivation which must otherwise have pressed upon me; while the gratification of this passion scarcely leaves leisure for despondency, at the same time that it supplies me with inexhaustible means of enjoyment. When I entered the naval service I felt an irresistible impulse to become acquainted with as many parts of the world as my professional avocations would permit, and I was determined not to rest satisfied until I had completed the circumnavigation of the globe. But at the early age of twenty-five, while these resolves were strong, and the enthusiasm of youth was fresh and sanguine, my present affliction came upon me. It is impossible to describe the state of my mind at the prospect of losing my sight, and of being, as I then supposed, deprived by that misfortune of the power of indulging in my cherished project. Even the suspense which I suffered, during the period when my medical friends were uncertain of the issue, appeared to me a greater misery than the final knowledge of the calamity itself. At last I entreated them to be explicit, and to let me know the worst, as that could be more easily endured than the agonies of doubt. Their answer, instead of increasing my uneasiness, dispelled it. I felt a comparative relief in being no longer deceived by false hopes; and the certainty that my case was beyond remedy determined me to seek, in some pursuit adapted to my new state of existence, a congenial field of employment and consolation. At that time my health was so delicate, and my nerves so depressed by previous anxiety, that I did not suffer myself to indulge in the expectation that I should ever be able to travel out of my own country alone; but the return of strength and vigour, and the concentration of my views upon one object, gradually brought back my old passion, which at length became as firmly established as it was before. The elasticity of my original feelings being thus restored, I ventured, alone and sightless, upon my dangerous and novel course; and I cannot look back upon the scenes through which I have passed, the great variety of circumstances by which I have been surrounded, and the strange experiences with which I have become familiar, without an intense aspiration of gratitude for the bounteous dispensation of the Almighty, which enabled me to conquer the greatest of human evils by the cultivation of what has been to me the greatest of human enjoyments, and to supply the void of sight with countless objects of intellectual gratification. To those who inquire what pleasures I can derive from the invigorating spirit of travelling under the privation I suffer, I may be permitted to reply in the words of the poet,

Unknown those powers that raise the soul to flame,
Catch every nerve, and vibrate through the frame;
Their level life is but a smouldering fire,
Unquench'd by want, unfanned by strong desire.

Or perhaps, with more propriety, I may ask, who could endure life without a purpose, without the pursuit of some object, in the attainment of which his moral energies should be called into healthful activity? I can confidently assert that the effort of travelling has been beneficial to me in every way; and I know not what might have been the consequence, if the excitement with which I looked forward to it had been disappointed, or how much my health might have suffered but for its refreshing influence.

I am constantly asked, and I may as well answer the question here once for all, what is the use of travelling to one who cannot see? I answer, Does every traveller see all that he describes?—and is not every traveller obliged to depend upon others for a great proportion of the information he collects? Even Humboldt himself was not exempt from this necessity.

The picturesque in nature, it is true, is shut out from me, and works of art are to me mere outlines of beauty, accessible only to one sense; but perhaps this very circumstance affords a stronger zest to curiosity, which is thus impelled to a more close and searching examination of details than would be considered necessary to a traveller who might satisfy himself by the superficial view, and rest content with the first impressions conveyed through the eye. Deprived of that organ of information, I am compelled to adopt a more rigid and less suspicious course of inquiry, and to investigate analytically, by a train of patient examination, suggestions, and deductions, which other travellers dismiss at first sight; so that, freed from the hazard of being misled by appearances, I am the less likely to adopt hasty and erroneous conclusions. I believe that, notwithstanding my want of vision, I do not fail to visit as many interesting points in the course of my travels as the majority of my contemporaries: and by having things described to me *on the spot*, I think it is possible for me to form as correct a judgment as my own sight would enable me to do: and to confirm my accuracy, I could bring many living witnesses to bear testimony to my endless inquiries, and insatiable thirst for collecting information. Indeed this is the secret of the delight I derive from travelling, affording me as it does a constant source of mental occupation, and stimulating me so powerfully to physical exertion, that I can bear a greater degree of bodily fatigue, than any one could suppose my frame to be capable of supporting.

I am frequently asked how I take my notes. It is simply thus: I keep a sort of rough diary, which I fill up from time to time as opportunities offer, but not from day to day, for I am frequently many days in arrear, sometimes, indeed, a fortnight together: but I always vividly remember the daily occurrences which I wish to retain, so that it is not possible that any circumstances can escape my attention. I also collect distinct notes on various subjects, as well as particular descriptions of interesting objects, and when I cannot meet with a friend to act as my amanuensis, I have still a resource in my own writing apparatus, of which, however, I but seldom avail myself, as the process is much more tedious to me than that of dictation. But these are merely rough notes of the heads of subjects, which I reserve to expatiate upon at leisure on my return to old England.

The invention of the apparatus to which I allude is invaluable to those who are afflicted with blindness. It opens not only an agreeable source of amusement and occupation in the hours of loneliness and retirement, but it affords a means of communicating our secret thoughts to a friend, without the interposition of a third party; so that the intercourse and confidence of private correspondence, excluded by a natural calamity, are thus preserved to us by an artificial substitute. By the aid of this process, too, we may desire our correspondent to reply to our inquiries in a way which would be quite unintelligible to those to whom the perusal of the answer might be submitted. This apparatus, which is called the "Nocto via Polygraph," by Mr. Wedgwood, the inventor, is not only useful to the blind, but is equally capable of being rendered available to all persons suffering under diseases of the eyes; for, although it does not assist you to commit your thoughts to paper with the same facility that is attained by the use of pen and ink, it enables you to write very clearly and legibly, while you have the satisfaction of knowing that you are spared all risk of hurting your sight. It is but an act of justice to refer such of my readers as may feel any curiosity on this subject, to Mr. Wedgwood, for full particulars respecting his various inventions for the use of the blind.

Having given these personal explanations—rendered necessary by the peculiarity of my situation, and the very general curiosity which appears to exist on the subject, if I may judge by the frequency of the interrogatories that are put to me—will now conclude my preliminary observations,

Nor will I thee detain

With poet's fictions, nor oppress thine ear
With circumstance, and long exordiums here;

but place myself at once on board H.M.S. Eden, at Woolwich, on the 1st of July, 1827, having been previously invited to take a passage to the coast of Africa, by her captain, W.F.W. Owen, Esq., who was appointed superintendent of a new settlement about to be established on the island of Fernando Po. The commission with which this gentleman was charged, afforded him peculiar advantages, as he was to retain the command of his ship, independently of the Commodore on the African station, for the purpose of facilitating his operations in the island. I had resolved to visit Sierra Leone, and other places on the western coast of Africa, principally from an early anxiety I felt to explore that part of the world, and also, strange and paradoxical as it may appear, for the benefit of my health. That a man should visit Sierra Leone for the benefit of his health, seems to be as unreasonable as if he were to seek for the vernal airs of the south in the inclement region of Siberia. But, I am strongly inclined to believe, that the apprehensions of European travellers on this subject are often as fatal as the climate that produces them. In my own case, I was not only free from any apprehensions concerning fevers and those diseases which are incidental to a tropical climate, but, having been recommended to try the effects of a warm region, I anticipated an improvement in my general health from a short residence at a spot, which incautious modes of living, in addition to the insalubrity of the climate, have rendered fatal to so many of my countrymen. At the same time, I am not insensible to the fact, that all Europeans are more or less susceptible of those disorders which are prevalent within the Tropics; especially on the western coast of Africa, in Batavia, Trincomalee, and different parts of the West Indies; but it is equally certain that fear is a great predisposing cause of disease, and that the despondency to which most persons give way while they are under the influence of its effects, increases the mortality to a considerable extent. It has been generally observed, that those persons who happen to be so actively engaged in any engrossing pursuit, as to have no leisure for the imagination to work upon their fears, are less liable to the fever, and, if attacked, are better able to encounter its virulence, than the timid and cautious. In the event of an attack, if the patient keeps up his spirits, and prevents desponding thoughts from occupying his mind, there is every reason to hope for a favourable result—

The sons of hope are Heaven's peculiar care,
Whilst life remains 'tis impious to despair.

There are, of course, some constitutions more susceptible of the disease than others; and it may also be observed, that young people are more exposed to danger, than those who have passed the meridian of life.

We left Woolwich on the following day, July the 2nd, for Northfleet, where we remained a week, for the purpose of making observations, regulating the chronometers, &c. We also took in our guns, 26 in number, of the following calibre—18 32-pound carronades, 6 18-pound ditto, and 2 long 9-pounders, with a full proportion of shot. This quantity of metal alone (for the carriages had been previously taken on board and fixed at Woolwich) brought the ship bodily down in the water four inches, drawing, when on board, 15 feet 2 inches forward, and 15 feet 6 inches abaft. We also received, on the day after, as much powder as could be put in the magazines. On Monday, the 9th, we left our moorings, and proceeded down the Thames, anchoring for the night. On the following day we arrived in the Downs, where we remained for about six-and-forty hours, and from thence proceeded down Channel, and anchored in Plymouth Sound, on Saturday the 14th of July, immediately after which I accompanied my brother, Lieutenant Robert Holman, R.N., who came on board for me, to his house at Plymouth, where I spent a very agreeable time, amongst my old shipmates, relatives, and friends. For the last few days, indeed, my enjoyment was marred by illness, but that was merely the bitter, which a wise Providence mingles in the cup of life.

The period of my stay at Plymouth happened to be one of general congratulation and excitement, owing to the arrival of his present Majesty, then Lord High Admiral; who came there on a visit of inspection. His Royal Highness held regular levees, which were numerously attended. The opportunity to wait upon his Royal Highness was to me a source of sincere gratification, of which I gladly availed myself. But I must acknowledge that a faint hope arose in my mind, that the peculiar circumstances in which I was placed might interest his Royal Highness on my behalf, and lead to some change in my situation favourable to the objects I had so long cherished. I ventured to indulge in the thought, which, perhaps, I scarcely suffered myself altogether to define, that I might be relieved from the obligations of my appointment at Windsor, by which I am under restrictions, both as to time and space; and be permitted to enjoy some equivalent consideration, which would leave me free to prosecute the plans to which I had devoted the whole energies of my mind. As it was, I had only obtained permission to go abroad for the benefit of my health; but the remedy was in itself an incitement to further travel, so that I should no sooner have reaped the advantage of my leave of absence, and with renewed health, acquired an increased desire for exploring distant countries, than I should be compelled to relinquish my undertaking, and the apprehension of a sudden recall constantly presenting itself to my mind, checked in a great measure the enjoyment of my pursuit. But my sanguine wishes, and unconfessed hopes, faded like a dream; and I turned again to the sea, to contemplate the bounds that were placed to my ambitious projects. Had it been otherwise—could I have followed unchecked the course of my own impulses, I should not have circumscribed my plan to any precise limits, but would have pursued my travels, wherever the slightest point of interest encouraged me to proceed.

Possibly it is better as it is. I have much reason to be grateful for the protecting hand of Providence that preserved me throughout my wanderings;

and, had I been less restrained by the force of circumstances, I might not now, perhaps, possess the power of recording the results of my researches.

In consequence of having been confined to my bed by severe indisposition, I was unable to walk to the boat when the Eden was ready to sail, and had nearly lost my passage; but my anxiety to proceed overcame all my difficulties, and ill as I was I saved my distance by hastening in a coach to the waterside, where Captain Owen had kindly provided a boat for my reception.

On the 29th we got under weigh at 9 A.M., with a fresh breeze from the eastward.

> Gallant before the wind she goes, her prow
> High bearing and disparting the blue tide
> That foams and flashes in its rage below.
> Meantime the helmsman feels a conscious pride,
> And while far onward the long billows swell,
> Looks to the lessening land, which seems to say, 'farewell!'

We did not long enjoy our easterly breeze, for in the evening the wind became variable, the rain fell in torrents, accompanied with lightning and thunder, and the night was dark and dismal, with an irregular sea, which made the ship very uneasy; then followed one of those scenes of confusion which can be witnessed only on shipboard; the creaking of timbers as they were strained by the conflict of the elements, the uproar of a multitude of voices, the ludicrous accidents arising from the pitching and rolling of the vessel, things breaking loose in all directions, chests flying from side to side, crockery smashing, people hallooing, others moaning and groaning, accompanied with frequent evomitions, and occasionally a general scream, from some extraordinary crash. With tumultuous noises of this kind I was entertained as I lay on my bed, not from sea-sickness, but from previous indisposition. Towards morning the wind settled in the N.W., blowing very strong, and the Eden continued rolling a great deal the whole day. This breeze fortunately kept up the two following days, when the weather became very fine, and the wind light and variable. The whole of this day (Thursday, August 2nd) we were in sight of Cape Finisterre. On Sunday the 5th the weather was very fine and warm, with a moderate breeze; we had eleven sail of vessels in sight, the greater part of which, from their regular order of sailing, were supposed to be the experimental squadron under the command of Sir Thomas Hardy. Divine service was performed by the Rev. Mr. Davy, a Church Missionary, who, with his wife, was bound to Sierra Leone, to perform the duties of a missionary and teacher to the liberated Africans; his wife taking upon herself to instruct the female part of that community. The following day, in 36-1/2 deg. N. lat., we saw several flying fish, which I mention merely because it was thought to be very unusual to see them so far to the northward.

On Wednesday, the 8th of August, we came in sight of Porto Santo. The first appearance of land always produces a degree of interest in the ship even to sailors, but to passengers it is generally the cause of great excitement. In the afternoon we saw Madeira, [1] and on the following day we rounded the west end of the island, and stood for Funchal Roads, having passed along the north side in order that Captain Owen might ascertain its length, which he found to be thirty-four miles; this was precisely the same distance that he had calculated it to be on a former measurement. He had taken this trouble a second time, in consequence of some navigator having expressed a different opinion on the subject. In the evening we anchored in thirty-six fathoms water, the Loo Rock bearing N. by E. We found a Portuguese sloop of war and several small merchant vessels lying here. The next morning I went on shore with the surgeon and purser of the Eden, both of whom have since died of fever on board the same ship.

The general landing place for ships' boats is at the Loo Rock on the west side of the bay, which is at the extremity of the town on that side, and you have more than a mile to walk over a very badly paved road before you arrive at the centre of the town; you may, however, land on the beach near the custom-house, from whence you immediately enter the best part of the town, but the surf is sometimes so rough that you cannot attempt this point without risking a ducking, or the upsetting of your boat, which you must immediately haul up on the beach or keep outside the surf.

Notwithstanding we had left England in the height of summer we found a great difference in the climate, the weather being exceedingly hot. On the following day I was invited to dine and take up my residence at Mr. Shortridge's during our stay at Madeira. We met a large party at dinner, consisting of Captain Owen, with some of his officers, the Rev. Mr. Deacon, and a number of the most respectable English residents. Madeira is so frequently visited by ships from different parts of Europe, and has been so fully described, that it may, perhaps, appear superfluous to attempt any further account of a place already so well known; but as all men are supposed to possess a certain portion of vanity, and as travellers are proverbially accused of laying claim to the discovery of some facts which had escaped the observation of their predecessors, I venture to throw together, into as brief a compass as possible, the result of my inquiries, in the hope that I may add something to that which is already known, and, at all events, with a strong confidence in the accuracy of my remarks.

The wine, being of vital importance to the prosperity of the island, presents the first claim to the attention of a stranger. A sort of controversy, with better reasons on the one side than the other, prevails, respecting the relative qualities of the wines produced at the north and the south sides of the island; in which the vineyards at the north side have suffered what appears to be an indiscriminate and injudicious censure. The grape chiefly grown there is the Virdelho, which the most experienced planters allow to be productive of the strongest and most esteemed of their wines; and when it is of the growth of the southern vineyards it is held in the highest estimation. It must, however, be

---

[1] Madeira received its name in consequence of being covered with wood; the word "madeira" in the Portuguese signifying timber.

admitted that the northern aspect is unfavourable to the grape, and that the greater proportion of the wines from that side are only fit for the still. The cause of this may be referred to a variety of circumstances; such as the marked difference in the soil and aspect and the mode of cultivation, the vines being trained upon trees; whilst on the south side the more approved system is practised of training them upon horizontal trellis work, raised two or three feet from the ground, by which the plant is supported and the fruit exposed to the full influence of the sun. A great superiority of flavour is, no doubt, thus obtained: on the north side, the grapes are entirely of the white kind, whilst on the south there is a great variety, but chiefly of the red, from which it is said the finest wine is made. The famed vineyards of the Malmsey and Sercial wines, are towards the west end of the south side. There is but a very small quantity of either grown on this spot of the first rate quality, or indeed of any value as a characteristic wine, for on the easternmost part of this situation there is a constant flow of water rushing from the summits of the rocks, that greatly deteriorates the value of the growths over which its influence extends. The practice of plucking the leaves of the vines to admit the genial heat of the sun to the fruit, as well as a free circulation of air, has been found most beneficial in bringing the fruit to perfection. This process is also a source of emolument to the planter, as the leaves form an excellent food for fattening cattle destined for the shambles, giving also to the meat a fine and delicious flavour.

The wines of Madeira generally may be divided into three denominations, and may be thus described.

Tinto is a red wine, the produce of the Burgundy grape, transplanted to Madeira. It is drank in perfection in the second and third years, before it has deposited its extractive matter, after which it becomes a full bodied Madeira wine, of the usual colour and flavour.

Sercial is the produce of the Hock grape: a pale, lively, and very high-flavoured wine. It ought not to be drank in less than seven years, and it requires a much greater age to reach perfection.

Malmsey, when genuine, is a rich and highly cordial wine. There is a variety of it called *green Malmsey*, bearing some resemblance to Frontignan.

The first quality of the Madeira wine is certainly equal to the finest production of the grape in any part of the world, for its aromatic flavour and beneficial effects: therefore it is much to be lamented that so small a quantity of it, in its pure state, should find its way to foreign markets: and that its character should be sacrificed to the sordid speculations of any unprincipled traders. Wine drinkers in England are very commonly deceived into the idea that a voyage to the East or West Indies is sufficient to ensure the excellence of the wine; but this is an obvious fallacy, for if the wine were not of a good quality when shipped from the island, a thousand voyages could not make it what it never had been. It is well known to every merchant in Madeira, that a great proportion of the wines so shipped are of an inferior quality, and are purchased in barter by persons who are commonly known by the name of truckers.

I may here observe, as a general remark, that fine Madeira wines are equally improved by the extremes of heat and cold, and that damp is always hurtful to them.

Burgundy vines have lately been introduced into Madeira. The generally received opinion that the wines of Teneriffe and the Azores are brought here for the purpose of giving them the Madeira flavour, and sending them to foreign markets as the produce of the island, is very erroneous. Although smuggling is openly carried on, and to an extent that ought to set at rest so fallacious an opinion, any one acquainted with this island must be aware of the utter impossibility of introducing foreign wines with a view to exporting them again as native produce; for, in the first place, the whole of the inhabitants would be likely to resist such an attempt, from a conviction that the introduction would militate against their own interests, and from the obvious apprehension that the increased quantity as well as the inferior quality of the adulterated wines, would injure the character and reduce the price of their own.

The great increase too, which it would occasion in the amount sent out of the island, would render it very difficult for the speculators in the spurious wines, to avoid detection. It is, therefore, much more reasonable to suppose, that these mixtures take place in the markets to which the wines are sent: the great demand for them tempting the persons engaged in the traffic, to embark in an imposition which has had the effect of deteriorating the wines so materially, that at last they began to lose their previous character, to get out of fashion, and, consequently, to fall off in demand as well as in price. This system of intermixing different wines, to swell the quantity of some favourite wine, is known to prevail to a great extent in those of France and Portugal. The Clarets of the London market, are principally prepared for the purpose, and, in the transit, lose much of the pure nature of the original production: and the quantity of adulterated Port that is sold in England is almost incredible. It is also a well known fact, that there is more Tokay [2] sold on the Continent and in England, in one year, than the limited space where it is grown, on the mountains of Hungary, could produce in twenty years.

But there is also, independently of this vitiation to which the wines are liable, another cause for the inferior quality of those wines which are really the produce of the islands. A few Englishmen, and other foreigners, of a grade very different from that of the respectable English merchants who have been long established here, hit upon the expedient of exporting wines instead of attending to the business which they had originally established on the island. They thought it would turn out profitable to buy up cheap, and, of course, inferior wines, for the purpose of sending them to the European markets, under the impression that any thing would sell that was known to be the genuine production of Madeira. By this method of enlarging their business, the worst description of the native produce got abroad, and was substituted in place of the best. There are, of

---

[2] The vine of Italy was originally introduced to the mountain, of Tokay, in the fourteenth century, by Louis I. of France.

course, a great variety of qualities; but there is not a greater quantity of the first quality than is required to flavour their inferior wines; and it is only by appropriating it to that purpose, that they could be enabled to furnish a sufficient quantity for the immense demand in the various markets which they have to supply.

It will be seen from the following account of the exportation of wine from Madeira, that the demand was rapidly decreasing in 1825, 6, and 7, owing to the causes above mentioned.

1825.

	Pipes of 110 Gall.	Hds. of 55	Q.C. of 27-1/2	1/2 Q.C. of 15
January,	1367	1	0	0
Feb.	751	1	0	1
March,	1915	1	0	0
April,	2463	0	1	0
May,	1252	1	1	0
June,	1112	1	1	0
July,	1329	1	1	1
August,	677	1	0	0
Sept.	741	0	0	1
Oct.	1338	1	1	0
Nov.	881	1	1	0
Dec.	599	0	0	1
	14425	9	7	4

1826.

	Pipes, old Measure	Hds.	Q.C.	1/2 Q.C.
January,	1092	1	1	1
Feb.	420	1	1	1
March,	905	1	1	1
April,	777	1	1	1
May,	1826	1	1	1
June,	866	0	0	1
July,	488	1	0	1
August,	978	1	0	0
Sept.	317	0	0	1
Oct.	730	1	1	1
Nov.	703	1	0	1
Dec.	289	1	0	0
	9391	10	6	9

1827.

	Pipes	Hds.	Q.C.	1/4 Q.C.

January,	371	1	0	1
Feb.	573	0	0	0
March,	252	0	1	1
April,	958	1	1	1
May,	1539	0	1	0
June,	535	0	1	1
July,	567	1	1	0
August,	279	0	1	1
	5274	2	6	5

I am informed, that smuggling is so common a practice in this island, that there is no difficulty in procuring any prohibited article you may desire: among the most abundant are French brandy and Dutch gin. The former of these articles continued to be smuggled, in large quantities, for some time after the prohibition, from an idea that it was the best spirit they could use, and under an apprehension that the wines could not maintain their character without it:— experience, however, has shewn them, that they can not only do without French brandy, but that the spirit which is made on the island, is much better adapted to their purpose.

An extensive seizure of gin was made during our short stay at Madeira, under the following circumstances: A boat went off to a Dutch vessel, on the same evening that she left the port, which, no doubt, had been previously arranged, and took 300 cases of gin, which she landed at the N.E. side of the island. She remained there that day, and proceeded, under the obscurity of the following night, towards the town of Funchal; but on her way she struck, and must have been wrecked but for the assistance of a fishing-smack that happened to be near at the moment. The fishermen were, as a matter of course, easily bribed to assist the smugglers in landing and depositing the illicit store in a cavern at Prior Bay, a little to the westward of Funchal. The next day, however, a most unfortunate accident revealed the whole proceeding. Two lovers had formed an arrangement to make an excursion from Funchal to Kama de Loba, and leaving the former place in a small boat, were in due time landed at Prior Bay. They had not proceeded far, before they discovered the cave, and tempted, by its coolness and its solitary situation, they entered it, when, to their surprise, they saw a man lying in a remote part of the interior. As he appeared to be sleeping very soundly, they ventured to look farther in, when they perceived a great number of cases deposited in an obscure corner; and, suspecting that they were placed there to elude the vigilance of the revenue officers, they immediately communicated the fact to some persons in the Custom-house, in the hope of being rewarded for their zeal. The Custom-house people, who were probably already aware of the circumstance, did not appear to be very anxious to interfere, and told the disappointed informers that they might take a few cases for themselves, and say nothing more about the matter. Shortly afterwards, however, the affair reached the ears of the Governor, who immediately sent a military party to seize upon the illicit deposit, the contents of which were demonstrated by the potent effects which they had upon the soldiers.

The stone fruits of Madeira are in general of a very inferior quality, arising from mere want of attention to their cultivation; for where the trees have been planted in a favourable situation, and otherwise attended to, the produce is excellent; but they are generally scattered about the vineyards, and treated with the utmost carelessness, being very rarely pruned or dressed. It is supposed that they are permitted to grow in this irregular way for the purpose of attracting the lizards, insects, and grubs from the vines, as it was found that they always preferred the more solid nutriment of the stone fruit, especially the peach. These grubs are so numerous, that they will scarcely allow a single apricot or peach to ripen unperforated, consequently, the planters are obliged to pluck, in a green state, what they would otherwise desire to see expanding to full maturity.

Query.—Why do the insects prefer the peach tree to the vine? Is it from the resinous quality of the former?

There is also an abundance of apples and pears, but of a bad quality, occasioned by the same causes. The mulberry, fig, and guava, succeed better; they are both abundant and good, but there are not any plantains or bananas. On the higher lands, that is, above the general height of the vineyards, the walnut and chesnut grow most luxuriantly, and are both ornamental and useful. The chesnuts are so plentiful that, in the fruit season, they form a considerable article of food amongst the lower orders of the people. The fine old forest trees, the original occupiers of the soil, are disappearing rapidly, even from the deepest ravines; in situations easy of access they have been long since destroyed by the lawless and thoughtless despoiler.

I must not omit some reference to the vegetables of Madeira, and in particular the potatoe, which grows as fine here as in any part of the world. The cultivation of this edible has of late so much increased, as in some districts to constitute the chief food of the natives. The apparently unfavourable situation on which it is principally planted, affords a convincing proof of the superiority, in habits of active industry, of the peasantry of this island over the Portuguese peasants in general. Instead of being indolent and supine, and indisposed to embrace the means of ameliorating and improving their condition, they are, on the contrary, enterprising, hardy, and persevering. The potatoe is chiefly reared on the ascent of Pico Rueva, at an elevation of 6,000 feet above the level of the sea, and many of the beds are within 300 feet of the summit. [3] The ground above a certain height belongs to Government, and the people have only a trifling tax to pay for any portion that they choose to cultivate. Onions, pumpkins, melons, cucumbers, &c. &c. are in the greatest abundance. Beef, mutton, and poultry, of good quality, are to be obtained at moderate prices, and fish in the greatest abundance.

---

[3] In the mountains of the Caraccas the potatoe grows wild, and in great abundance; but as they are left unnoted, they are usually not much larger than the ordinary gooseberry.—See *Humboldt*.

Madeira may be said to be in general very healthy; but in the autumn diarrhoea is a common complaint amongst the lower orders, caused by eating bad and unripe fruits, and drinking the washings of the wine-press, a beverage made by throwing water on the husks of the grapes, after the operation of pressing out the wine has been performed, and then submitting them to a second pressure.

It is not an infrequent occurrence, that parts of the crews of ships that touch at the Island, suffer from eating unripe fruits, which are often incautiously allowed to be brought on board, particularly the peaches, which the commanding officers of vessels would do well to prohibit by every means in their power. The Portuguese boats are always ready to bring off great quantities of such trash, which no one can eat with impunity. The changes of the weather, for which the inhabitants are not sufficiently prepared by clothing, may be added as another cause of disease.

The planting of coffee has lately become very general in the vicinity of Funchal, chiefly in gardens and places not favourable for the culture of the vine, and this plant generally presents a most thriving appearance, producing a berry which is highly esteemed, and is in such demand at Lisbon that there is no doubt that the cultivation of it, will, hereafter, become an object of some consideration; and I may here observe, that it is already gradually extending. The quality of this berry is so superior as to have rendered it an article of exportation, and the people more readily resort to this new branch of culture, from the decline in the demand for the secondary wines. Our Consul has recently introduced the tea plant at his seat up the mountain, from which some favourable specimens have already been obtained.

The manufacture of sugar has also been tried on the island, but although the cane succeeds uncommonly well, the expense of conveying it to Funchal, together with that of the process of extracting the juice, and the want of skill in granulation, has rendered the experiment too costly, it being found that Brazilian sugar can be had cheaper than the native production.

Sunday, August 12th, 1827.—I accompanied Mr. Shortridge to the English Chapel, where the congregation was small, in consequence of the absence of the merchants and their families in the country, during the summer months. The service was performed by the Rev. Mr. Deacon, who is a member of the Established Church, and holds the appointment of Chaplain to the English residents, of whom there are a great number, consisting of merchants, shop-keepers, servants, and a few invalids. I do not, however, consider it the best place in the world for the last description of visitors. Bermuda is well known to be a much more healthy climate; from the land not being so high, the weather is less variable, and the temperature, of course, more equal. Madeira, notwithstanding, has two advantages over Bermuda, worthy of consideration; it presents more agreeable and better society, and offers greater facilities of intercourse with England; so that the accounts from home are more frequent and recent.

I left town in the afternoon, to dine with Mr. Webster Gordon, who resides at the mount near the Church of Nostra Senhora del Monte, about three miles in the country; where I was invited with Captain Owen and some of his officers. They went on horseback, while I, being still rather an invalid, hired a palanquin by the advice of my friend, Mr. Shortridge. Having heard a good deal of the luxury of palanquin travelling in the East, I thought it would be a very pleasant mode of conveyance on a hot day; but instead of finding it swing loftily, like a hammock, as I expected, I discovered much to my mortification, that, when on the shoulders of the bearers, it was raised only about eighteen inches from the ground, and consisted of a solid frame of wood, suspended from a pole with two iron stanchions, and covered on each side by a cloth flung over the pole, to serve as a curtain. In this I was placed, in a half sitting, half recumbent posture, which I need scarcely observe was not very agreeable. When I got out to call at a gentleman's house, before I reached my ultimate destination, I found that the cramp in the calves of my legs had so disabled me, that I could scarcely stand, and it was a considerable time before I could walk unaided and free from pain. I anticipated every moment that my bearers would have complained of the road, which was badly paved, and very steep the greatest part of the way; but they were fine, hardy, muscular men, and quite indifferent to a toil with which habit had rendered them familiar. Each bearer carries a long stick in his hand, which assists to support and steady him, over the uneven ground.

On arriving at Mr. Webster Gordon's, I was agreeably surprised to find that I had been previously acquainted with Mrs. Gordon and her mother in Italy.

The population of the town of Funchal is said to be about 25,000; and that of the whole island, including Funchal, 120,000.

Invalids have, latterly, more facilities for obtaining lodgings than they had in former years, the inhabitants finding it their interest to direct their attention more to that particular. The resident British may be estimated at about 250, including children; and since my return to England, I have been informed, that, during this last year, there were upwards of 100 invalid visitors from America.

I passed the short time the ship remained very pleasantly, and I could have wished that it had been longer; not only on account of the salubrity of the climate, but for the advantage of being enabled to collect more information. Some of the officers went to the Coural, a celebrated part of the island for extensive and beautiful scenery. In the afternoon of *Tuesday, August 14th*, we embarked, and sailed out of Funchal Bay on the same evening, directing our course for Teneriffe. Our consort the Diadem, transport, had left the bay a few hours before. From Funchal, Madeira, to Santa Cruz, Teneriffe, the course is S. 6 deg. E.; distance 252 miles.

CHAP. II.

Teneriffe—Town of Santa Cruz—Female Costume—Incident at a Ball—Bad Roads—Climate—Productions—Population of the Canary Islands—Imports and Exports—Various Qualities of the Wines—Fishery—Leave Santa Cruz—Crossing the Tropic of Cancer—Shaving and Ducking—General Remarks—Make St. Jago—Anchor at Porto Praya—Sickly Season—Death of the Consul and his Wife—Consul's Sister—Governor's Garden and Watering-place—Population of the Island—Produce—The Orchilla Weed, its growth, uses, and varieties—Cause of Fever—Departure for Sierra Leone

Wednesday, 15th.—Fresh breezes and cloudy, with the wind and a swell from the eastward. At sunset passed within six or seven miles to the eastward of the Great Salvage Islands.

Thursday, 16th.—At daylight saw the island of Teneriffe, [4] and at nine anchored in Santa Cruz Roads, in nineteen fathoms water; the flag-staff on the mole bearing W. by N. We saluted the Spanish flag with thirteen guns, which was returned.

Mr. M'Gregor, our Vice-consul, came on board, when he immediately recognised me, as having seen me at Hamburg about three years before. On his returning to the shore he was complimented with a salute of seven guns, according to regulations. I accompanied some of the officers on shore to take a ramble over the town. I regretted to learn from Mr. M'Gregor that Mr. Bruce, our Consul-General for the Canaries, was in England. This circumstance was a serious disappointment to me, as I had a letter of introduction to that gentleman from a friend of his at Madeira, who assured me that he possessed so vigorous and intelligent a mind, and was so intimately acquainted with the island of Teneriffe, where he had long resided, that I could not fail to obtain much valuable information from him that was not generally known.

My friends were very much pleased with the cleanly appearance of the town and good pavement, affording a striking contrast to Funchal, which, like most Portuguese towns, was dirty and badly paved. There was another agreeable sight; the Spanish women, who were generally handsome, with an interesting character of expression in their faces, which is much heightened by their beautiful dark eyes and jet-black hair. Their dresses are remarkable for their neatness.

The town of Santa Cruz stands near the sea, on a plain of about two miles square, at the foot of the mountains. The population amounts to about 6,000 souls. It has a well fortified sea-line of defence, and a mole protected by a fort. It was on landing at this mole that Nelson lost his arm, and Captain Boscawen his life. The English colours taken on that occasion are preserved as trophies in the

[4] This island was named Thenariffe, or the White Mountain, by the natives of Palma; Thenar, in their language, signifying a mountain, and Ife, white—the Peak of Teneriffe being always covered with snow.

principal church. Few persons are seen walking about during the day, and those only of the lower orders. The women wear large shawls thrown over their heads, hanging very low down, and a round black hat with a high crown. A friend of mine once visited the island in one of H.M. ships at the time of the Carnival, and on the last day of the festivities there was a public ball, to which the officers of the ship were invited. They went early to see as much as they could of the inhabitants, and their opinion of the ladies was, that they looked more like English than Spanish women in almost all respects, except their remarkably black eyes and hair. Before the dancing commenced the ladies were all blindfolded, and each provided with a stick, when they were conducted to one end of the room, where a jar full of *bon bons* was suspended, which they were desired to break, but the blows from their delicate hands were not able to accomplish it, and one of the gentlemen at last performed this task for them, when there was a general scramble among the gentlemen, from a desire to procure some of the contents to present to their fair partners.

The Diadem transport anchored here soon after us.

Friday, 17th.—The York, East Indiaman, was lying off this place in the forenoon whilst her boat went on shore with letters. Some of the officers took horse this morning and went to the town of Laguna, which is about six miles from Santa Cruz. They found the road in a terrible state, from a quantity of large stones and rubbish, which a late hurricane, with heavy rain, had brought down from the higher lands. Their ride was a very cheap one, for they only paid half a dollar for each horse, including a guide—a rare occurrence for Englishmen to find any thing cheap in a foreign country. Port Oratava, which lies on the opposite or north side of the island, the principal town for commerce on it, is 21 miles by land from Santa Cruz; and it is said to be 36 miles from Oratava to the summit of the Peak, a journey of at least two days' ascent from the latter place, which is the starting point.

Our visit to this island was too short to be of much interest to a traveller, for it would have required at least a week to have visited the Peak only and returned to Santa Cruz, which I certainly would have done if the ship had remained a sufficient time; as I also wished to have visited Porto Rueva, at Madeira, but on my arrival at that island I had not sufficiently recovered my strength after the indisposition I experienced on leaving England.

They have at Teneriffe, (besides horses, asses, and mules,) camels, which are much in use as beasts of burden. Smoking is a very general practice here, and consequently there is no want of ordinary cigars; but I was surprised to find that Havannah cigars are very difficult to be procured. They can be obtained, however, but at un exorbitant rate, in consequence of the risks attending the smuggling. Tobacco is a royal monopoly, and the duty is so high, that it amounts almost to a prohibition, and consequently affords great temptation to smuggling. They have ice at their command here in abundance, which is a great luxury for a hot climate. They bring it down from the mountains, and use it very commonly in lemonade, creams, and for many other purposes. It is desirable to call here on your way to a hot climate, if it were only to procure a few good drip stones, the best of which are brought from Grand Canary, and which are to be had in great plenty, and very cheap, from one to three Spanish dollars each, which is the most current coin of this island.

Teneriffe, in climate, soil, produce, and general appearance, strongly resembles Madeira, from which it is distant 240 miles, due south. The principal towns are Port-Oratava, Oratava, Realexo, and Caracheeo, on the north side of the island; and on the south, Santa Cruz, Candilaria, and Adexi; besides the inland towns, Laguna, (the capital) about two leagues from Santa Cruz, Metanza, and Victoria, all on the road between Santa Cruz and Port-Oratava, which arc at an elevation, varying from 3,000 to 5,000 feet above the level of the sea. This affords a considerable variety of climate, and choice of residence. Teneriffe, however, possesses but little English society, consequently there are few comforts or inducements for invalids. There is an extensive plain of table land and corn country round Laguna, which is a bishop's see, with an income of 30,000 dollars per annum. The governor of the province resides at Santa Cruz. There is also a bishopric at Grand Canary (where the audience, or supreme court is held), worth about 50,000 dollars a-year.

Teneriffe, from its great elevation, and gradual slope to the sea, possesses every variety of vegetation from the tropic to the frozen regions. In the first or lower region are found the date, palm, pine-apple, alligator-pear, and sugar cane, tea and coffee trees, lemons, citrons, oranges and grapes; the next region is that of grain and fruits, and trees of temperate climates; next follow the chesnuts, pines (Pinus Cananensis), and other hardy Alpine trees; then the region of heaths, laurels, and other evergreens; and at the extreme limit of vegetation, a considerable distance from the summit, the white broom (Spartium Nubigenum.) The population of the Canary Islands is about 200,000, viz. Teneriffe, 80,000; Grand Canary, 60,000; Palma, 25,000; Lanzerota, 15,000; Forteventura, 10,000; Heirro, 4,000; Gomera, 6,000.

The exports, exclusive of the coasting trade, are wines, barilla, orchilla weed, rock-moss, safflower, (hay-saffron,) and silks. The imports are sugar, cocoa, oil, tobacco, paper, &c. from Cadiz; earthenware, from St. Lucia; brandy, from Catalonia; dry goods, cloth, iron, and hardware, from England; and staves, soap, candles, and rice from the United States of America.

The volcanic nature of the soil of the Canary Islands renders it extremely favourable to the cultivation of the vine, which grows luxuriantly in Teneriffe, where more than three-fourths of all the wines exported from the Canaries is produced. The Teneriffe wines are of the same description and varieties as the wines of Madeira, namely, Tinto, Verdelho, Gual, Listan, Malvasia, [5] &c., but they are not equal in quality to the fine wines of the south side, yet superior to the wines of the north side, of that island. They are distinguished by what may be called the generic denominations of dry and sweet. The dry is well known by the name of Vidonia, and the sweet as Malvasia. The first quality of the former

---

[5] Malmsey, or sack.

can only be obtained from the most respectable merchants, it being a very common process to convert it, by admixtures, into a counterfeit of Madeira, or sherry, and occasionally to drug it with port. The strongest quality of the celebrated wine called sack, [6] is made in Teneriffe, Grand Canary, and Palma.

Carbonate of soda is obtained from the *sal sola soda*, extensively cultivated at Lanccrota and Forteventura. It is gathered in September, dried, and then charred or fused into a ringing, hard, cellular mass, of a greyish blue colour. A small quantity is made also at Grand Canary. The barilla of the Canary Islands has been sold in England so high as 80l. a ton, and as low as 6l.; at the present time, (December, 1833) it is worth 9l. 10s. a ton. The depreciation is caused chiefly by kelp, and other substitutes found in the British alkali, a French chemical discovery, manufactured from sea salt, from which, the other ingredients are detached, by combination with sulphur, and acids subjected to heat. The imports of barilla from the Canary Islands to this country are about 3,500 tons a-year. The United States of America, and of late years, Brazil, also, take off a few cargoes of this article. Lancerota produces, annually, about 300 tons of barilla; Forte ventura about 1500 tons.

Rock moss (Parmelia perlata) is worth about 70l. a ton, and is one of the innumerable lichens common to the Canary Islands; it is used in the manufacture of cudbear for the dyers. There is also a spurious kind, with difficulty distinguished from the good.

Silk is chiefly produced at Palma. There is but little exported from Teneriffe. It might, however, be produced in immense quantities, the white and red mulberry tree being indigenous and luxuriant in the middle region of the island, and the climate so mild, that the insect could be hatched and reared under wooden sheds, without any difficulty. The great defect in the Teneriffe silk is the coarseness of the fibre, from want of dexterity in winding it off the cocoons, and in regulating the heat to which it ought to be subjected during that separation.

A considerable emigration used to take place annually from the islands, and particularly from Lancerota and Forteventura, to the Spanish Main, and to Cuba, where those islanders were much in request, as labourers and muleteers; and often prospered so well as to be enabled to return home enriched: but the practice has been prohibited since the declaration of independence of Spanish South America.

There is a considerable fishery carried on from the Canary Islands, on the coast of Barbary, for a species of bream, which is salted in bulk, and sold very cheap, and in great quantities. This trade is pursued in decked schooners, or lugger-rigged vessels, of from 60 to 70 tons burthen, which rum down before

---

[6] This word is erroneously supposed to be a corruption of "sec," or *dry*, but both Canary and sherry sack of old times (as well as the present) was a *sweet* and *rich* wine, and the name could not, therefore, have been so derived. The term *sac* is more likely to be a contraction of the word "saccharine," or it may have been adopted in consequence of the wine being made from half-dried grapes.

the trade wind to their station, where they remain until they procure a cargo, when they beat up to the island, take in a fresh cargo of Cadiz salt, and again return to their station. They have very little intercourse with the Arab tribes of that coast, but they sometimes bring back a few lion, tiger, and leopard skins, and ostrich feathers. I am happy to learn that our knowledge of the natural history of these islands is likely to be soon very much increased, by the indefatigable exertions of P.B. Webb, Esq., a gentleman well known to the scientific world, who is now engaged at Paris in publishing the result of his researches in different branches of natural history.

In the afternoon we took in some oxen and wine, and left Santa Cruz roads at seven in the evening. From Santa Cruz to Porto Praya, St. Jago, the course is S. 26 deg. W. 920 miles.

Monday, 20th.—Having crossed the tropic of Cancer last evening. Captain Owen granted the ship's company permission to perform the customary ceremony of shaving and ducking all those who had not previously passed the tropic. Whenever a ship is intended to enter the southern hemisphere, this marine exhibition is not performed until she reaches the equinoctial line. Although this ceremony has been frequently described, I do not think it right to pass it over altogether unnoticed; I will therefore make a few general observations by way of comment on the practice.

A sea voyage is at the best a monotonous life, and a long voyage is only to be wished for by the few whose health it is calculated to improve; therefore, any little variety, that produces even but a temporary excitement, is desirable; and in this point of view only, is the old custom of shaving and ducking (which, by the bye, is a barbarous one) at all excusable.

When it is permitted to be practised, it should only be under certain regulations, as the consequences have frequently been very serious, for want of some salutary restrictions; in some cases the harmony that has existed amongst the society on board has been destroyed; actions at law, and duels, fevers from exposure daring the day's amusement, have ensued: it is, therefore, imperatively necessary that the law should take cognizance of this custom, and enforce some rigorous rules for the government of all commanders of vessels, whenever circumstances should permit the indulgence of this indefensible practice. In the first place, the ship should be always put under snug sail; and that part of the vessel, in which the scene takes place, should be completely screened in, and no cruel or offensive practices permitted. The Captain should always have the power of protecting his officers and passengers from being compelled to submit to the demands of old Neptune, by paying a small fine for the exemption: say cabin passengers, five shillings, steerage passengers half-a-crown. The sum total of these fines should be divided among those sailors who had previously crossed the line; and, if any of the sailors on board should be found to throw water, rope yarns dipped in tar, or in any other way insult, or annoy, persons who do not take a part in their proceedings, they should be punished as they would for a similar breach of discipline at any other time. There is one example, which I feel at liberty to quote, and which was nearly the occasion of a court-martial on the senior lieutenant of one of H.M. ships that arrived in Simon's Bay during my residence at the Cape of Good Hope. The circumstance was as follows:—The purser of the ship had shut himself up in his cabin, determined to resist any forcible attempt to make him undergo the ceremony of shaving; but those who were engaged in it, were resolved that he should not be permitted to escape: they accordingly forced the door of his cabin, from which they got him out, dragged him on deck, and performed the ceremony, in spite of his efforts and remonstrances. The charge against the first lieutenant was, I understood, for encouraging the persons who committed this act of violence. This formed the grounds of an application for a court-martial, which was only prevented from taking place by the intercession of some officers of rank. It is satisfactory to be enabled to add, that this barbarous and unworthy custom is rapidly falling into disuse.

Wednesday, 22nd.—A moderate trade wind, and all sail set. At daylight saw the island of Sall, bearing E.S.E. 15 miles. At half-past 5 in the afternoon saw the island of St. Jago, [7] when I went to the fore top-mast head, for exercise and amusement, while others went to see the land. At 11 brought the ship to the wind, and stood off the land at a convenient distance for going into Porto Praya on the following day.

At daylight, made all sail, and stood towards the anchorage, with a light breeze and very fine weather. At noon anchored off Porto Praya, in 12 fathoms water and sandy bottom. Extreme points of the bay from W. 3/4 S. to E. 3/4 S. Garrison flagstaff N.N.W. 1/2 W.

Our Consul-General for the Cape de Verds (Mr. Clark) waited on Captain Owen, from whom we learnt, that His Majesty's ship, North Star, sailed from this port five days before, and that a very heavy gale of wind arose from the S.W. on that night. We were also informed, that this is the most sickly part of the year, in consequence of its being the rainy season, which commences at the beginning of August, and continues to the end of October; during which time the winds are frequently from the southward and westward, making it hazardous to anchor at this port in those months. The whole of this time is generally very sickly, so much so that the principal authorities are glad to leave the island, and repair to Fuego, which is the highest, and also considered to be the most healthy of all the Cape de Verd group. The Chief Justice and his family left Porto Praya, for Fuego, in a Portuguese sloop of war, on the day we entered it, the Governor having previously left for the same destination.

There were many of the inhabitants suffering from fever, while we were at St. Jago, and two of the Consul's family were among the number, and I lament

---

[7] The islands of Mayo, Bonavista (or St. Filippe), and St. Jago, were the first of the Cape de Verds discovered, in May 1461, by Antonio de Nolle, a Genoese in the service of Portugal; and St. Jago, was the first settled. The remaining seven were also discovered the same year, by Portuguese subjects, namely, St. Antonio, St. Vincent, St. Lucia, St. Nicholas, Sall, Fuego, and Bravos.

to relate, that not long after our departure, both the Consul and his wife fell victims to this too commonly fatal fever of St. Jago, leaving his sister, an amiable and accomplished young lady, dangerously ill of the same disease. The case of this lady was one of the most melancholy interest. She was entirely unprotected by the presence of any country people of her own, except a gentleman, who, happening to call there on his way from England to Sierra Leone, was induced to remain on the island, at the request of Mrs. Clark, for the purpose of acting as Vice-Consul, during the severe illness of her husband. This gentleman, after performing the painful duty of reading the burial service over the Consul-General and his lady, was himself attacked by the same fever, and after struggling for a length of time against it, was, at last, sent off to the island of Mayo, just in time to save his life, leaving the Consul's sister behind, reduced to the last extremity of the disease, with scarcely any symptoms of life remaining, and attended only by her Portuguese friends, and any occasional English visitors who landed incidentally from their ships for refreshments, on their way to other parts of the world. At last, however, she happily recovered, but after a very severe struggle, and a protracted illness, and then she could not return direct to England, but was obliged to go to the Brazils, in a French schooner, before she could procure a passage home. I shall give, hereafter, some further details of this young lady's history, leading to the attachment which afterwards sprung up between her and her medical attendant, who fell in love with her during a second attack of illness, and there is no doubt that her fortitude and good sense had a great share in the admiration with which she inspired him.

Friday, August 24th.—Soon after breakfast I accompanied Captain Owen, the Rev. Mr. and Mrs. Davy, and some of the officers of the ship, to pass the day at the Consul's. We took a walk before dinner, to visit the few places that were worthy of any notice; we first went to the fort. This fort was forty-seven paces long and seven broad, where the only objects of interest were the graves of two Captains in the Navy. One of them contained the remains of an old shipmate of mine, Capt. J. Eveleigh, who was mortally wounded when commanding the Astrea, in company with the Creole, during an engagement with two French frigates, the Etoile and Sultane, on the 23rd of January, 1814, off the Cape de Verds. I sailed in the same ship with this officer when I first went to sea. He was then junior lieutenant of the Royal George, bearing the flag of Lord Bridport. I met him some years afterwards, when he was lieutenant of the Isis, bearing the flag of Admiral Holloway, on the Newfoundland station, in which ship I was a passenger from England to Newfoundland, on my way to join the Cleopatra, as lieutenant, on the Halifax station. The other grave was that of Capt. Bartholomew, of the Lieven frigate, who died while he was occupied in the survey of these islands. The late Consul-General had been purser of that ship, and, poor fellow, both his grave and that of his wife were made near his former captain's.

From thence we went to visit the Governor's garden, which lies in a low swampy situation, much below the town, and not far from the sea, where the boats are obliged to land to procure water, subject to the inconvenience of the surf, which sometimes renders it very difficult to get the casks off. The water at this island does not deserve the bad character given of it by some persons. It is, in fact, very good, and it must, therefore, have been from negligence in procuring it, either by disturbing it too much, or by using bad bungs, which allowed the salt water to get in while floating off, that it acquired its unfavourable reputation. It is supplied by several springs, issuing from the side of the hill at the back of the town, which unite into one stream, and as it approaches the sea, expands and forms into a basin, the nearest part of which is forty yards from the beach. As this is rarely dry, ships may be easily watered, by landing their casks through the surf; and, when filled, floating them off to the ship. However, when it is dry, or nearly so, as was the case when we were there, you are obliged to roll the casks a considerable distance from the beach to a well in the Governor's garden, from which they must be filled. This mode is both tedious and laborious, while the sailors are almost sure to get drunk on a bad spirit called *aqua dent*, which is sold to them secretly by the blacks, who are ever on the watch to elude the vigilance of the officers employed in that service.

During the time of the former Governor, (the present one not having been long in command,) this garden received great attention, and was kept in excellent order; but the present Governor does not take any interest in it himself, and, consequently, it is very much neglected; indeed, there appears to be such a general apathy in all the people at Porto Pray a, that it seems more like a place allowed to go to decay, than a colony under an European Government, visited so constantly by vessels from all parts of the globe.

The population of Villa de Praya is about 4,000, and that of the whole island about 28,000, which are principally blacks. A large proportion of the male population of St. Jago, are enrolled in the militia, and armed with boarding pikes; 300 of whom are compelled, in rotation, to attend every Sunday, at their own expense, for the purpose of exercising at Villa de Praya. The regular troops do not amount to more than 400 for the whole of the islands.

This place owes its support entirely to the ships that call here for provisions; and the quantity of stock, fruit, vegetables, and water, that is purchased annually at the island is immense. A considerable sum of money is also spent by passengers, who go on shore for their amusement.

The landing at St. Jago is, at all times, indifferent, and in the rainy season frequently very bad, both on the rocks, and on the beach, for there are two distinct places of debarkation. Yet, with a little attention, and a small amount of labour, a more secure landing-place could very easily be made, by cutting a few steps in two or three favourable situations, that would readily admit of the improvement; whereas now you are obliged to watch the swell, and step out on pointed rocks, or an irregular surface, at the risk of falling back into the boat or the water; or bruising yourself severely on the rocks. Captain Owen and myself once fell, when he was kindly assisting me out of the boat. The best time for landing on the rocks is at half-tide. I was informed that materials have been collected for constructing a pier, a project, for which nature has provided an excellent site; but, from the poverty of the government, or some other cause, it has been postponed. This is the more extraordinary, as the Portuguese government has hitherto been in the habit of transporting to St. Jago convicted felons, by whom public works could have been cheaply accomplished. Angola, however, has latterly been adopted as the principal convict settlement of the Portuguese.

Hides, goat skins, and salt, are exported from these islands, but the chief and most valuable produce is the orchilla weed. It is a government monopoly, and is at present farmed out to a man named Martiney.

As the orchilla weed is a production, the practical application of which in various ways is diffused over a large surface of utility, and as its peculiar properties are not very generally known, a minute description of its nature and uses, which I have procured at some cost of time and research, may not prove uninteresting.

The orchilla is a delicate fibrous plant, springing up in situations that are apparently the most unfavourable to the sustenance of vegetable life. When gathered it has a soft delicious odour, which it retains for a great length of time. Mr. Glas, in his history of the Canary Islands, gives so clear and accurate an account of its growth, that I will avail myself of his description, as being not only the best I have met with, but as containing all the necessary particulars. "The orchilla weed," he observes, "grows out of the pores of the stones or rocks, to about the length of three inches: I have seen some eight or ten inches, but that is not common. It is of a round form and of the thickness of common sewing twine. Its colour is grey, inclining to white: here and there on the stalk we find white spots or scabs. Many stalks proceed from one root, at some distance from which they divide into branches. There is no earth or mould to be perceived on the rock or stone where it grows. Those who do not know this weed, or are not accustomed to gather it, would hardly be able to find it, for it is of such a colour, and grows in such a direction, that it appears at first sight to be the shade of the rock on which it grows."

Mr. Glas adds, that the best sort is of the darkest colour, and nearly round; and that the more white spots or scabs it exhibits the better. It is found in considerable quantities in the Canary Islands, the Cape de Verds, the Azores, and the Madeiras, and such are the nice varieties and properties incidental to the different soils, (if they may be so called,) or climates, that although the above clusters of islands are at no great distance from each other, the difference in the produce makes a very considerable difference in the value of the article. It is also found on the coast of Barbary, and the Levant, and on that part of the coast of Africa, which lies adjacent to the Canary-Islands; but, owing to the want of seasonable rains, the produce of the latter is not rapid or abundant, although the quality is excellent. It has been suggested, that the orchilla was probably the Gertulian purple of the ancients; a conjecture which is strengthened by the fact, that the coast of Africa, where the orchilla abounds, was formerly called Gertulia. That the vivid dye which resides in this weed was known to the ancients, does not admit of any doubt.

The plant belongs to the class Cryptogamia, and order Algae, of the Linnean system, and to the class Algae, and order Lichenes, of the natural system. Professor Burnett, in his Outline of Botany, informs us, that "Roccella, a corruption of the Portuguese Rocha, is a name given to several species of lichen, in allusion to the situation in which they are found; delighting to grow on otherwise barren seaward rocks, that thus produce a profitable harvest. Tournefort considers that one species at least (R. tinctoria) was known to the ancients, and that it was the especial lichen (Greek: leichaen) of Dioscorides, which was collected on the rocky islands of the Archipelago, from one of which it received the name of the 'purple of Amorgus.'"

Of all the known varieties of orchilla, that which is grown in the Canary Islands stands the highest in estimation, and brings the greatest price. In the collection of the weed, which is always performed by the natives, the risk is imminent: they are obliged to be suspended by ropes over the cliffs, many of which are of stupendous height, and loss of life frequently occurs in these perilous efforts to contribute to the luxury of man. Such is the esteem in which the orchilla of the Canaries is held, that it has recently reached the enormous value of 400l. per ton. That from the Cape de Verds is next in quality, but of much greater importance, in reference to the quantity produced. Madeira and the Azores produce the next qualities. The same plant, though of a very inferior character, is found in great abundance in Sardinia, in some parts of Italy, and also on the south coast of England, Portland Island, Guernsey, &c. but of so poor a kind that it would not reward the expense of collection.

The original mode of preparing orchilla, that which was practised by the ancients, is said to have been lost, and many chemical experiments exhausted in vain for its recovery. In 1300, however, it was rediscovered by a Florentine merchant, and from that period preserved as a profound secret, by the Florentines and the Dutch. It appears that the Florentines were not satisfied with keeping the preparation of orchilla a mystery from the rest of the world, but that they endeavoured to lead all inquiry into a false channel, by calling it tincture of turnsole, desiring it to be believed, that it was an extract from the heliotropium or turnsole: the Dutch also disguised it in the form of a paste, which they called *lacmus* or *litmus*. The process is now, however, generally known, and simply consists of cleaning, drying, and powdering the plant, which, when mixed with half its weight of pearl ash, is moistened with human urine, and then allowed to ferment: the fermentation, we are informed by Professor Burnett, "is kept up for some time by successive additions of urine, until the colour of the materials changes to a purplish-red, and subsequently to a violet or blue. The colour is extremely fugitive, and affords a very delicate chemical test for the presence of an acid. The vapour of sulphuric acid has been thus detected as pervading to some extent the atmosphere of London."

I understand—and for some valuable particulars I here beg to tender my acknowledgments to Mr. John Aylwin, merchant of London—that the great object obtained from this vegetable dye, is the production of a red colour, without the aid of a mineral acid. But the utility of the orchilla is not confined to the purposes of manufacture. It has been successfully employed as a medicine in allaying the cough attendant on phthisis, and in hysterical coughs. It is also variously used in many productions, where its splendid hue can be rendered available, and imparts a beautiful bloom to cloths and silks.

The introduction of the weed into England came originally through the Portuguese. The Cape de Verd Islands having long been a possession of the crown of Portugal, orchilla became a royal monopoly, and was transmitted in considerable quantities to Lisbon, where it was sold by public auction; from Lisbon it gradually found its way to England, France, Germany, &c. The recent political contest in Portugal, caused a total suspension of the shipment of orchilla at the islands. About six months ago, there were two cargoes at Bona Vista waiting for orders, one of them (a vessel of about 66 tons) put to sea, and arrived safe at Lisbon only a few weeks before Admiral Napier's naval victory. When the news of the result of that battle reached the island, the holders of the remaining cargo proposed to hand it over for a consideration to certain parties in the interest of Donna Maria, and it was accordingly consigned to a Portuguese house in London. The vessel in which it was sent was called the Saint Anne, of 60 tons, and sailed under British colours: the cargo consisted of 564 bags, [8] each containing 2 cwt., and the whole sold for 15,000£. I mention this circumstance as an occurrence worth being recorded; the arrival of a vessel to England direct from the islands being a great novelty, accounted for, in this instance, by the political events which threw the trade out of its regular channels.

The principal manufactories of orchilla in England are London and Liverpool, but there are many others in different parts of the country. The chief manufacturers are Messrs. Henry Holmes and Sons of Liverpool, and Mr. Samuel Preston Child of London. The manufactured orchilla is frequently shipped to Germany, Holland, &c. in its fluid state, with a small proportion of weed in each cask for the satisfaction of the purchasers. The inferior qualities of the weed, and also a variety of mosses that have the same properties as the orchilla, only in a minor degree, are dried and ground to a fine powder, which is denominated cudbear, and is applicable to the same purposes as the weed itself.[9]

It is a curious illustration of the importance that is attached to the weed generally, and to the weed of the Canaries in particular, that, within the last twenty years, the latter production was considered in London as a remittance

---

[8] The bags in which the weed of the Cape de Verds is packed, are marked with the initials of the island of which it is the produce, and indicative of its quality which is at all times uniform.

[9] A regular trade with Sweden for moss has been long established. A variety of mosses, different in their growth, but all producing the colour found in orchilla, are to be met with on the hills and rocky places, at a distance from the sea, in every country where the weed itself is indigenous.

equivalent to specie, and was invariably quoted in the usual channels of commercial intelligence with the price of gold and silver, thus:—

Doubloons	per ounce
Dollars	ditto
Orchilla Weed	per ton

A bark called the Cape Packet, bound on a whaling voyage in the Pacific, arrived and sailed again to-day. Our consort the Diadem transport arrived this afternoon, and sailed the following evening, being *Saturday 25th.*

Sunday, August 26th.—The Consul General, with his wife and sister, came on board to attend divine service, and pass the remainder of the day.

Monday, 27th.—Very fine weather. At 7 in the morning, I accompanied the Rev. Mr. Davy to pass the day with the Consul's family. A bark from England, bound to the Cape of Good Hope, anchored in the roads to-day. A brig, loaded with timber, bound from Sierra Leone to England, was cast away on this island some time since, and the wreck was purchased by our Consul. He accordingly made an agreement with some people for the purpose of having it broken up, with the understanding that he was to retain the copper bolts, and they were to have the wood for their labour. I fear that this did not prove a good speculation on the side of the Consul, as he found it necessary to be nearly always on the spot, from a very reasonable suspicion that the workmen would steal some of his bolts. It is not unlikely, that so great an exposure to the sun as this occasioned him, had no small share in predisposing him for the fever that afterwards attacked him.

The cause of so much fever at St. Jago, may be traced to the peculiar situation of the town, which stands on an elevation between low swampy grounds, the exhalations from which pass over it as they arise.

There are a great number of horses, horned cattle, goats, pigs, &c. bred here. There was formerly an extensive traffic in slaves carried on between these islands and the coast of Africa, which I was informed is not yet wholly abolished. The best anchorage among the Capede Verds is at St. Vincent's. What should prevent the Portuguese giving it up to us, so that we might form an establishment for any ships to call there, instead of going to St. Jago, where they so often make fever an accompaniment with their refreshments? His Majesty's ship Tweed, visited this place on her way to the Cape of Good Hope station, and a great proportion of the young officers who slept on shore, died within a fortnight afterwards.

The bay abounds with fine fish, yet there are not many taken, therefore the town is badly supplied, owing entirely to the indolence of the inhabitants.

At 5 in the afternoon we made sail out of Porto Praya, leaving it without regret, except what we felt in parting from the Consul and his family. There was also a Consul for the United States, but he was not on friendly terms with Mr. Clark. Their differences, however, were very soon settled by the great pacificator, death, for they were not long after interred near each other in the fort. Visiting the Portuguese was quite out of the question, as very few of them had the power of entertaining strangers, excepting one old woman known by the name of English Mary, and she was well paid for her civilities. She could give you a sort of dinner with bad wine, bad spirits, and fruit. You could also get your things badly washed here, that is, wetted and well beaten for money. The Portuguese troops vary from black to white, with all the intermediate shades, in ragged party-coloured clothing: but a truce with the Colonial Portuguese:—I am now bound to an English colony, where I fear I shall not find every thing as it ought to be, and that is Sierra Leone, which bears from Porto Praya about S.E. by E. 1/2 E. 720 miles.

P.S. The port charges at St. Jago are not heavy, as they do not exceed sixteen dollars for a vessel of any size or nation.

CHAP. III.

Arrival at Sierra Leone—Mr. Lewis—Black Washerwomen—Visitors on
board—Capture of Leopards—Mortality—Funeral of Mr. Lewis—
Education of Native Children—Regimental Mess—Curious Trials at a
Quarter Sessions—Depredations of the Kroo-men—Causes of
Unhealthiness—The Boollam Territory—Lieut. George Maclean's
Mission—Election of a King—Regent's Speech—Macaulay Wilson—
Ceremonies of the Coronation—Character of the Boollams—Christian
and Mahommedan Missionaries—Aspect of the Country—Cession of
Boollam to Great Britain—Extraordinary Trial for Crim. Con.—News of
the Death of Mr. Canning

Saturday, September 1st, 1827.—There was a moderate breeze from the S.W.
and fine weather to-day. At noon, lat. 9° 20' N. lon. 16° 6' W. Cape Sierra Leone
S. 73° E. 173 miles. Imagining that I was avoiding a lady who was intentionally
advancing to address me on the quarter deck to-day, I stepped back and
measured my length across the gunroom skylight, which, fortunately for me, had
a piece of wood lengthways in the middle of it, to rest the sashes on, or I must
have paid the officers a visit in their mess-room in a very unceremonious
manner; I had however the good luck to escape with a slight bruise.

Sunday, 2d.—At six in the morning we got soundings in 50 fathoms of water,
and at eight in 29 fathoms. Lat. 8° 29' N. lon. 13° 56' W. Cape Sierra Leone S.
81° E. distant thirty-six miles. At three in the afternoon we saw the land, and at
the same time a schooner, (which we afterwards learned was the Joseph and
Mary from Sierra Leone bound to England.) Soon after this we saw the brig Ark
coming out of the harbour of Sierra Leone, which returned into port on the 7th,
and sailed again on the 14th of the same month. This brig had the Aid-de-camp
of the late Sir Neil Campbell on board, who died nearly three weeks before our
arrival, and this officer was the bearer of despatches relating to Sir Neil
Campbell's death, &c. Shortly before midnight we anchored off the town of
Sierra Leone in 14-1/2 fathoms water, and found that our consort the Diadem
transport had arrived only a few hours, although she left St. Jago three days
before we started. We had not any visitors from the shore that night, in
consequence of the lateness of the hour at which we came to anchor; but we had
a great number on the following day to make up for it.

Monday, September 3rd.—At 7 in the morning Mr. Lewis, the agent; victualler,
came on board to see Captain Owen, and some of his old friends, whom he had
previously known on board H.M. ship Leven. This gentleman, however, had
another motive for coming on board at so early an hour; he had felt unwell for
several days, and having boasted a good deal about his infallible method of
keeping off the fever, namely, by the use of brandy and water and cigars, he did
not choose to apply to any medical man on shore, knowing that the
circumstance would be immediately spread among his acquaintances; he
therefore applied to the surgeon of the Eden for some medicines, which of

course he obtained; but mark the result—on that day week the officers of the ship were invited to attend his funeral.

About 8 o'clock the ship was crowded with black women, who came on board to procure clothes for washing. Some brought a little fruit, and all brought a very long tongue, for there was such a clatter that it was almost impossible to catch one word that was said, and they clustered round our breakfast table without any ceremony, which was not very pleasant, in consequence of the variety of odours they carried with them, from the delightful one of fruits and flowers, to the broadly contrasted smells which I suppose were peculiar to their colour.

In the course of the forenoon Colonel Denham, Mr. Kenneth Macauley, and many other gentlemen, came on board to wait on Captain Owen, and the officers. We found that Colonel Lumley, the Commandant of the troops, had assumed the reins of government on the decease of Sir Neil Campbell, (August 14th) with the title of Lieutenant Governor. We learnt that the place was still very sickly, but the rainy season was drawing to a close, and sickness diminishing.

Tuesday, 4th.—The two previous days had for a wonder been fine, but the usual weather for the season returned to-day, namely, frequent and heavy showers, with a bright sun at intervals. Took a ride on horseback with Mr. Campbell before dinner, and afterwards dined with that gentleman, in company with Dr. Burn.

Mr. Campbell had two leopards, which he purchased with the intention of sending to England, secured in one of the out-buildings in his yard. They were brought from the Rio Pongas, about 80 miles to the northward of Sierra Leone, and were taken, near that river in the following manner:—Some black fellows having discovered a leopard's den, about a dozen of them, armed with muskets, placed themselves to watch the departure of the dam in quest of prey. When they went to examine it they found two young ones, not larger than good sized cats, which they immediately bagged, and conveyed to the town. They were soon followed by the dam, but she would not venture to attack so great a number of persons; she continued, however, to hover about the town for several weeks, before she despaired of recovering her young.

Wednesday, 5th.—Continued heavy rain in the morning, and showery throughout the day. We hired 30 Africans, called Kroomen, [10] who are always ready to serve as seamen on board of a man of war, or any other vessel, so long as they continue on that coast. They are usually entered as supernumeraries on the ship's books for provisions and wages, in the same manner as British seamen. They are employed on any service which would expose Europeans too

---

[10] Although these men are hired under the denomination of Kroo men, they are generally Kroo, and Fish men, who inhabit the country between Sierra Leone and our settlement of Cape Coast Castle.

much to the climate, such as wooding, watering, pulling in boats, &c. I shall hereafter give further particulars of these people, and their country.

Saturday, 8th.—I accompanied Mr. Macaulry, to wait on his honour, the Lieutenant Governor, Colonel Lumley, who continued in his Commandant's quarters at the barracks, situated on a hill, which at first rises gradually from the town, but becomes much steeper as you ascend. We then accompanied Captain Perry and Mr. Green to the regimental mess, where we lunched. It is worthy of remark, perhaps, that three out of four of these gentlemen, namely, the Lieutenant Governor, Mr. Macauley, and Mr. Green, whom I was in company with at the barracks this morning, died long before my return to England. Dined at Mr. Reffells, the acting Chief Justice, where there was a large party, consisting of the Lieutenant Governor, and all the principal official characters of the place, Captain Owen, &c.

Monday, 10th.—Notwithstanding the heavy rain to-day, a large party of the friends of the late Mr. Lewis, (agent victualler, who died last night at 11 o'clock,) assembled at his residence near King Tom's point, to witness his interment, under a large tree not far from the house. It was distressing to observe a favourite dog of the deceased gentleman howling about the grave of his late master. He offered so much resistance to those who attempted to remove him, that it was with great difficulty he could be prevented from throwing himself into the grave after it had received the coffin.

Mr. Miller, who was a volunteer serving for a commission in the Royal African Corps, died to-day from the effects of fever.

Tuesday 11th.—Some slight showers in the forepart of this day, and fine in the afternoon, when the Rev. Mr. Davy took me to visit a school for free black children under the charge of Mrs. Taylor, widow of a late missionary in this colony. Although this is but a day-school, there is a probability of its doing some good with all who attend it, and a great deal of service to a few. But it is in vain to attempt to civilize savage nations through the medium of book instruction alone. Previous habits exercise so powerful an influence over the mind, that the value of precept is hardly felt. The good impressions which arc made by the teacher in the morning, are obliterated by the example of ignorant parents in the evening; so that the result of an education imparted in this way, is merely to sharpen the natural cunning of youth, and give them an increased power of evil, by the fragments of information they thus acquire. If we would have our efforts to improve their condition, really effective, we should deal with them as with foundlings. They should be removed from the contagion of their former intercourse, and apprenticed out to persons who would look after their morals, and whore they would have no bad examples set them, so soon as they were capable of applying their faculties to objects of utility. The instances are very rare where these African children have fulfilled the expectations of their benevolent benefactors; I am persuaded that an establishment for a limited number, in which the end proposed should be the completion of the work of civilization, would be incalculably superior to the attempts to accomplish that desirable purpose with great numbers in so imperfect a manner.

Wednesday, Sept. 12th.—Heavy and frequent showers, from last evening till near noon to-day, when it cleared up, and continued fine all the afternoon. This forenoon, I accompanied Mr. Kenneth Macauley to the Court House, and attended the opening of the general quarter sessions. [11]

Friday, 14th.—Attended the Court to-day with Mr. Macauley, where I heard various cases of petty larceny. The morning was fine, but it became cloudy in the evening, and very dark with much lightning. The latter is a strong intimation of the expected tornadoes, with which the rainy season terminates, as well as commences. Captains Owen and Harrison, Lieutenant Woodman (agent for transports), and myself, dined with the Governor at his regimental mess. There were also present, all the principal officers of the civil establishment. Could our friends in England have witnessed the hilarity that prevailed at that banquet, in such a country, and at that melancholy season of the year, they would have scarcely credited what they saw and heard. Many who were seated there on that day, are now no more! The assistant surgeon of the North Star, who was serving on hoard a schooner, that was tender to that ship, died to-day. His death was supposed to have been much accelerated by the gloomy apprehensions that entered his mind from the moment he was seized with the fever.

Saturday, 15th.—Attended the Court, and heard some amusing trials for house-breaking, and stealing therefrom; in one case there were Kroomen against Kroomen:—Tom Coffee and Bottle of Beer—against another Bottle of Beer.

Sunday, 16th.—Very fine day. Accompanied the Rev. Mr. Davy on board the Eden, whore he performed divine service: after which we dined with Captain Owen, and returned on shore in the evening, when I accompanied him to a chapel in the parish of St. George's, Freetown, where he performed the evening service. There are a great number of Independent chapels in the town, supported by the free black population, and with black preachers. I unfortunately witnessed a trial in the Court, that did not redound much to the credit of one of these preachers. As it is very novel, and not a little amusing in its way, I think I cannot do better than to give, in its proper place, the opening speech on the day it occurred, as delivered in the Court by the plaintiff's counsel, who was a black gentleman. It was the first cause of the kind that ever was tried in this colony, where morality does not appear to be so highly appreciated as in some countries of Europe.

Monday, 17th.—Very fine warm day. I attended the Court as usual to-day; and heard two trials of the same nature as most of the others; distinguished also by the same difficulty of obtaining the truth from most of the witnesses, who are quite indifferent to the responsibility of an oath, because they have no qualms of conscience; but if their priests were to fetish them, it is probable they might be

---

[11] There were only nineteen prisoners in the calendar, one of whom was a soldier, Patrick Riley, for a desperate attempt to murder a serjeant with his bayonet. The rest of the prisoners were principally Kroomcn, and other black fellows, for house-breaking, stealing, &c. &c.

induced to give their testimony more honestly. Sentence was this day awarded to all the prisoners that had been tried, as follows:—

> John Rhode, a native of the Rio Pongas, for petty larceny.
> Grando, a Krooman, for assault.
> Yellow Will, a Krooman, for receiving stolen goods. [12]
> Peter, a Krooman, for stealing from a dwelling-house.
> John Testing, a discharged soldier, for ditto.
> Jim Johnson, a liberated African, for grand larceny.
> Ben Kroo, a Krooman, for ditto.
> Jack Freeman, a Krooman, for receiving stolen goods.
> John Freeman, a Krooman, for ditto.

Several other prisoners found "not guilty," were discharged by proclamation, and the sentence on Patrick Riley, a private soldier in the Royal African Colonial Corps, for maliciously stabbing with intent to murder, was respited on the motion of counsel, until a reference should be made as to the application to this colony, of the statute under which he was indicted;—the 43rd Geo. III. cap. 58th, commonly called Lord Ellenborough's Act.

It is some gratification to know, that, notwithstanding these sessions have been unusually heavy, still, that out of 19 prisoners in the calendar, only two were liberated Africans, although this class of persons forms nine-tenths of the community of the colony, and that but one of them was found guilty; whereas, the time of the Court was taken up with the crimes committed by Kroomen, 13 of whom were tried for various offences. The evidence disclosed in these cases, afforded the strongest grounds for the measure now in progress for reducing the number of such strangers, by sending all above 600 from the colony; and more particularly what are termed headmen. These fellows, who perform no kind of work, it would seem, from what transpired in two or three of the robberies brought to light before the public on this occasion, live on the labour, and proceeds of plunder, obtained by the younger hands, who first leave their country under the protection of these headmen, and who are the mere instruments of this privileged class, contenting themselves with planning the felonies committed by their dependants, and thus generally escaping the consequences of detection; while, at the same time, they *alone* benefit in the pecuniary advantages of this criminal course of life. The organization of professional criminals, and the presence of the principle of co-operation amongst rogues, who live by the commission of a variety of depredations on society, are not confined to such places as London and Paris. The schemes and resources of the headmen, considering the limits and differently constituted sphere of their operations, are quite as admirable as those of the more practised thieves of the modern Babylon.

---

[12] In these cases the principal felons remained unknown.

Tuesday, September 18th.—About one o'clock this morning, we had a violent tornado, which we had expected, from the frequent lightning of the last four or five days; also, from the near approach of the termination of the rainy season. The morning was very fresh and clear after it; but, in the afternoon, it became cloudy and close. Burglaries are frequently committed by the Kroomen in Sierra Leone, under cover of the storm, it being a favourable time, from the difficulty of hearing their operations, as well as from the disinclination the inhabitants feel to go out in such heavy rain and wind, to examine their stores and out-houses.

Wednesday, 19th.—Heavy rain from last evening till nine this morning. Attended the Court, where I heard the trial of an action brought by a house-carpenter against the executors of an estate, for work, forming part of a contract that he had made with the late Tascoe Williams, Esq.; the executors objecting to pay any part, because the whole of the contract had not been performed, although it appeared, that he was ready, but they were not willing, that he should complete it: a verdict was, of course, given for the carpenter.

At three in the afternoon, I accompanied Capt. Owen to dine with Capt. Arabin, on board the North Star, which was to sail for the Gambia on the following day, taking a detachment of the Royal African Corps thither, under the command of Lieutenant Nott. There was, at one period, so much sickness at Sierra Leone, that this young man (then an ensign) was the COMMANDING OFFICER IN BARRACKS!

Thursday, September 20th.—Very fine weather. Accompanied Mr. Macauley in a ride on horseback, through the grass-field, to a village called Portuguese Town, and round Barrack Hill, passing the new, and afterwards the old burying-ground, &c. The grass-field is said to be that part of Sierra Leone, which is the principal cause of the unhealthiness of the town, it being, in heavy rains, partly covered with water; however, there are other causes in addition to this, that are said to contribute to the unhealthiness of the place. One of these is a belt of wood on the hill above the town; which must considerably impede the current of air, and, if this was cleared and cultivated, it would greatly improve the salubrity of the place; but, I fear, the greatest evil of all is insurmountable, under existing circumstances, as it is not within the control of the colonists. This is the low marshy land that lies on the other side of the bay, and directly opposite the town, called the Boollam shore, where a friend of mine (Lieutenant George Maclean, Royal African Corps, who is, at present, at the head of the Council at Cape Coast) went a few months before my arrival, on an important mission from the Governor of Sierra Leone, to be present at, and thereby countenance and confirm their choice in, the election of a king.

The origin of the connection between our colony at Sierra Leone, and the natives of the Boollam territory is very interesting, and will form an appropriate introduction to a sketch of Lieutenant Maclean's visit during the election of a King.

In the year 1804, the colony of Sierra Leone was attacked by the Native Powers, and a body of blacks to the northward of the Boollam territories was put in motion for the purpose of assisting the other native tribes in overwhelming the white population at Freetown. The King, or Chief of the North, (or, as they call themselves, the Sherbro Boollams,) who has since been known by the name of King George, and through whose territories the hostile tribes must needs pass, being a firm ally of the King of Great Britain, declared that on no account whatever would he permit them to pass through his country to attack a British settlement: and he carried his point so effectually as to render the expedition fruitless. In consequence of the determined and friendly conduct of this Prince, a deputation of whites from Freetown was despatched to him, with an invitation to visit Sierra Leone, which invitation he accepted. While at Freetown, he was crowned with all solemnity by the name of King George. He continued on the most amicable terms with the Government of Sierra Leone until his death, which took place the 19th of May, 1826, at the advanced age, it is said, of upwards of one hundred years, a point which it would be difficult to ascertain accurately, as these people are entirely ignorant of their own ages. Since this period the throne of the Boollams has been vacant; it being now, however, the intention of the people to proceed to the choice of a King, according to their custom; and it being deemed of considerable importance from the vicinity of Boollam to Sierra Leone, that a person should be elected who was known to be friendly to the English settlement, it was determined by his Excellency the Governor that a person should be sent as a commissioner to be present at the election and coronation; whose duty it should be to support the claims and secure the election of a person known to the English by the name of Macaulay Wilson, who, being a near relation of the late King George, and having been educated in England, being also a man of considerable abilities, was deemed in every way worthy of the throne.

The election of Macaulay Wilson having been accomplished, it would then become the duty of the Commissioner, on the part of the English Government to use every means in his power to induce the new King, with the numerous chiefs and head men, to accede to, and sign, a convention, whereby the sovereignty of Boollam was to be ceded to the King of Great Britain, under certain limitations and restrictions specified in the treaty. The attainment of this point, would, of course, be attended with great difficulty; but it had become of the utmost importance for the suppression of the slave trade that the attempt should be made; for slave dealers who were actually carrying on their traffic in Freetown, upon the least alarm, removed to Boollam with their unfortunate victims, and being then out of British territory were in perfect security. The following is Lieutenant Maclean's personal narrative of his mission.

"*Yougroo, Boollam, March 3rd, 1827.*

"I left Freetown tins morning in the Government barge, with Mr. S. (a person appointed to accompany me as interpreter) and arrived in the course of the evening at the Boollam shore. On landing I proceeded to Yougroo, called by the late King, George Town, where I was received by the King *(esse)*, by Dalmahoumedii, a powerful Mandingo chief, with a number of other chiefs, and headmen.

"There was a very good house (constructed after the country fashion) assigned us as a place of residence. After taking possession, I was visited by the different chiefs and head men, who came to pay their respects, or, as they phrase it, to do service to me, as representing the Governor of Sierra Leone. These consisted principally of Boollam chiefs, who had seldom left their own country; and a few, notwithstanding their vicinity to a white colony, who had scarce ever seen a white man before. There were, also, not a few Mandingo chiefs, who had acquired property and influence in Boollam, and which was daily increasing. These Mandingoes are possessed of considerable intelligence and great cunning, by which means, and by the genius of their religion (Mahommedan), they invariably, though gradually, acquire the superiority over the native rulers of those countries in which they choose to settle. In Boollam this was becoming very apparent; and as the Mandingo chiefs are all either covertly or openly, supposed to be engaged in the slave trade, and consequently opposed to the English Government, I was instructed particularly to guard against, and to oppose their interest in the election of the King. Dalmahoumedii, whom I mentioned above, is the principal Mandingo chief in Boollam, and is by far the best informed man that I had seen here. He is even well conversant in European politics. He is a man of large property, and has a town of his own, called Madina, inhabited entirely by Mandingoes.

"For the ground-rent of this town and neighbourhood, he pays a nominal duty to the king of the Boollams, as his superior, although, in fact, his power and influence in the country is nearly equal to the king's own. On the day of my arrival, he sent me, ready cooked, in the European style, an excellent dinner, of which I, of course, could not do less than ask him to partake. Although a Mahommedan, he drank wine freely, in compliment, as he said, to me, although I could perceive that he enjoyed it exceedingly. He told me, in the course of conversation (carried on principally through an interpreter) that he had, at that time, no fewer than 85 wives. His brother, who had died some time previously, left 75 wives, all of whom he was entitled, by the custom of his country, to have married; he told me, however, that he only chose 45 of them, all of whom he wedded in one day. In the evening a number of these ladies favoured us with their company, some of whom were very fine women. They also seemed to drink their wine with great relish.

"Rejoicings commenced at sunset, and continued during the whole night. I had a guard of honour placed over my residence, to prevent intrusion during the night; which, however, I found it impossible to prevent altogether, as during the election and coronation of a king, the laws 'sleep,' nor can any crime, short of murder or an attempt to murder, be punished during that space of time, which generally extends to 14 or 16 days. The natural consequence of this is, that all the most idle and worthless of the neighbouring nations, or tribes, flock to a place where they can practise all manner of crimes with impunity. Many persons, particularly minstrels, or bards, had walked upwards of 400 miles from the interior, to be present at the election about to take place at Yougroo.

"The town of Yougroo, I was told, generally contained but about 500 or 600 inhabitants, although, during the election, &c. there must have been, at least, 5000 or 6000 persons present.

"The mourners for the deceased king, of whom there are 16 in number, are the most extraordinary figures that can possibly be conceived. One half of their faces (the upper half) is painted white, forming a hideous contrast with their black countenances. The mourners (literally 'makers of the cry,' i.e. lament) are appointed immediately on the death of the king, [13] and continue their functions until the election of a new king takes place, however long it may be before that event may happen. They are generally girls of from ten to fourteen years of age, and are, while mourners, held sacred and inviolate.

"*Sunday, March 4th.*—This day was appointed for the formal election of a successor to the throne of King George. By noon, the whole of the chiefs and headmen were assembled in the Palaver House, when the Regent, or person appointed to administer the government during the *interregnum*, proposed, in a speech of some length, John Macaulay Wilson to be the future King of the Boollams. Previous to this, a deputation had been sent requesting my presence. I accordingly attended in full dress, along with Mr. S———. The Regent's speech, as literally translated by my interpreter, and immediately after noted down by me, was as follows:—

"'We have now met, headmen and brethren, to perform a great duty, and to exercise a great privilege. It becomes our duty to elect a successor to our vacant throne, "the cry" (i.e. the mourning) being about to close. We have now no king; if we look to his hearth, there is no one there; if we call upon our king, no one answers; thus are we, as children without a father; as a family without a head; whom then shall we choose to sit in

---

[13] King George was the first king of Boollam, that had been allowed to die a natural death, through fear of getting 'a palaver,' as they term it, with Sierra Leone. Previous to this, they always despatched their kings when they considered them about to expire, sacrificing two human victims, whom they buried in the same grave.

the seat of our late venerable king? Who shall walk in the footsteps of him, whose sayings were the sayings of wisdom, and out of whose mouth proceeded justice: whom, I say, shall we elect, but his own son[14], who listened to him when alive, and who will not forget him now that he is dead?

"'You have long known this person; and you know that he will not bring disgrace upon your choice; but that he will do those things which a King of the Boollams ought to do; that he will discourage wickedness, encourage the righteous, and do justice to all men; I therefore propose that John Macaulay Wilson be elected King of the Boollams.' [15] The speaker of the above was an old man, highly respected by all classes, named, 'Nain Banna.' It becomes his duty, immediately on the king's death, to assume the government as Regent; he is, however, on that account ineligible for the throne.

"After some conversation among the chiefs, consisting principally of tributes of praise to the late king, it was formerly announced to me, 'that John Macaulay Wilson was elected King of the Boollams:—that he held the Boollam Country in the palm of his hand:—and that the scales of justice hung upon his finger,' I was also entreated to report to his Excellency the Governor of Sierra Leone, the choice they had made, and their hopes that it would meet with his approbation. The people expecting that I should address them, I rose, and by my interpreter, said, 'that I should not fail to report to my master, His Excellency the Governor of Sierra Leone, the good order and unanimity which had prevailed in the assembly; that I had no doubt but His Excellency would approve of the object of their choice that day; that from what I had heard of their new king, I had no doubt, but that he would justify the confidence they had placed in him; and I trusted that the same good sense and attention to the true interests of their country, which they had shewn that day, would guide all their future deliberations. In conclusion, I begged leave to congratulate them, on having chosen such a ruler; and to congratulate their king, on the distinction that day conferred upon him.'

"The day closed as usual with every manner of licentiousness.

---

[14] Meaning that the late king loved him as a son.

[15] It is but right to state, that the above speech was read over sentence by sentence, to the person who spoke it, and that he deemed it to be almost literally reported, and seemed much astonished that it could have been taken down.

"*Monday, March 5th.*—This being the day appointed for the inauguration of the new king, it was ushered in with the firing of musketry and other demonstrations of joy. At 10 A.M. the chiefs and headmen assembled, and immediately proceeded to the performance of certain mysteries, which take place in the depths of the bush; and to which the initiated only are admitted.

"At noon they emerged from the bush, having the new king with them; whom they now regarded as a complete stranger, providentially sent them from heaven to be their ruler.

"A deputation now requested my presence at the Palaver House, to which they were then conducting the king; the headmen and people dancing around him, as he passed through the streets, in the most fantastic manner. On my arrival the late Regent pronounced a very long harangue in the Boollam language, which was repeated sentence by sentence in the Mandingo and English by the respective interpreters. In this speech, which however I did not note down, Nain Banna rehearsed what had from time immemorial been the practice of the Boollams, in cases such as the present, and declared that all the rites and mysteries proper for the occasion, had been duly performed. He then pronounced a long encomium on the virtues of their late king, and concluded by paying his respects to the new king, and myself, respectively, which he ended with the highest term of respect which the Boollams know:— 'May you live for ever.'

"He then requested permission to introduce to the assembly, a stranger whom they were in future to revere, 'King Bey Sherbro;' [16] after which, Bey Sherbro received the homage of his subjects. During this time a number of minstrels played upon their several instruments, some of which were very ingenious and musical. Those in particular, who had come a long distance from the interior, executed with spirit and taste some very beautiful airs; much finer, indeed, than any native music I had yet heard. They accompanied their instruments with extempore recitatives in praise of those chiefs whom they knew. I was, of course, included, as they expected that I would be inclined to reward them handsomely. Each minstrel of any repute had a person attached to him by way of fool or jester, several of whom acted their parts very well, and strongly reminded me of Shakspeare's clowns.

"Dalmahoumedii was in the assembly, surrounded by a number of followers, but he appeared to feel that he had lost ground. He took no part in the proceedings.

---

[16] The new appellation of John Macaulay Wilson.

"If it were fair to estimate the character of a people, by their conduct during a period of unbounded license, I should say that they were generally, almost universally, a nation of thieves, idlers, and drunkards. It was with difficulty, indeed, I could preserve my own private stock of wines, &c. I was assured, however, that such is not their general character, although they are, no doubt, like all Africans, extremely indolent and attached to the old customs of their country. To even the most absurd and superstitious of these, they cling with such tenacity, that it would be a work of incalculable labour, and of many years, to induce them to abandon them altogether, even after they should be made conscious of their absurdity and barbarity. The European Missionaries of the present day would never do it. It was attempted some years ago with much zeal, but there is not at this moment, I believe, a single convert to Christianity in Boollam, to reward the labour, or repay the expense, which was lavished on that object. But a very different success has attended the efforts of the disciples of Mahommed in propagating the doctrines of the crescent. Not only in Boollam, but in all the neighbouring districts; even in the Peninsula of Sierra Leone itself, there are twenty converts to the crescent, for one to the cross; and the reason is obvious; the Christian Missionaries begin at the wrong end; they insist upon first making people Christians, and then morality and civilization, they say, follow as matters of course: and they present Christianity in its most inattractive form, to men accustomed to the uncontrollable indulgence of their passions. The Mahommedans know the genius of the people better, and without altering the spirit of their religion, they exhibit it in a manner exactly suited to that genius, as far as regards externals; and in such a form, that the adoption of it even flatters the vanity of the convert. Thus, in the article of dress, the Mahommedans have a peculiar or distinguishing cap; to be entitled to wear which, is, in itself, a matter very flattering to the vanity of the young worshipper of the crescent; and I am convinced, that were it incumbent upon Christians to wear in public a red cross on the shoulder or hat, that it would be the means of drawing many to listen to the doctrines of Christianity: and really I can see no sin in the means thus adopted.

"This evening I despatched the barge to Sierra Leone, with an account of our progress, and requesting the Convention to be immediately transmitted, together with the usual presents to be given to the new King and chiefs. In the mean time every measure was taken, and argument used (with occasional presents), to induce the chiefs and headmen to consent to the cession of the sovereignty of the country to Great Britain.

"*Tuesday, March 6th.*—This morning I walked out to make a few observations, and to form some idea of the capabilities of the Boollam country. What struck me, in the first instance, was the great fertility, and natural beauty of the surrounding country, which it was really painful to contrast with the extreme ignorance and indolence of its inhabitants. There is not, perhaps, a country under Heaven more calculated to repay the exertions of industry, from the richness and fertility of the soil; as also from the flatness of the country, which would prevent the soil from being carried away by the rains when cleared of the bush. It is in my opinion far more adapted for agricultural purposes than the Sierra Leone side of the bay. Spices of almost every description grow naturally and in abundance; and it would require but little capital, with industry, to make the soil produce sugar, coffee, tobacco, and indigo in great plenty. In short, the produce of the Boollam country might, without very great labour be made to rival that of either our East or West India possessions, in fact almost every article imported into Great Britain from either is indigenous to this soil. The indolent and lazy natives, however, cultivate little excepting rice. The articles procured from the British settlement at Sierra Leone, such as fire-arms, gunpowder, tobacco, rum, &c. are got in exchange for timber, and occasionally labour.

"During my residence in Boollam, it frequently struck me, that a British Settlement on the Boollam coast would be highly desirable, say at Madina. For the reasons stated above, I am almost certain that practical agriculture would soon become prevalent, inasmuch as it would soon become profitable. Another, and a very strong inducement to settlers would be, that Madina, and indeed the whole range of the Boollam coast, is very healthy. What is called the *country fever* in Sierra Leone, is scarcely known in Boollam.

"To-day five or six of the mourners came to do service to me, which they performed by bending their heads to the earth, and, in that position, moaning in a low tone the praises of the deceased King, mixed with compliments to myself.

"At midnight I received letters from Sierra Leone, by which I had the satisfaction of learning that His Excellency approved of my measures.

"*Wednesday, March 7th.*—This day I succeeded in removing the numberless evasions and objections urged by the chiefs against the treaty.

"In effecting this measure Mr. S——'s exertions were of the greatest service.

"In the evening we were a good deal amused by the natives fishing on the beach. They caught a great number of fish, such as snappers, cat-fish, soles, sharks, &c.

"*Thursday 8th.*—This day the convention arrived, and the blanks being filled up, and the treaty solemnly signed and ratified, I had the satisfaction on *Friday, March 9th, 1827*, of hoisting the British flag, and of taking possession of Boollam in the name of His Britannic Majesty."

Such is the narrative of Lieutenant Maclean, respecting a people whose habits are as peculiar as his account of them must be interesting to Englishmen.

September 21st, 1827.—On this day I attended the Court, to hear the trial to which I have already alluded. It was a case of adultery, and the parties were all free blacks. The action was brought by a carpenter against the Rev. Samuel Thorpe, a preacher at one of the Independent chapels, for criminal conversation with his wife; and, as I have a copy from the records of the Court, I think it will be much more satisfactory to insert the document in full, than to supersede it by any desultory remarks of my own. It will give a clear and characteristic idea of the state of society amongst these people. The occurrence was so unusual, that it created no small astonishment, that such a case should be brought into Court. The following is the address of the plaintiff's counsel, and the verdict.

BERNARD *v.* THORPE.

"Gentlemen of the Jury,

"I bespeak your attention and indulgence. I am not only this day the advocate of my client, but I am lending my humble efforts to defend, perhaps I ought to say, assert, the divine right and sacredness of the social compact of marriage, the palladium of every married man's family, happiness and comfort. I will remind you, gentlemen of the jury, that this is the first action of the kind that has been tried on these boards since the colony has been ceded to the British crown.—Among you, gentlemen of the jury, I see fathers, brothers, and husbands, to all I appeal this day on behalf of my client, and of this colony. Shew the world this day, by your verdict, that you will not suffer with impunity the foul crime of adultery to be committed in the face of a rising family; shew the value in which you hold the solemn engagements of your female relatives; let your verdict warn the seducer that he dare not trespass on any man's honour, or blight with apathy, for one moment, any pleasure or gratification of his conjugal tenderness.

"It has been too common in actions of this kind, for the defendant to treat with contumely the humble situation of the injured prosecutor. I do not apprehend much from any such attempt in this cause. I acknowledge, gentlemen, that my client is a very humble individual, but he is a respectable and an honest man, by trade a carpenter. I see, gentlemen, on your countenances, that his humble lot shall not deprive him from having his happiness considered as dear to him as to any man, and equally inviolate; for you need not be told, that the comforts and happiness of the rich and the poor originate from one source: as it is not necessary to be rich to feel with acuteness the pain to which our weak frames are subject, or to enjoy with zest the most pleasurable sensations, so the poor possess the same advantages; indeed, it is the poor to whom family happiness must be the greatest solace! the rich have various resources to derive comfort from; the poor seldom more than centres in their family. But before I attempt to describe to you the sufferings of my client, I shall enter rather minutely into the actual situation in life in which the plaintiff and defendant in this action are placed: if unnecessary to some of you, yet there may be others who naturally demand this explanation should be given; I trust this will be admitted as my apology.

"I will begin with the defendant; because, indeed, gentlemen, he is the more highly favoured man; I mean, gentlemen, that Providence has blessed him with a much greater share of this world's goods; he is known to man by the solemn designation of the Rev. Samuel Thorpe; yes, gentlemen, the defendant in this action, for criminal conversation with the wife of my client, is, or very lately was, a preacher of morality; an expounder of that divine doctrine which inculcates the precept, 'Do unto others, as you would have others do unto you;' he is a gentleman, who, beholding with horror the degeneracy of the times, and believing, no doubt, it required some extraordinary exertions to recall us unto virtue, has voluntarily, for no idea of gain, or means of livelihood, publicly devoted his talents to the pulpit. Such conduct, if we had not other most opposite circumstances to disclose, would have called forth our admiration and applause; for, gentlemen, the pulpit, in the sober use of its legitimate peculiar powers, must stand acknowledged, while the world shall stand,

"The most important and effectual guard,
Support and ornament of virtue's cause.

"The defendant, gentlemen, is also a rich man; he is, to say the least, in very easy circumstances; we see, in this colony, several valuable possessions of his; and we behold, at one of his houses, a store from which is retailed valuable merchandise. The defendant, gentlemen, I am instructed to say, is verging towards the decline of life; to have arrived at those years, when the hey-day of the blood might well be expected to have gone by, and that, while he preached morality, he would find no constitutional impediment to prevent his practising it. I am persuaded, gentlemen, that, if a cause of the present nature had been brought before you, in which the defendant had been a young unmarried man, you would have made some allowance for the infatuation of his youthful passions; but when, as in the present instance, we find experienced age; the well-informed man; the promulger of that divine law, which denounces everlasting punishment to the adulterer, is brought before you, charged, although a married man, with this offence, I feel I must, indeed, commit an act of injustice to you all, if I did not declare, that, in such a case, I am convinced your feeling's cannot be otherwise than aroused to visit such a criminal with your vengeance.

"My instructions suggest to me more than I will utter; yet, I must confess, that I have been struck with the sacred profession of the defendant, and the pertinacity with which it appears he committed the offence against my client, for which you are now called upon to award him the only remuneration the law allows; I cannot refrain from asserting my belief, that the defendant's feelings must have been strangely perverted; he, doubtless, made his full calculation upon his outward profession, and his inward inclinations, and, I believe, I do him no more than justice, when I put into his mouth, and suppose by him uttered in his private moments, the expression used by an arch hypocrite of former days:

> "I sigh, and with a piece of scripture,
> Tell them God bids us do good for evil:
> And thus I clothe my naked villany
> With odds and ends stol'n forth of Holy Writ;
> And seem a saint, when most I play the devil.

"I regret, very much regret, gentlemen of the jury, I am thus obliged as a faithful advocate before you; but I have still another feature to disclose, and here I must declare, that it has astonished me more than I shall attempt to describe. I alluded before, gentlemen, to the circumstance of the defendant's being a married man. Yes! He has a wife living in Freetown, whom (from fear she should take a right from his substance) he has turned out upon the world! to the generosity—the kindness—of the stranger! surely we may infer that he may be left at home with more ample means to gratify his passions. He has also no children; this I am sorry for on his account; surely he would have paused before he would have offered them such an example; before he would systematically set about the seduction of a woman, surrounded even by her grand-children.

"I turn now to my client; but, indeed, I have little more to add respecting him. He is poor, because he has many claims on his industry; his wife has born him several children; and some of these children are grown up, and married, and in their turn have children; the connexion between the plaintiff and his wife has therefore been of long standing, in fact on their entrance into life they became attached to each other. The connexion was not for several years sanctioned by the rites of our religion, but it was not less a marriage; the assent of the heart was complete, and it has been sanctioned by what the parties thought binding; further ceremony could only add more publicity to the engagement. Yet after many years mutual intercourse, they resolved to give that intercourse every tie, and were consequently legally married according to the rites of the Church of England. I mention these particulars because I apprehend my learned friend will set about pulling their family history to pieces, and endeavour to shew that my client and his wife might have had some little family jars; be it so, gentlemen, let him make the endeavour: I will tell him that their jars are the pleasures of the married life; they are the tornadoes of the marriage state, which clear away the mists and fogs, that, alas, will at times intrude themselves, to make the succeeding calm more susceptible of enjoyments; I warn you I speak by experience; and my learned friend Samo, on this sacred subject, can offer nothing but theory; think, gentlemen, how dearly they must have valued each other, when after a lapse of many years—after all their little storms of life—they yet resolve to make their union indissoluble, by adding thereto the celebration of those rites of our church, which has for its maxim 'that those whom God has thus joined together no man shall put asunder.'

"Contrast this with the conduct of the defendant, his own wife an exile from his bed and board, for no cause, except the lordly will of the defendant. A woman, against whom scandal has not yet dared to whisper; still, (although she has suffered much from the violent conduct of her husband) still, I say, striking for personal attractions and accomplishments; and is avowedly of an unspotted character. Let the defendant, therefore, but attempt to pry further than he has done into the private habits of my client, as regards his wife, and I shall not hesitate still further to tear down the beautiful appearance of adopted sanctity, simplicity, and innocence of deportment, with which he has hedged himself round.

"My client had been often led to believe that all was not right between his wife and the defendant, even before the time of the criminal conversation now prosecuted for. I am aware that my learned friend may allege that:—

"Trifles light as air,
Are to the jealous confirmation strong
As proof of holy writ;

"But, gentlemen, can you for a moment believe that there was no art, no perseverance, no continued attention, no working on the passions before the criminal moment; but that the victim fell at once into the commission of the adulterous intercourse alleged? Human nature forbids such an idea. The female mind, always timid, would think of her ties—her husband—her children—her grand-children; and prevent her, before, at least, all her fears. I challenge the defendant to name, even in one slight instance, any thing in the conduct of my client's wife, that such a ready compliance could be expected.

"On Thursday night, the 17th of May last, between nine and ten o'clock at night, the defendant sent his lad to call Mrs. Polly Bernard to his house. You must know, gentlemen, that Mr. Samuel Thorpe then lived (and for aught I know does now) in the same street, and within a short distance of the dwelling of my client, but which was then exclusively occupied by his wife. The object of thus sending for Mrs. Bernard by the defendant, is alleged, I am informed, for the simple purpose of making his bed. It is really astonishing that this gentleman could not be content to have his bed made by some of his men servants; that he did not hire a female, considering his ample means. Now the real object for which Mrs. Bernard was thus called to the house of the defendant became soon apparent. After her ingress the light ceased to throw its shade through the casement—the windows and doors were closed upon the guilty pair. Too much cunning generally defeats its own intention: not far distant from this scene of unhallowed pleasure stood the keen eye of jealousy, watching the progress of the night in order to preserve what custom had made her consider as her own. Yes, gentlemen, Mrs. Samuel (another intimate acquaintance of the Rev. Samuel Thorpe,) some time after Mrs. Bernard had entered the house of the defendant, rushed to the house—knocked at the door and got admittance. On getting inside, the only object she sought was Mrs. Bernard. Although in the dark she called her by name—what eye so keen as that of a jealous woman: she attacked Mrs. Bernard, as Mrs. B. sat on the bed of Mr. Samuel Thorpe. Both females exerted themselves to the utmost; one to the assault, the other to repel such violence. Only conceive, gentlemen, what a fine figure for the painter and the moralist was here exhibited; at the dark hour of night, two married women fighting most lustily in the bed-chamber of the pious defendant; while he (taken by surprise) kept pacing his piazza, unable to recollect what he had best do, and trembling with fear that the indiscreet uproar would lead to his exposure. I will pass over the effects of excited passion, and merely inform you, that to identify the person so as to leave no subterfuge, Mrs. Samuel carried away as trophies of her resentment, some handkerchiefs and an ear-ring, she had taken from Mrs. Bernard.

"Well then, gentlemen of the jury, you see the defendant, detected in connection with the wife of one man, by the wife of another, whose passions he had raised to jealousy by prior intercourse—whether criminal, or not, I leave to your judgment—that is not, to-day, my duty to decide.

"Mrs. Samuel, in the excited feelings of the moment, smarting under the seeming neglect and vacillating conduct of the defendant, as regarded herself, flies from house to house, spreading the dishonour of the plaintiff; the news soon reaches the injured husband; his wife has absconded from consciousness of guilt—he seeks her out, charges her with her crime—she confesses it—and now, gentlemen, he is forced to fly to you, to redress his wounded sensibility and affection."

The Jury, having heard counsel on the other side returned a verdict for the plaintiff, damages Fifty Pounds.

The schooner Thomas arrived from England this morning after a passage of 35 days. By her we heard of the death of Mr. Canning, which caused an extraordinary sensation. A warm discussion sprang up among the Freetown politicians, as to who should form the next Ministry, each person, of course, electing a Prime Minister for himself, and making a Cabinet after his own taste.

CHAP. IV.

Auction at Sierra Leone—Timber Establishments in the River—Tombo, Bance and Tasso Islands—Explosion of a Vessel at Sea—Liberated Africans—Black Ostlers—Horses Imported—Slave Vessel—Colonial Steam Vessel—Road and Street Repairs—Continued Rains—Suggestion for preserving the Health of European Seamen—General Views of the Colony—Population—Parishes—Supply of Provisions—Description of Freetown—Curious Letter from Black Labourers—Original Settlers—Present Inhabitants—Trade with the Interior—Strange Customs of Native Merchants—Anecdote of Sailors—Injurious Example of the Royal African Corps—Vaccination of Natives—Medical Opinion—Departure from Sierra Leone

Monday, Sept. 24th.—Still stronger signs of the breaking up of the rainy season, more frequent heavy showers, with thunder and lightning for the last two days. A fine morning, but squally and showery in the afternoon. There was an auction held to-day of the effects of the late Tasco Williams, Esq.; one peculiar feature of which is worth noting. The persons who had assembled were hospitably entertained with bread and cheese, and abundance of wine and spirits, with a view, no doubt, to increase the animation and excitement of the scene. Whether the bidders became extravagant in consequence, I do not know, but I think it very likely; at all events I suspect that the auctioneer was trying an experiment on the animal spirits of the company. This custom, although by no means familiar to Englishmen, is very generally practised in the north of England. It is probably a relique of ancient manners.

I left Freetown, about five in the afternoon, with Mr. McCormack to visit his timber establishment at the island of Tombo, a distance of twenty miles up the river, which we made, with a slight breeze, in about three hours. We passed two similar establishments, the one on Tasso, and the other on Bance Island, of the former of which Messrs. Babington and Macauley are the proprietors, the latter belonging to Mr. Williams. The account I received of Mr. McCormack's enterprise was full of interest.

When that gentleman first visited Tombo, he found the interior covered with a dense jungle, and the shores choked up with mangroves. There was only one solitary hut on the island near the beach, which was used as a resting place for boats trading up the river. At that time there was a slave factory in full occupation at Bance Island. It would be very difficult to compute the expense, and almost impossible for persons who are not practically acquainted with African mangroves and jungle, to estimate the exertion and perseverance which must have been necessary to bring this place to its present state of improvement. The wildness of the surface has given way before the hand of industry, and that which was some years before a wilderness of underwood, now presents an aspect of cultivation. The whole of this point is as clear as the streets of Freetown; and on a fine open situation, where the breeze plays from almost every point of the compass, an excellent stone house, with out-offices, has been erected. The site is well chosen and the building is scarcely inferior to the best houses in Freetown. The upper part is used as a private dwelling, and the lower part is appropriated to storage. A good boat-house, a saw-pit, upwards of twenty plastered huts, for the mechanics and labourers employed on the spot, and a well cut through the solid rock, from whence excellent water is obtained, complete the conveniences of the establishment.

Mr. McCormack does not fell any timber in the island; he merely uses his location here as a depôt for the wood which is brought down the rivers Rokelle and Porto Logo from the upper countries. For this trade he contracts with the natives inhabiting the lands lying near the shores of the rivers, and the wood is floated down on rafts to Tombo, where ships come to take in their cargoes. The African oak is so heavy that the natives are obliged to raft it on wood of a much lighter specific gravity. This trade is of considerable benefit both to our colonists and the native tribes. It not only promotes a friendly intercourse between them, but affords constant employment to great numbers of the latter, by which they are enabled to secure many of the comforts of civilized life, of which they must otherwise have been destitute. It has also had the happy effect of releasing them from vassalage, which formerly prevailed universally, and which was in some degree necessary as a protection against the arbitrary power of the different chiefs during the existence of the slave trade.

A statement of the annual export of timber from Tombo, since the commencement in 1816, will shew with what rapid strides the trade has increased.

In	1816	716	logs.
	1817	7,087	do.
	1818	1,341	do.
	1819	2,251	do.
	1820	6,271	do.
	1821	4,454	do.
	1822	1,429	do.
	1823	4,593	do.
	1824	10,093	do.
	1825	22,206	do.
	1826	24,456	do.

There is a mud bar across the river about one mile and a half below Tombo; and as the depth here is not more than 14 feet at high water, vessels ought not to load more than 13 feet before they drop below.

Tuesday, Sept. 25th.—Heavy rain in the night, but a fine warm day. Soon after noon I left Tombo, and visited Bance Island. The only objects of interest that presented themselves were the remains of an old slave factory, and a burial ground. The road to the latter place was by a path through a lime and orange plantation, which grew so luxuriantly that it quite obstructed our way, and we were compelled to have a black pioneer, who went before us with a sword to cut down the thorny branches. In this remote and lonely place I found the following epitaph on a tombstone, which appeared to me so curious that I caused it to be transcribed.

Here lies The Residue of The Honourable Sea Captain, GEORGE ANDREW HIORT, Born in Denmark, the 6th of September, 1746, Married January 8th, 1766, to the virtuous Lady Mary Catherine Schive, who, extremely sorrowful, with two good-natured Daughters, deplores the too early Death of this now eternally-blessed Person.

Died on the Coast of Guinea, the 15th October, 1783. His Body reposes here, waiting for a glorious Resurrection, whilst his Soul is in the hands of GOD, where no pain can reach.

In this place we discovered a tombstone of the date of 1680, but unfortunately the inscription was illegible.

We made an excursion to the island of Tasso before dinner, and returned to Bance Island where we passed the night. On approaching Tasso, we saw a large alligator, which Mr. McCormack fired at, but apparently without any effect. It is a well-known fact that the scales of these creatures will turn a bullet. They abound in the river, and are very fearless and ravenous. Some of the men belonging to the timber rafts, who incautiously trusted themselves in the water, have been on several occasions seized by the alligators and carried off, sometimes escaping with the loss of a leg or an arm; at other times, when the people on the rafts happened to sit at the sides, with their feet hanging over, the alligators have been known to seize them by their legs and drag them into the water. They have been taken of the enormous length of 18 feet.

Wednesday, Sept. 26th.—The night being very fine, we got up at half-past two, and left Bance Island to return to Sierra Leone, where we arrived in less than four hours, pulling the whole way, having a very fine boat belonging to Mr. McCormack, with a crew of able bodied blacks.

Mr. McCormack related to me the following circumstance which occurred to him in a vessel trading along the Gold Coast, and by which he was placed in a situation of great peril. In the middle of the night he heard a sudden cry of "Fire," and at the same moment a volume of flame issued from the fore-hatchway; in a few seconds after another burst forth from the main hatchway; so that before he had time to collect his thoughts as to what ought to be done, the whole of the middle of the vessel was in a blaze. The crew were thrown into consternation, and speedily crowded the deck in a state of confusion, bordering on frenzy. The despair of their situation was increased by a knowledge of the fact, that a great quantity of gunpowder, which had been embarked for the coast trade, was stowed below, while there was but one available boat to get off the men before the ship should be blown into the air, which they momently expected. But there was no time for reflection: each man looked to his own safety, and a rush took place, through the fire, towards the after-part of the deck, to reach the boat. The poor fellows who thus risked a passage through the flames, that now curled up fearfully, and swept the whole surface of the vessel, were dreadfully burned, and looked more like demons than men. But, at last, after much difficulty, they succeeded in lowering the boat into the sea. Those, however, who got in first, seeing that the whole crew must inevitably perish if they suffered a greater number to crowd the boat than she could with safety contain, pushed off from the ship as speedily as they could. If they had yielded to the impulse of their feelings, every soul must have perished; for, although they might have escaped from the fire, they must, of necessity, have swamped the boat. Fortunately, however, the boat got off in safety; but she had made a very short distance when the vessel blew up. Several poor wretches, seeing that their fate was not to be averted, had leaped into the sea, and were drowned; while others, who clung despairingly to the vessel, were annihilated by the force of the explosion. One poor black boy, nerved by desperation, flung himself overboard, and swam after the boat, which, with great exertion, he overtook. Through Mr. McCormack's interposition he was taken on board. The crew of the boat, so sudden was their resolution taken, had not time to provide themselves with a supply of provisions, although they were a considerable distance from the shore: they snatched up such trifling articles as happened to be at hand in the hurry of their departure, and trusted themselves to Providence for the rest. This melancholy accident was occasioned by the insubordination of some of the sailors, who forced their way through the bulk-head into the fore-hold, to get at a cask of spirits.

In the evening I accompanied Mr. Macauley in a drive to the village of Kissey, one of the settlements of liberated Africans. Its population is nearly a thousand souls, composed of the descendants of natives of Aco, who were taken from a slave vessel on the river Lagos in the Bight of Benin. The immediate neighbourhood of this village, which is about five miles from Freetown, supplies a great part of the grain and vegetables that are brought to that market. We called on the Doctor of the village, who was a black man, and we afterwards went to the chapel, where we heard a liberated African preach to his black brethren.

Thursday, September 27th.—I dined with a party at the house of Colonel Denham, the celebrated African traveller. I would gladly offer a tribute of admiration and respect to the memory of this distinguished gentleman, but the language of panegyric is superfluous.

Our party consisted of the Lieutenant-Governor, Captains Owen and Harrison, of the navy; Dr. Barry, of the medical staff, &c. &c.

Friday, September 28th.—Soon after noon I accompanied Captains Owen and Harrison, Mr. Reffle, the acting Judge, and the Rev. Mr. Davy, all mounted on good steeds, to visit some of the villages established for the liberated Africans. The first part of our journey was very hilly. We passed through Gloucester and Regent Town, on our way to Bathurst, near which we were overtaken by a thunder storm; but, before the heaviest part of it reached us, we got into good quarters at Mr. Davy's residence, where we found Mrs. Davy expecting us, and prepared to entertain us in a most friendly and hospitable manner. This lady undertakes to instruct the African females, of all ages, not only in the mere education of letters, but in all the moral duties of civilized society. As a proof that her efforts were not altogether unavailing, it may be observed, that her domestics consisted of some of her pupils, whom she had selected for the performance of the household duties. Morality here is at a very low ebb amongst the adult native population, and infidelity in the married state is a common occurrence. During our short stay, a poor fellow came to complain to Mr. Davy that his wife had gone to live with another man, and that when he went to demand her restoration, the guilty paramour and his friends turned him off with a sound beating. The circumstance did not seem to excite much surprise, although Mr. Davy gave every possible attention to the poor fellow's case, as he never omitted any opportunity of exerting his influence for the moral benefit of the community.

In the course of the day I had an opportunity of examining a snake which a Timmanee black carried, as ladies wear boas in England, round his neck, which is a common practice. It was about a yard long, and six inches in circumference. The blacks frequently extract the teeth of these reptiles, even those of the most venomous species, a process which renders them harmless. In the evening we returned to Freetown. The black ostler, who is generally a Krooman, performs in this country a double duty, for he not only attends the horse in the stable, but accompanies him on his journey, keeping pace with the animal at whatever rate his master pleases to ride. This would be a very good punishment for some of our ostlers who are in the habit of cheating the horses out of their corn. To compel the rogues to share fatigue with the animal, might teach them to treat them with more humanity. Horses are sometimes brought to this country from St. Jago, but they do not live long. A smaller and hardier breed comes from the Gambia, and the climate seems to agree very well with them. Neither English nor St. Jago horses live long at Sierra Leone, and the cause assigned for this is, that the coarse grass, which grows so rapidly in this country, has too little nutriment in it to support the animal under the exhausting effects of such a climate; and it is observed that he is continually though gradually wasting away, notwithstanding his appetite is most voracious; that at length he partially loses the use of his hind legs, becomes weak across the loins, and for the want of nervous energy, a paralysis ensues, and the horse ultimately dies. But if he is given more stimulating food there is a chance of his doing well; or at any rate of his living much longer than he otherwise would on such poor food as he usually gets.

Saturday, September 29th.—The Henri Quatre, a beautiful brig, arrived yesterday afternoon from the Bight of Benin, with 548 slaves on board, a prize to H.M.S. Sybille. This vessel was afterwards fitted out as a tender to the Commodore's ship, and well known, as the celebrated Black Joke, for her success in capturing other slavers. To-day I accompanied the Rev. Mr. Davy on board. A multitude of slaves crowded her deck in a state of nudity. The spectacle was humiliating in every sense, and the immediate effect upon the olfactory nerves was excessively disagreeable and oppressive. We found the officer who had charge of the vessel confined to a small space in the after-part of the deck near the tiller. The pressure of this dense mass of human beings was suffocating, and the crowd was so great that one poor slave who had fallen overboard in the night, on the voyage, was never missed until the following morning.

From the Henri Quatre we went to visit a steam-vessel called the African, which was to sail this afternoon, with 300 persons on board, and as much provisions as she could stow. Her immediate destination was Cape Coast Castle, where she was to wait the arrival of the Eden. She had formerly been employed in the Colonial service on this coast, but had lately been laid up for want of repair. Captain Owen, however, being desirous to forward a number of mechanics and labourers belonging to the free population of Sierra Leone, to the new settlement at Fernando Po, thought that this vessel might answer his purpose, and save Government the expense of chartering a ship expressly for that service; he therefore applied to the Colonial Government requesting that he might be allowed the use of her; which, after many preliminary arrangements, occasioning much delay, was at last granted. One condition was, that he should send her to England after she had completed the service required of her. He therefore ordered Lieutenant Badgeley, with a small party of men, to clear her out and prepare her for sea, as she was at that time half full of mud and water, and employed some mechanics to repair her engines, which were completely out of order.

At five this afternoon I went to the race course, to be present at a private match between two gentlemen's horses. Besides these private sports, there are regular annual races at this place.

The roads, which are very much cut up during the rainy season, are always repaired on its termination, commencing immediately after Michaelmas. I found that there were gutters, which had been cut by order of Sir Neil Campbell, (three or four feet deep, and from one to two wide) in various directions, to carry off the quantity of water occasioned by the heavy rains. The utility of these gutters in drawing off the water was sufficiently obvious, but they were found to be very dangerous both to men and horses in the dark; accidents frequently occurred, and on one occasion a horse had his legs broken. They were also dangerous to wheel vehicles, whenever it became necessary to cross them: indeed, the inconvenience of these drains, without bridges, was considered to be so much greater than the advantage, that it was determined they should be filled up, and that the rain should be left to take its own course over the surface of the ground, as before. The magistrates, who are elected annually, are obliged to superintend the repair of the roads, both in the town and its neighbourhood, in addition to their ordinary duties; and all offenders who are sentenced to labour on the public works, or to confinement in the house of correction, are compelled to assist in the necessary repairs. The expense of keeping the roads in good order is defrayed by a tax of six days' labour on every inhabitant of the towns and villages in the colony, which, however, may be commuted to a fine of seven shillings and sixpence.

After the race, I went to Mr. Barber's to dine. This gentleman has a small plantation of ginger and arrow-root, which succeeds uncommonly well; also some plants of the blood orange from Malta, and some young cinnamon trees; which, I should observe, are by no means uncommon in this colony.

Mr. K. Macauley has also a small plantation of coffee, which prospers very well. In fact, all the tropical fruits and plants must succeed here, if proper attention be paid to them.

Sunday, September 30th.—The morning was fine, but the afternoon showery; rain, indeed, appears to be quite a matter of course, either in the morning or evening. I had now been upwards of a month in Sierra Leone, and I found that it rained without fail in some part of the four-and-twenty hours, and sometimes throughout the whole day and night; yet, the rainy season had nearly exhausted itself when I arrived, and some short time before, it had rained for three weeks without intermission. These alterations of the weather, however, had no effect whatever on me, for, rain or shine, I went about, at all hours, as much at my ease as if I had been in England; and instead of suffering any illness or annoyance from the fluctuations and uncertainty of the season, I really found my health improved.

The brig Atalanta came down the river this morning, and anchored off Freetown, having taken in a cargo of timber at Bance Island. There was not a single vessel left up the river, which was remarked as an extraordinary circumstance, for since the year 1816, when the contract for African timber commenced, such an event had not taken place.

From the observations I made while I remained at Freetown, it occurred to me that a plan might be adopted, with good effect, for improving the management of the timber trade. I should recommend that an old ship be moored in the river, a little above Freetown, and housed over for the purpose of receiving the crews of such vessels as go up the river to take in their cargoes. The object of this arrangement would be to give the crews an opportunity of refitting, rigging, and repairing the sails of their own vessels, or of any others that might require assistance, while the Kroomen were employed loading the ships under the direction of the mates, or such other persons as might be appointed to that duty. [17] By this plan (with a proper check to prevent the sailors from going on shore too often, every reasonable indulgence being allowed them on board the hulk) many valuable lives might be saved, and those delays averted which now occur so often, from the difficulty of procuring hands for the homeward bound voyage, to supply the place of those who had been carried off by fever.

Tuesday, Oct. 2nd.—On calling at the barracks this morning, to take leave of the officers of the Royal African Corps, from whom I had received some very kind attentions, I was sorry to learn that Lieutenant Green, who had always been one of the most cheerful of the party, had been taken ill with the fever that

---

[17] All the headmen understand enough of English to perform any labour under the direction of Englishmen, and the Kroomen are a hard-working body of men.

morning, and that, from the great depression of his spirits, serious doubts were entertained of his recovery.

Wednesday, 3rd.—The ship Redmond arrived to-day from England, bringing letters from thence up to August 23rd. His Majesty's ship Eden, received on board to-day 60 black soldiers, of the Royal African Corps, to perform garrison duty at Fernando Po, under the command of Lieutenant Mends.

A gentleman in charge of the ordnance died this afternoon.

Before I take leave of Sierra Leone, a few general retrospective glances at the colony may not be without interest. First, of the population. There are not exceeding 110 Europeans in the colony, two-thirds of whom are under 30 years of age. This may, probably, in some degree, account for the great mortality that prevails amongst them.

In Freetown alone, there are between 5000 and 6000 coloured men, all of whom are free.

In the village of Kissey, three miles and a quarter from Freetown, are contained 1,100 souls, all liberated Africans.

In Wellington, six miles and a quarter from Freetown, about 800, composed principally of liberated Africans, with a few disbanded soldiers from the 2nd West India regiment.

In Allen town, three miles from Wellington, about 150, all liberated Africans.

In Hastings, twelve miles from Freetown, 600, composed of liberated Africans and disbanded soldiers.

In Waterloo, nine miles from Hastings, 900, composed of liberated Africans and disbanded soldiers.

In Wilberforce, two miles and a half from Freetown, 100, all liberated Africans.

In York, twenty miles from Freetown, about 600, composed of liberated Africans and disbanded soldiers.

In Kent, twelve miles from York, about 500, composed of liberated Africans and disbanded soldiers.

In Gloucester, three miles from Freetown, 700, all liberated Africans.

In Leicester, one mile from Gloucester, 100, all liberated Africans.

In Regent Town, one mile and a half from Gloucester, 1000, all liberated Africans.

In Bathurst, two miles and a half from Regent Town, 1000, all liberated Africans.

In Charlotte, three quarters of a mile from Bathurst, 900, all liberated Africans.

In Bassa town, three miles from Charlotte, 130, all liberated Africans.

In addition to these there are about 400 inhabitants at the island of the Bananas, 100 at the village of Calmunt, and many others of whom no correct amount can be given, residing at various little villages along the coast, perhaps their entire number may be about 200; if so, it will make the population of the

whole colony about 15,000. The names of the parishes to each town are as
follows:

St. George's	in	Freetown.
St. Patrick		Kissey.
St. Arthur		Wellington.
St. Francis		Hastings.
St. Michael		Waterloo.
St. Paul	in	Wilberforce.
St. Thomas		York.
St. Edward		Kent.
St. Andrew		Gloucester.
St. Charles		Regent Town.
St. Peter and James		Bathurst.
St. John		Charlotte.

Freetown is well supplied with fish every afternoon at sunset, most of which
is brought in by boats that go outside the harbour in the morning, and return in
the evening. Unfortunately, there is an immense number of sharks generally in
the harbour, which sometimes commit great depredations.

Sierra Leone is about six miles within the cape of that name, and lies at the
entrance of the river. The town is laid out with great regularity, and the streets
are spacious. It is two miles in length near the water-side, and about one mile in
width, gradually ascending from the beach to the hills at the back of the town.
The intervening space between a short distance beyond the extremity of the
town and the summit of the hills is principally unreclaimed forest land, which
was originally portioned out amongst the first settlers in the colony. From want
of means, however, or some other cause, the colonists never cleared those
grounds, nor did they offer them on sufficiently reasonable terms to enable
others to do so. This is the more extraordinary, as it is generally supposed that if
the wood were removed, it would greatly improve the salubrity of the air in the
town and neighbourhood, as well as open a new source of profit to the
proprietors, it being already well known that all tropical productions thrive most
successfully in this soil. Coffee, cocoa, arrow-root, sugar-cane, &c. have been
tried with the utmost success. The houses of the Governor, several of the
respectable merchants, and some of the natives, are built of stone. There is a
church also, on a very magnificent scale; indeed, so ambitious was the design of
this building, that the Colonial Government do not appear to have been able to
afford the expense of furnishing the interior, and have accordingly run up an
ugly brick wall in the centre, for the purpose of appropriating one half of it to
religious duties, and the other to public offices. The church, as it was built, was
evidently too capacious for the congregation that was likely to attend the service
of the established religion, particularly as a great portion of the population
consists of Dissenters, who have men of their own colour and way of thinking
for preachers. I have heard some of their black divines, but cannot say that I was
much edified by their discourses.

The following extraordinary letter from two master workmen, free blacks, who were employed on the church, received by a Member of Council, while I was on a visit to him, will serve as a specimen of the advancement in education that some of these poor fellows have made. The letter is given literally from the original.

"*Sierra Leone, Sept. 18th, 1827.*

"Honourable Sir,

"I have the honour of sendin to you this morning with humble manner I was to the Honour D. Denney yesterday, about the trouble what I have, I was take work from the church-yard, and I finish it, the gentlemen I must made petition and I cannot tell who will go to please to help me from this trouble if I will get the money from the gentleman. Shew me the way for get the money by your Honour all the people what I hired I do not know how to do with myself—only you one I know because I was under your brother if any trouble to much for me I cry to you with humble manner I am poor black man—

"I remain
Your affectionately and obedient servant,

"JOSEPH RICKETT and GEORGE DUNE,
Sierra Leone Labourers.

"*To the Honourable
K. Maccauley, Esq. M.C. &c.
Freetown.*"

The original settlers of this colony, we learn from "Murray's Historical Discoveries," consisted of about four hundred blacks, and sixty whites, (the latter chiefly women of abandoned character,) who arrived at Sierra Leone the 9th of May, 1787. These blacks, as is well known, were part of those that went to Great Britain; having been sent with the white loyalists, among the Bahama Islands, Nova Scotia, and England, at the conclusion of the American war: and twelve hundred more of the same description of American blacks agreed to leave Nova Scotia for Sierra Leone, on terms proposed to them by the Sierra Leone Company, where they arrived in March, 1792: and in December, 1793, Lieut. Beaver arrived at Sierra Leone, with the few survivors that had abandoned the colony of Bulama.

The present inhabitants arc principally composed of negroes of a variety of nations; Maroons from Jamaica, negroes who were captured or had deserted in the American war, some from England, some from Nova Scotia, some from disbanded West India regiments, and many prize slaves, that come under the name of liberated Africans, who from their industry and prudence have saved a little money and settled at Freetown in various capacities. There are besides a great number of persons residing here in succession under the denomination of strangers. These are people from various parts of the interior of Africa, namely, Timmanees, Foulahs, Mandingoes, &c. &c. There are also a great number of Kroomen, formerly upwards of a thousand, but a late order in council reduced them to 600, with the intention of introducing and encouraging the liberated Africans to come forward as labourers, fishermen, mechanics, sailors, soldiers, &c. &c.

Sierra Leone has a large market-house, with a market held daily, where the inhabitants may be well supplied with most of the tropical fruits and vegetables, and some from Europe. Poultry is abundant and reasonable. Beef and mutton are in most common use. The animals are small, a quarter of beef weighing on an average between 50 and 60 lbs. and a quarter of mutton from 5 to 8 lbs. Pork and lamb are seldom sent to table, and I never met with veal. The colony is principally supplied with stock, (viz. bullocks, sheep, and fowls,) by the Foulahs, Mandingoes, Sousoos, and Timmanees. They carry the fowls on their head in a large basket, and their necessaries in a sheep-skin bag fastened on the top of it. Perhaps the reason why veal and lamb are but rarely seen at table is in consequence of the bullocks and sheep having to travel a considerable distance, and fresh pork is almost too gross a food for a hot country.

The trade with the nations of the interior is chiefly confined to the Foulahs and Mandingoes, who bring small quantities of gold with them, which they exchange for European articles to carry home. Their mode of travelling to the colony is not a little curious. They first appoint one of their number as head man, who is referred to on every occasion, and who is answerable for the conduct of the whole. They generally come down in numbers of from six to thirty, and sometimes more. Each man carries on his head a kind of basket, made of the rattan cane, in which is contained his shirt, a calabash, some rice, and a bag made of sheep-skin, which holds the alcoran, some rice, bread, a knife, scissors, and other useful articles; also a small pouch in which they carry their gold, averaging about 5l. sterling each person. They secure the bag by fastening the sides of the basket together, and binding it round with strong twine which they make from grass. On the top of the basket they tie their bow and quiver of arrows loosely, so that they can get at them readily, in case they should be attacked in the woods by wild animals, or by any of the different tribes whose settlement they pass through in coming down. They also carry a bamboo cane about six feet long, and three inches in circumference, with a piece of iron, about six inches long, and sharp at the point, fixed into the end of it; this they make use of as a spear. They also carry a long knife or sword, which is slung over the arm by a belt. They partly live on the wild fruits of the country, and occasionally get something at the villages through which they pass; generally walking between the hours of six and ten in the morning, and two and six in the afternoon each day. When they arrive at Porto Logo, (which place is the termination of their land journey) they engage a canoe to take them to Freetown, for which they used to pay four dollars a head, but it is now reduced to one, and this charge they are accustomed to levy afterwards upon the merchant with whom they intend to deal, looking upon it as a bonus included in the traffic. They also apply to the merchants in Freetown, for accommodations during their stay, which is from ten days to a month. They will not trade either on the first or second day, but go round the town examining the different goods in the shops, and ascertaining the prices. In this preliminary proceeding they are assisted by their countrymen, who have been long resident in the colony and are acquainted with the English language. These interpreters make their living by cheating in every possible way, both the poor traveller and the merchant.

When they begin to trade it takes one day for the head man to settle the investment of the gold in the merchant's hands, which he has received individually from his companions, giving a separate receipt to each: after which they all assemble to choose their goods to the amount of each person's portion. This is an affair of three or four days. They do not, however, think it necessary to leave the colony so soon as their business is settled, but remain some time after idling about the streets. Two or three days before they really intend returning by the canoe to Porto Logo, the whole party call and say that they are going, which is intended as a hint to prepare some present for them. They repeat their visit the next day, and if they do not receive a present from you, they address you in the following manner. "Friend," (calling the merchant by his name, and holding out his hands with extended arms,) "do you see my hands? do you not see that they are empty? When I go back to my country, my countrymen will ask me if I have seen the great merchant! they will say they doubt me, asking me, at the same time, where are your presents? and if I have nothing to shew they will call me a liar, saying that the great merchant never allowed any one that went to see him, to go away empty-handed. I came from my country on purpose to see you. True, I have brought you but little trade this time, but when I go back to my country, and say I have seen the great merchant, and shew them the presents I have received, then they will all want to come, and bring plenty of trade." This of course concludes with a present to propitiate the grasping spirit of the African petty dealer.

The goods principally preferred by the Foulahs and Mandingoes, are powder, muskets, fowling-pieces, flints, swords, spear-pointed knives, India blue baft, India white baft, India scarlet silk taffety, red cloth, beads, and tobacco, which they make into snuff, being the only manner in which they use it.

The following amusing dialogue occurred between two sailors who happened to be on the military parade when the soldiers were at drill, going through the evolution of marking time,—a military manoeuvre by which the feet, as well as the whole body of the person, are kept in motion, presenting a similar appearance to that which they exhibit when they are actually marching. One observed the other watching the movements of the corps very attentively, with his eyes fixed and his arms akimbo: "What the h-ll are you looking at?" he inquired. "Why, Jack," replied his companion, "I'm thinking there must be a d—d strong tide running this morning." "Why?" said he. "Why?" answered the other, "why, because these poor beggars have been pulling away this half hour, and have'nt got an inch a head yet!"

The custom of sentencing soldiers to serve in the Royal African Corps, must naturally be attended with bad consequences, not only to the soldiers themselves, but to the natives. If we desire to enlighten a savage race, we could scarcely devise a worse plan than that of sending amongst them the refuse of a civilized country, who carry into the new community, the worst vices and crimes of an old country. These soldiers consider themselves to be exiled for life from their native land, and as they entertain no hope whatever, under such forlorn circumstances, of redeeming their character, they abandon themselves to debauchery, and give a free vent to the most debasing tendencies of their nature. The influence of this injurious example, which is a thousand fold more powerful than all the precepts of the preachers, upon the minds of the Africans, must be obvious. It weakens the effect, even if it does not altogether obliterate the impressions of that morality which we so studiously labour to inculcate. The African says, "The white man tells us not to do those things which are wicked in the sight of God; yet, in the same breath, he commits the very guilt against which he warns us. The white man tells us that drunkenness is a crime in the eyes of God, yet he drinks until his senses become stupified; he tells us not to curse and blaspheme; yet the most terrible oaths are on his lips. Which are we to follow? the white man's words or his actions?" If we wish to command respect, and to impress upon the savage the real advantages of civilization, we should send out only such persons as would be likely to secure a complete influence and ascendancy over the uninstructed people, and so demonstrate to them, by the force of actions, the purity and stability of the Christian faith, the importance of education, and the practical benefits of social organization. If it be necessary, as no doubt it is, to send out Europeans to serve in the African Corps, they should be sent in the capacity of officers, or non-commissioned officers: privates of good character might be selected, who would volunteer to go out on certain conditions, perhaps on some such terms as these: to serve as corporal for a limited period, after which time, if their conduct had been unimpeachable, to be advanced to the rank of serjeant, when, having served in that rank for a prescribed period, they might be permitted to return home on a pension. Two years might be assigned as the first period of service, and three as the second, making altogether a service of five years in Africa, which, considering the opinion that is popularly entertained respecting the climate, might be deemed of sufficient duration. I am aware that this suggestion is liable to one objection arising from the prejudice that is generally entertained against the climate, namely, the difficulty that would arise, in the first instance, in obtaining volunteers; nor am I entirely prepared to say, that the objection is without force. But the plan might be tried, and the temptation which would be held out, by the certainty of promotion, might, probably, be considered an adequate compensation to the risk: and, in case any individual should have conducted himself throughout the whole period of his service, to the entire satisfaction of his officers, and should subsequently wish to remain at the colony, it might be adviseable to offer him a small government appointment, or, in some cases, the reward might be extended to a commission in the Colonial Corps. If this could be carried into effect, it would certainly be attended with considerable advantages; it would procure respect for the British name, recall the savage from his life of recklessness, and put a final stop to those disgraceful scenes of profligacy which are so frequently witnessed in the streets of Sierra Leone.

Having requested my friend Dr. Barry, who was at the head of the Medical Staff at Sierra Leone, to procure me what information he could on the subject of vaccination and small-pox, in Africa, he most obligingly forwarded me the following document, which, for the sake of perspicuity, is put in the form of question and answer.

Replies to Dr. George Gregory's Queries on Vaccination and Small-pox, Sierra Leone, 24th September, 1827.

1st. Is vaccination generally practised among the infant negro population?

2nd. Whence do they derive their stock of lymph?

3rd. What is the degree of confidence placed in it?

Vaccination is not at all practised among the negro population, by native vaccinators; it is, however, practised among certain branches of the negro population by European surgeons; the negro population of Sierra Leone consists of Nova Scotian, and Maroon settlers, liberated Africans, and several of the aboriginal African tribes, namely, Timmanees, Mandingoes, Soosoos, Boollams, Sherbros, &c. &c. &c. The three first mentioned of these branches of the negro population, having greater intercourse with Europeans, are better acquainted with European customs, and have, of course, imbibed more of European notions and prejudices, on such subjects as the one now under consideration, than the aboriginal inhabitants of this part of Africa; vaccination, therefore, is, and has been, practised among them to a considerable extent, the stock of lymph being derived from, and kept up by, frequent renewals from England. That their confidence in it, as a measure preventive of small-pox, is great, I judge from the anxiety which they shew, and the eagerness which they manifest to have their children vaccinated when the small-pox is raging around them; while, under ordinary circumstances, and when their fears have been lulled by the absence of this fatal epidemic, an absence which they well know is probably but temporary, they exhibit such an unaccountable apathy regarding vaccination, that a stranger might well suppose they had no faith in it as a prophylactic measure; notwithstanding this, I believe they have great confidence in it, although, from circumstances to which I shall presently allude, that confidence has declined considerably.

4th. How soon does the arcola arrive at its greatest height in those countries?

The arcola surrounding the vaccine vesicle is, I think, at its greatest height about the eleventh or twelfth day after vaccination, if the lymph used has been genuine.

5th. Does small-pox prevail there?

6th. Does small-pox prevail there after vaccination?

Small-pox prevails occasionally, and there are instances of its having occurred even in a confluent form after vaccination: one genuine instance of this kind came under my notice in the year 1824, in the person of a liberated African girl, of about sixteen years of age; vaccination had been performed in this case, by the late Dr. Nicol, Deputy Inspector of Hospitals, and was considered satisfactory; the case proved confluent; the secondary fever was accompanied by a severe diarrhoea, which carried off the patient about the thirteenth day. Another well authenticated instance of the same fact, occurred in the early part of the present year, in the family of a respectable Nova Scotian settler; other cases of a similar nature have been reported by the inhabitants; but I do not consider that, in these cases, the proofs of a pure previous vaccine disease have been satisfactorily established; when vaccination has been carried on for some time, from the same stock of lymph, the disease is apt to degenerate and become spurious, from which cause we require a frequent renewal of lymph from England, in order to keep it in continuous and successful operation; the spurious disease, on the fifth day, generally shews itself in the form of a small globated papula; on the eighth day, it presents sometimes an ash-coloured pustule, containing purulent matter; at other times, and less frequently, a brown-coloured scale, having a small quantity of purulent matter under it, capable of producing, by innoculation, a disease similar to itself; the great prevalence of a disease among the negro population, called "craw craw," is considered as materially influencing that change in the properties of the pure vaccine lymph, which has been just noticed: that apathy and indolence of which I have already accused the negro population, leads them to consider the appearance of disease in the arm, after vaccination, as the test of safety from small-pox, great as the difficulty sometimes is, in getting them to bring forward their children for vaccination, it is still greater to procure the examinations in its progress and maturation; the mere appearance of disease in the arm, is supposed to carry along with it immunity from small-pox; and, on the occurrence of the epidemic at an after period, it may be easily foreseen how wretchedly and how fatally this confidence in the spurious disease may be misplaced; I, therefore, do not consider, that, in all the cases spoken of among the inhabitants, as cases of small-pox occurring after vaccination, there existed satisfactory proofs of the patient having previously undergone the genuine vaccine disease; yet, I am sorry to say, that from such occurrences as these, vaccination has rather lost ground in the opinion of the negro population.

7th. Is small-pox an increasing malady?

Small-pox is not an increasing malady; it is generally introduced here from the slave cargoes of vessels detained by the squadron, and sent here for adjudication; were this source of its renewal removed, I am persuaded that small-pox would, in the course of a few years, be almost unknown in this part of Africa.

8th. Can the vaccine virus be retained on points and glasses, so as to be fit for use?

The vaccine lymph, if taken on points, will not retain its virulence seven days in this country: this observation is established by repeated trials; if taken on glasses, I would not be disposed to depend on its activity when kept longer than fourteen or sixteen days, though I have known it sometimes to retain its original properties for four or five weeks; if preserved in glass bulbs, hermetically sealed, in the manner practised by the National Vaccine Institution, I have known its properties unimpaired after keeping for three months; repeated trials have convinced me of the excellence of this mode of preserving the vaccine lymph, and, I believe it to be the best and surest that has been yet devised of transmitting the lymph from England to tropical countries: next to this method, I believe the crusts have proved the most successful.

9th. Are the young negro population pitted with the small-pox?

The negro population are pitted with the small-pox in the same manner as Europeans.

10th. Are there periodical vaccinations of large districts? or, is each child vaccinated soon after its birth? if the latter, how soon?

The practice, in these cases, is, as long as the vaccine lymph continues to produce a genuine disease, to keep it up by the weekly vaccination of all comers. Children are rarely vaccinated under four weeks old; but there is no rule observed on this head.

11th. What sort of scars are usually left in the arms?

The scar bears the shape of the original vesicle, and is slightly depressed below the surface of the surrounding skin; the surface of the scar is marked by a number of small depressions of various shapes, corresponding, I believe, with the cells in the original vesicle.

12th. Is vaccination, in hot countries, attended with feverish symptoms? and, if it is, on what day do they begin?

Vaccination is, sometimes, in this country, attended with feverish symptoms; but, in the most marked cases, so far as I have seen, these symptoms have been so slight, as almost to escape common observation. I have not remarked on what day they begin.

13th. Is vaccination ever followed by any eruptions?

I have seen only one case of this: an eruption appeared on the sixth day after unsuccessful vaccination; it was diffused over the whole body, and is now in progress.

W. FERGUSON, *Assistant Surgeon, Royal African Corps.*

N.B. The case alluded to, in the last of the above replies, was, in the first instance, papular eruption; the base of each papula being surrounded by an inflamed ring; the eruption was thickest on the thorax, and on the arms; in its progress, the eruption became pustular, the pustules being in circumference about half the usual size of the vaccine vesicle; on the twelfth day, the crusts had dropped from some of the smaller pustules; and, by the seventeenth day, they had all dropped off, leaving a mark, but not in any manner pitted; and which, I think, promises to be permanent.

W.F.

Thursday, October 4th, 1827.—At length the day arrived when I was to quit Sierra Leone, and I might say with some regret; for, during my residence there, I had been very hospitably and agreeably entertained by the principal government officers, as well as by several of the most respectable merchants; and I had found a sufficient variety of objects of interest, to yield ample occupation for the mind. I could have desired to remain sometime longer, particularly as the fine weather, and what is called the healthy season, was fast coming on, which would have afforded me more time to examine and reflect on what was of interest to the colony as well as to the mother country; but I was conscious of a feeling of still deeper regret, and of a different character from that of mere curiosity;—it was the pain of parting from those whose kind sympathy had led them to take more than a common interest in my pursuits, and to whose friendly and constant attentions I was indebted for the advantages I enjoyed while I remained in the colony.

The apprehension, too, which was afterwards fatally realized, that many of us should never meet again, was calculated to embitter my leave-taking, even more poignantly. Of the friends who were then around me at Sierra Leone, the greater number are now no more; the principal persons amongst whom are the following: Colonels Lumley and Denham; Mr. K. Macauley (member of council); Mr. Barber, Mr. Leavers, Mr. Reffel (acting judge), Mr. Magnus (clerk of the court), Lieutenant Green, R.A.C., and several gentlemen volunteers of the same corps.

At daylight in the morning, just as the ship was preparing to get her anchors up, a heavy tornado came on, and the rain continued for some hours after the violence of the wind had subsided. Notwithstanding the rain, however, Colonel Lumley, the Lieutenant-Governor of the colony, and his private secretary. Lieutenant McLean, R.A.C., came on board at eight o'clock for a passage to Cape Coast, where the Lieutenant-Governor was going for the purpose of delivering the fortress of Cape Coast Castle into the hands of the British merchants, who were to take possession of it with a militia force, which they were permitted to organize for their own protection: the Government allowing them a stipulated sum to support the necessary establishment, at the same time withdrawing the troops of the Royal African Corps, and all the government stores, part of which were to be sent to Fernando Po, and the rest to Sierra Leone or England.

At ten o'clock we got under weigh, and made sail out of Sierra Leone harbour. The Horatio, a schooner, which Captain Owen had purchased to take provisions, mechanics and labourers to Fernando Po, was to have sailed in company with us, but from some unaccountable delay, she did not join us till we got to Cape Coast. [18] At noon, Cape Sierra Leone bore E. 1/2 S. distance seven miles; and the Banana Islands S. 1/2 E. The afternoon cleared up, and the wind was very light. From Sierra Leone to Cape St. Ann, the course is S. 57°. E. distance 86 miles. From Cape St. Ann to Cape Mesurada the course is S. 60 degrees E. distance 123 miles.

---

[18] Fenao Gomez, a Portuguese, was the first person who rented a monopoly of the trade of the Coast of Guinea, on consideration of his paying 300 milreas per annum for five years; and he was to discover 100 leagues of coast per annum, beginning at Sierra Leone. He finished his discoveries at Cape St. Catherines.

CHAP. V.

Cape St. Ann—Dangerous Shoals—Old Sailors—Liberia—Origin and History of the Colony—Failure at Sherbro Island—Experiment at Liberia—Difficulties Encountered by the Settlers—Differences with the Natives—Final Adjustment—Improving State of the Colony—Laws and Morals—Remarks on Colonization

Friday, October 5th.—There was a moderate breeze from the westward, and fine weather. At eight o'clock, finding, by our calculation, that we had rounded the shoals of Cape St. Ann, we altered our course more towards the land, intending to run along the Gold Coast, within sight of the shore. These shoals are the most dangerous part of the west coast of Africa; and there is good reason to believe that many vessels have been wrecked on them, particularly in former times. There is but little doubt that H.M. (late) ship Redwing was lost here, for there has been no trace of her since the day she sailed from Sierra Leone, (the afternoon of which was very squally) excepting a small mast that was picked up on the coast, to the northward, with her name on it; and as she was bound from Sierra Leone to Accra, she had occasion to go round these shoals, which commence about 30 miles from Cape Sierra Leone. But there is an additional cause for apprehending that such was her fate, for I was informed by an officer, that he heard Captain Clavering say, that he did not believe in the existence of these shoals; it is not improbable, therefore, that, with an idea of shortening his passage, he might have attempted to have gone nearer to them than prudence would justify, and thus tempted the danger which he held to be apocryphal. They might also have neglected to sound sufficiently often, an error which I have frequently witnessed, and which arises from a mistaken wish to save trouble and time—a poor excuse for risking the loss of lives and property. I am sure this will not be the case with Captain Owen, for I believe he knows the ground under water where his ship is in soundings, as well as that which he sees above it; and among the jokes of the crew of his ship, there was one on his late surveying voyage, uttered by an old sailor, who said, that as soon as he was paid off, he would set up a public-house in Wapping, with the sign of The Bag and Nippers, [19] and the words "Watch, there, watch!" written underneath. Notwithstanding this poor fellow's joke, he entered a second time with Captain Owen, on board the Eden, for an equally hazardous voyage, which he did not survive. I was near him in his last moments, when the fatal signal of ebbing life—the rattles in the throat—fell on the ear like the melancholy sound of the muffled drum in a dead march.

Sunday, 7th.—Light airs and variable, with rain at times. Cape Mesurada in sight great part of the day. Under the eastern side of this Cape is the American

---

[19] This is a small bag filled with air, for the purpose of floating nippers that are attached to it, through which the line passes, being intended to fasten itself to the line on the surface of the water the moment you check it on perceiving the lead strike the bottom, by which means more correct soundings are obtained.

settlement of Liberia. The origin and progress of this colony present so many points of interest, that I am induced to lay before my readers a succinct account of its early history. I am chiefly indebted for the materials of this sketch to a pamphlet, which I procured in Sierra Leone, published a short time before in Washington.

The first efforts of the American Colonization Society were directed to Sierra Leone in 1818, when two Agents were sent there to purchase land for a new colony; on their arrival at their destination, two men of colour, well acquainted with the coast, accompanied them on a voyage of exploration. Having examined all the places which appeared suitable for their purposes, they finally made arrangements for forming the new colony on Sherbro Island, about 100 miles south of Sierra Leone, when one of the agents returned to America, the other having died on his passage. The Society now resolved to fit out an expedition immediately, in which they were greatly aided by the President, the object seeming to be well calculated to promote the political advantages of the United States. The first colonists left America in February, 1820. They consisted of two government agents, one from the society, and eighty-eight persons of colour. These emigrants were very unfortunate: they arrived just at the commencement of the rainy season, the *damps* of which were much increased by the unhealthiness of the low, marshy ground of the Sherbro. The result was that all the agents, and a great number of the colonists died; the remainder wisely abandoned a speculation so fruitful of risk. Those people remained at Sierra Leone until new agents were sent out, and another spot selected lor colonization. The new scene of operations was Liberia.

The territory on which the first settlement, of the colonists of Liberia was made, forms a tongue of land of twelve leagues extent, in no part more than a league in width, and in some parts contracted to half that distance. This peninsula is so connected with the main land, as to represent a scale beam, the narrow isthmus answering to the pivot; which isthmus is formed by an acute angle of the Junk river on the eastern side, that falls into the sea at the S.E. extremity of the peninsula and an acute angle of the Montserado river on the western side, which falls into the sea at the N.W. extremity. Thus the N.E. side of the peninsula is washed by the above rivers; and the whole of the S.W. side by the sea. The north-western termination of this linear track of country is Cape Montserado, which towards the extremity rises to a promontory, sufficiently majestic to present a bold distinction from the uniform level of the coast.

The town of Monrovia is situated on the inland side of the peninsula, on the S.W. bank of the river Montserado, about two miles within the extremity of the Cape. The original settlement approached within 150 yards of the water, and occupied the highest part of the spiral ridge, which traverses a large part of the peninsula, and rises at this place to about 75 feet. At the time this territory was purchased by the agents of the American Colonization Society, in December 1821, this tract of land was covered by a dense and lofty forest, entangled with vines (a very large description of parasitical plant, so called) and brushwood, which rendered it almost impervious to new settlers.

Opposite the town, are two small islands containing together less than three acres of ground. The largest of these islands is nearly covered with houses built in the native style, and occupied by a family of several hundred domestic slaves, formerly the property of an English factor, but now held in a state of qualified vassalage (common in Africa) by a black man.

This little community lives so entirely within its own resources, that the individuals composing it are little known by their neighbours; their utter indifference to whose politics, however, does not preserve them from their dislike and envy, which, without the protection of the American colony, would soon be converted into acts of oppression.

There are four tribes in the neighbourhood of this coast, viz. the Deys, who extend along the coast twenty-five miles to the northward of Montserado, to the mouth of the Junk about thirty-six miles to the south-eastward. Next, towards the interior, the Queahs, a small and quiet people, whose country lies to the east of Cape Montserado. The Gurrahs, a more numerous and toilsome race, occupying the country to the northward of the upper part of the St. Paul river. And further into the interior, the Condoes, whose warlike character renders them the terror of all their maritime neighbours.

On the beach, one mile to the north of the new settlement, there is a small hamlet belonging to the Kroomen, a people entirely distinct in origin, language, and character, from all their neighbours. They originate from the populous tribe, whose country is Settra Kroo near Cape Palmas, and are well known as the pilots and watermen of the country. The number of families belonging to this hamlet, scarcely exceeds a dozen, and may comprehend fifty individuals.

The purchase of the Montserado territory being effected, it was first occupied by such American emigrants as could be collected early in the following year, at which time the indications of hostility exhibited by the Dey people, demonstrated but too distinctly the insincerity of their engagements with the new settlers, the first division of whom, consisting chiefly of single men, were met with menaces, and positively forbidden to land. This purpose they, however, effected upon the small island of Perseverance, situated near the mouth of the Montserado, where they were kindly received by Mr. S. Mill, an African by birth, who was at that time occupant, and from whom the island had been purchased by Dr. Ayres on behalf of the Society.

After many ineffectual attempts to conciliate the friendship of the Deys, the ferment of opposition seemed to have subsided, and Dr. Ayres received an invitation to meet the chiefs at a friendly conference in King Peter's town. This amicable appearance, however, proved to be a mere *ruse de guerre*, and the doctor found himself a prisoner in the hands of his faithless allies. Nor could he obtain his freedom until he consented to receive back the remnant of the goods, which had been advanced to the natives the preceding month in part payment for their lands, but, in according this enforced compliance to their wishes, he contrived eventually to elude their purpose of ejectment, by pleading the impossibility of removing the emigrants until vessels could be procured for their use.

The individuals at this time upon the island of Perseverance, did not exceed twenty persons. The only shelter for them and their store was that afforded by half a dozen diminutive native huts; the island itself was a mere artificial formation, which being always becalmed by the high land of the Cape, was extremely unhealthy; it was also entirely destitute both of fresh water and firewood—which circumstances, added to the insalubrity of the air, and the closeness of their dwellings, soon produced a sensible effect upon the health of the settlers. Happily at this critical juncture a secret arrangement was concluded with King George, (a monarch who claims the right of jurisdiction over the northern district of the Peninsula) and by virtue of his authority the settlers were permitted (in consideration of certain presents, consisting of rum, trade-cloth, and tobacco) to cross the river and commence clearing the forest for the site of their intended town. Being stimulated to exertion, by the union of interest and self-preservation, their labours proceeded with surprising rapidity, and in a very few weeks presented the skeletons of twenty-two dwelling houses, ranged in an orderly manner to form the principal street of their town. Unfortunately, at this period, so promising to their hopes, and so honourable to their assiduity, a circumstance occurred that interrupted their avocations in the most painful manner, and plunged them into a disastrous war with the natives.

A small vessel, the prize of an English cruiser, bound to Sierra Leone, and having on board about thirty liberated Africans, put into the roads for water, and had the misfortune to part her cable and run ashore below George's town, where she was in a few hours beaten to pieces by the heavy surf. She was immediately claimed by the natives on behalf of their king, whose alleged rights they came forward to maintain by the force of arms.—In attempting to board, however, they were opposed and beaten back by the prize-master and his crew. The American settlers, perceiving the extreme danger of their English visitors, hastened to their relief, bringing with them a brass field-piece, which they turned against the assailants, who, terrified by so unaccustomed a mode of warfare, hastily retreated towards their forest-bound hamlet, leaving the English officer, his crew, and the Africans at liberty. The damage on both sides was, however, considerable; on that of the natives it consisted of many wounded men and two killed; on that of the strangers, in the total loss of their vessel, with most part of their stores and property; but on that of the settlers the injury sustained was fatally severe, it consisted of the destruction by fire of their most valuable and requisite stores, amounting in actual worth to three thousand dollars: a loss incalculably increased by their necessities.

The accident arose from some mismanagement of the fusee, used for the cannon, a spark from which communicating with the thatch of the public storehouse so rapidly spread into a flame, that it was only by the most daring courage that the powder, some casks of provisions, and a few other stores were rescued from the devastating element.

The natives meanwhile, exasperated at the interference of the settlers, and maddened by the sight of their wounded and dead brethren, were only restrained from taking summary vengeance by the dread of the artillery. Even this fear could not prevent their occasionally venturing near enough to fire upon the settlers and their new allies,—these furtive and for the most part futile indications of malignity, were, however, always easily repelled by a single shot from a four or six-pounder, which usually put the assailants for the time being to an immediate flight. But it was not to this mockery of warfare with King George's warriors that the annoyance of the settlers was limited. Many and various were the vexations to which the hostility of the Deys subjected the unhappy adventurers; in the mere act of obtaining water (for which purpose they had to pass through the enemy's town) their obstacles were endless. While the demolition of their unfinished houses, secretly accomplished by their persecutors, and similar injuries constantly practised, ultimately compelled them to discontinue their principal work. At length the vigilant hatred of their savage enemies, resolved itself into a mode of attack which robbed the settlers of all present means of resistance.—Watching their opportunity when the boats went up the river Montserado, in search of water, they sheltered themselves beneath the large trees and rocks which overhung the narrowest parts of the river, from whence they fired upon the boats at pleasure, alike without the possibility of receiving any injury, or of their victims avoiding the danger by a hasty retreat. In this adventure, one colonist and an English seaman lost their lives, and two other persons were slightly wounded.

The recurrence of such events did not fail to keep up a spirit of animosity between the Dey tribe and the colonists, whose principal crime in the eyes of the natives, was their aversion to the slave trade; an aversion which struck at the root of all the interest, fears, and prejudices of the Deys. Old King Peter, the venerable patriarch of the nation, and with whom the first treaty for the purchase of the ground had been negotiated, was capitally arraigned and brought to trial on a charge of betraying the interests of his subjects, by selling their country. The accusation was substantiated, and it became doubtful whether the punishment of high treason, would not be executed upon a monarch, whom they had been accustomed to venerate and to obey for more than thirty years.

Under these circumstances the settlers became seriously alarmed respecting the nature of the intercourse which might become necessary to the policy of Bacaia, the king of the larger island, and from whom they had received many proofs of friendship, in secret supplies of fuel and water. But as his plantations, with numerous detached bodies of his subjects, were entirely exposed to the power of the Deys, it seemed absolutely requisite that his friendship with that tribe should not be affected by any further acts of kindness to a people so inimical to their views. Hence the suspicions of the colonists became naturally excited against Bacaia. It appeared that the considerations which had been so painfully entertained on the part of the colonists, operated no less powerfully upon the mind of the chief; for he immediately summoned to his aid one of the most powerful and famous chiefs of the Condoes, by whose protection he had for many years been sustained in his dangerous contiguity to such quarrelsome neighbours.

King Boatswain, whose political influence over the maritime tribes of the country was nearly absolute, and whose name had long been the terror of his countrymen, replied to the request of his protegée with that prompt alacrity which characterized all his actions, almost immediately arriving in person, accompanied with an armed force sufficient to carry into effect any measure that might seem most desirable to their chief. He, with that apparent modesty in which extreme pride delights to dress itself, and which is but another way of exhibiting innate confidence, assured his allies,—that he came not to *pronounce sentence* between the coast natives and the strangers, but *to do justice to all*. He next convoked the head chiefs of the neighbourhood to a meeting with the American Agents, who were but just returned to the settlement, having been absent during the last mentioned events, and principal settlers, who on their part were required to set forth their grievances and the nature of their claims. These complained of the dishonesty of the Deys, in withholding the possession of lands which they had sold, and of the hostile acts committed against the colonists by King George's people. These charges were followed by a clamorous discussion on the part of the accused; which the haughty judge having heard, as long as his patience served, at length closed, by abruptly rising, with the remark, that, "as the Deys had sold their country, and accepted a part payment for it, they must abide the consequences of their indiscretion; and that their refusal of the balance due to them could not annul nor affect the sale. Let the Americans," said he, "have their lands immediately. Whoever is unsatisfied with my decision, let him say so."—Then turning to the Agents, "I promise you," said he, "protection. If these people give you further disturbance, send for me. And I swear, that if they oblige me to come again to quiet them, I will do it effectually, by taking their heads from their shoulders, as I did that of old King George on my last visit to settle their disputes."

The necessity of an acquiescence in this decree, being by common consent allowed, no farther opposition was offered by the natives, and the usual interchange of presents having been effected, the colonists resumed their labours with increased zeal and confidence.

On the 26th of April, the colonists took formal possession of the Cape, but unfortunately so much time had been lost in contesting with the natives, that, notwithstanding all their industry, the rainy and tornado season set in while the dwelling-houses were still roofless. In the island sickness began to make terrible ravages; both the Agents were among the sufferers, and it was soon evident, that unless a removal from their insalubrious situation should be speedily effected, the consequences would be finally fatal. Nor was this their only trial, for in the midst of this appalling visitation, the gaunt spectre famine reared its ghastly head, and threatened them with new terrors. In circumstances so dispiriting, where despair seemed about to crash the weakened energies of the labourers, and where nothing but activity could preserve them from the loss of life; it was perhaps more honourable to Dr. Ayres' benevolence than to his policy, that he proposed to convey the settlers back to Sierra Leone. It is, however, a fact worthy of record, as well as of admiration, that only a small part of the emigrants embraced this proposal. The rest, consisting of twenty-six persons capable of bearing arms, with a few women and children, together with Mr. Wiltberger, the Society's assistant agent, remained to combat the difficulties of their situation; thus nobly affording a pledge to find for themselves and their brethren a present home, and for the oppressed African, or the captured slave, a safe asylum on this once hostile coast.

The settled rains of the season now set in with unusual violence, and the struggles and hardships endured by this little band cannot be easily imagined. However, so great was their persevering industry, that before the first of May several dwelling-houses had been rendered habitable, with a small frame-house for the Agent; and a storehouse sufficient for their purposes had been constructed of servicable materials.

In the beginning of July the colonists completed their removal from the island, each took possession of the humble dwelling that was henceforth to constitute his home. The Agents had meanwhile both sailed for the United States, leaving the settlement under the management of one of the emigrants (Elijah Johnson of New York), who acquitted himself so much to the satisfaction of the settlers that he now enjoys one of the most respectable situations in the municipal government, conferred upon him by the people.

Still the most economical division of their rapidly diminishing store of provisions, could not enable them to exist through more than half of the rainy season, and as no present produce could be derived from the soil, their prospects continued dark and dispiriting, circumstances which derived no inconsiderable addition from the fact that their stores had been reported to the managers in the United States as sufficient for a twelvemonth's consumption. But, as though fortune, at length won to admiration of their heroic fortitude, had determined to recompense their sufferings, a vessel arrived, unexpectedly, with a moderate supply of stores, and thirty-seven persons patronized by the Colonization Society.

This vessel had encountered many difficulties on her passage, but she arrived safely off Cape Montserado on the 8th of August, being the middle of the rainy season; here Mr. J. Ashman, who had with a truly philanthropic feeling undertaken the direction of this expedition, received the first accounts of the departure of the Agents, and the disasters of the colony. A fresh difficulty now arose in providing dwellings for the newly arrived emigrants, as well as a larger and more secure storehouse for transport stores. And it was not until after four weeks of incessant labour that Mr. Ashmun had the satisfaction of seeing the passengers and property all safely landed, and provided with shelter to secure them from the rains of that inclement season.

He next lost no time in ascertaining the external relations of the settlement with respect to the temper of their neighbours, and for this purpose proceeded to conciliate those kings whose alliance he deemed most desirable. He encouraged them to trade with the colony, and sought to establish them in amicable bonds, by receiving their sons and subjects for the purposes of instruction in all those points which form the basis of civilization. Yet, notwithstanding these pacific measures, a hostile and malign spirit on the part of the Deys, could not be wholly concealed. These symptoms rendered it advisable that measures of permanent defence should be adopted, and on the 18th of August the present Martello tower was consequently planned and the building actively commenced.

Their military force was, meanwhile, extremely slender, consisting of not above thirty men capable of bearing arms. They had forty muskets, but out of six guns attached to the settlement, one only was fit for use, four of the remaining number being without carriages. There were no flints, and but little ammunition. It was soon perceived that a system of defence was to be originated, without either the materials or artificers usually considered requisite, but undaunted by obstacles like these, each difficulty seemed to stimulate the ingenuity of the colonists to fresh activity and untried resources.

With immense labour the guns were transported over the river, and conveyed to the height of the peninsula, where they were mounted on rough truck carriages. Thirteen African youths (attached to the United States Agency) were next exercised in the daily use of arms. A master of ordnance was also appointed to repair the small-arms, and to make up a quantity of cartridges, as well as to arrange minor details for service.

But their chief difficulties arose from the necessity of clearing the heavy forest from the neighbourhood of the town, and of keeping a constant nightly watch: a duty which required no less than the services of twenty men; but, arduous as these were, they were carried on with unremitting diligence by all whose health remained unaffected by the climate.

At the commencement of the third week after his arrival, the Agent was attacked with fever; and, a few days after, his wife, whose affectionate devotion had induced her to accompany him, was seized with symptoms fatally. The sickness, from this period, made so rapid a progress amongst the last division of emigrants, that, in a short time, there were but two of their number who were not on the sick-list.

Notwithstanding the domestic calamity, and the enervating debility which bowed the energies and spirit of the Agent, he continued, at every intermission of fever, to direct the operations of the colonists, and to organize such a plan of defence as he considered necessary to secure the safety of the settlement; so that, in the event of his death, they might not be deprived of their security.

To accomplish this purpose, five heavy guns were stationed at the different points of a triangle, which enclosed the whole town; each angle resting on a point of ground, sufficiently commanding to enfilade two sides of the triangle, and to sweep over a considerable extent beyond the lines. These guns were to be covered by musket-proof triangular stockades, of which two would be sufficient to contain all the settlers in their wings. The brass piece, and two swivels, mounted on travelling carriages, were stationed in the centre, ready to support the post exposed to the heaviest attack: these detached works were to be all joined together by a paling, intended to enclose the whole settlement; meanwhile, the Martello tower was to be carried on with all possible speed; and it was hoped that this, when completed, would almost supersede the necessity of the rest, and form an impregnable barrier to the efforts of any native force; while the tangled brushwood, and newly-felled trees, were to form a formidable and impracticable hedge forest side.

With all the details of this plan, the most intelligent of the colonists were made familiar, so that they might be carried into effect for the good of those who might happen to survive.

On the 8th of November, while these warlike preparations were still far from being completed, intelligence arrived at the colony, that King George, who, with his people, had previously evacuated the neighbouring town, and to whom the African youths had deserted, was advancing upon the settlement with a force, composed of such people, from among all the neighbouring tribes, as had the daring to set the authority of King Boatswain at defiance. Happily for the colonists, they had a means of acquiring intelligence of their enemy's deliberations and intentions, of which that enemy was little aware; a circumstance which enabled them effectually to guard against surprise, and of which the Agent took advantage to press the necessity of coolness and determination upon the attention of the men.

On the evening of November 10th, the army of King George made its appearance, at the distance of little more than half a mile to the westward of the settlement, where it encamped for the night. The number of warriors comprising this force, was generally estimated at nine hundred; but, as the chiefs were the only persons who could tell the exact amount, and each was afterwards interested to diminish the account of their individual subjects, it is probable that the force was much greater than it was allowed.

The most wakeful vigilance was kept up by the settlers throughout the night; but the out-piquet having imprudently ventured, in violation of their orders, to leave their station at the dawn of day, were immediately followed by the native force; who, suddenly presenting a front of ten yards in width, fired a volley, and then rushing forward, took possession of the post, towards which they had been so incautiously led, and from which the men were driven without having been able to discharge their guns. Had the enemy possessed the skill, or the self-denial to have kept their advantage, the colonists must have been utterly destroyed; but such was their avidity for plunder, that, abandoning every thing for the pillage of four houses in the outskirt of the settlement, they so far impeded and confused the main body of their army, that the colonists had time to recover from their panic, and, by keeping up a rapid fire with the brass field-piece, they brought the whole body of the enemy to a stand. A detachment of musketeers, with E. Johnson at their head, was, meanwhile, despatched round the enemy's flank, which considerably increased their disorder, and, in about twenty minutes, the main front of the assailants began to recoil, but from the numerous obstacles presented to their rear, the entire absence of discipline, and the difficulty of giving a reversed order, without method, to so large a body, and added to all, the delay arising from their practice of carrying off their dead, their retreat was, for a time, rendered impossible; and the violence used by those in front, to hasten this measure, only increased the difficulties of its accomplishment. The colonists, perceiving their advantage, quickly regained possession of the western post, and brought their long nine-pounder to rake the whole line of the enemy, who, pressed together into so dense a body, that a child might have walked on their heads from one end to the other, remained thus defenceless, and exposed to the destructive fire that was poured upon them by a cannon of great power, at no more than sixty yards distance; every shot from this tremendous engine did immense execution, and savage yells filled the forest with horrible echoes. These gradually died away, as the terrified host fell back. At eight o'clock the well-known signal for their retreat was sounded, and immediately after, small parties were seen running off in different directions. One large canoe, employed in carrying a party across the mouth of the Montserado, venturing within the range of the long gun, was struck by the shot, and several men killed.

On the part of the settlers it was soon ascertained that considerable injury had been sustained. One woman who had imprudently, and contrary to express orders, passed the night in a house outside the fortifications, and which happened to be at the point first attacked, received thirteen wounds, and had been placed aside as dead, (after incredible suffering she, however, recovered.) Another, flying from the house with two infant children, received a wound in the head, and was robbed of both her babes; but she herself providentially escaped. A young married woman, with the mother of five small children, finding their house surrounded, barricaded the door, in the vain hope of resistance. It was forced, when each of the women seizing an axe, held the barbarians in check several minutes longer; they were, however, speedily overpowered, and the youngest stabbed to the heart: the mother instinctively springing through the window to preserve her suckling babe, providentially escaped, but the babe recoiling through fright, was left behind and fell into the enemy's hands.

It was not possible to ascertain the number lost by the enemy, but it must have been very considerable, as it is calculated that the killed carried away by water alone amounted to not less than 150. Many others were conveyed along the beach on mats; and twenty-seven bodies were at one period found by a party of friendly Condoes employed by the Agent to remove them; and long after this action the offensive effluvia from the wood proved that the researches of these persons were still incomplete.

The numerical force of the settlers at this period amounted to 35 persons, including six native youths not sixteen years of age. Of this number, but one half were engaged. After this action it was determined to contract the lines, and to surround the central houses, and stores, with a musket-proof stockade, and before night more than eighty yards of this erection were completed.

The work was carried on with no other interruption on the following day, than the necessary one of burying the dead: and was so speedily completed that by the fourteenth of the month half the number of men were, by the contraction of the lines, relieved from camp duty: thus obtaining for each a larger portion of rest during the day, which enabled them to perform their night watch with renewed vigour. An additional gun was mounted and posted on the same day, and every hour witnessed some progress in the discipline or defences of the colonists.

It was at this period that a friendly message, accompanied by a small present, consisting of the country's produce, sent by Prince Tom Bassa, a chief of some distinction, inspired something like encouragement to the hopes of the desolate little band; but it cannot be denied that their despondency outweighed their hopes, on discovering that, exclusive of rice, there remained but fifteen days provision in store. Each individual was now placed on an allowance per diem, scarcely sufficient to sustain animal strength, especially when such constant demands were made upon their industry and vigilance. No supplies could be obtained from the natives, in whose hands seven infant children were retained as captives, added to which the enemy's troops, though repelled, had not dispersed, and the colonists remained in daily expectation of a fresh incursion upon their little territory; to complete all came the cruel conviction that their stock of ammunition was insufficient to maintain more than an hour's defence.

These considerations, as well as the fear that the infant captives might fall victims to their infuriated enemies, determined the Agent to make another attempt to open a treaty for peace with the hostile chiefs, and after great difficulty he succeeded in conveying a message to their council (then in the act of debating a second attack), descriptive of the wishes of the colonists to maintain peace, and of their equal determination to oppose an invasion, with measures still more destructive than those under which their assailants had already suffered. These negotiations being unsatisfactorily entertained for some time, a day of humiliation and prayer was set apart at the settlement, after which the preparations for resistance were carried on as before. Fortunately, at this juncture a trading vessel touched at the Cape, from which the most pressing wants of the people obtained relief, and a few days after, a still more bountiful supply was received through the disinterested kindness of Captain Brassey of Liverpool, who, unsolicited and without prospect of remuneration, nearly exhausted his own stores to relieve the necessities of the sick and wounded, and presuming upon a long acquaintance with the people of these parts, he undertook to negotiate for peace; his efforts were however not successful; and immediately after the departure of his vessel a considerable army advanced upon the colonists; they, however, on their part were better defended than on the former occasion, and although the force against which they had to contend was more numerous and better disciplined than before, yet as the forest in the neighbourhood of the town was now converted into a wide plain, the assailants were obliged to approach under a fire from the cannon, the rapidity of which to them appeared like magic.

The natives sustained these destructive measures with surprising fortitude and perseverance; several times throwing themselves on their faces to allow the shots to pass over them, and renewing their own fire immediately after each discharge. But a contest so unequal could not be long maintained—in seventy minutes from the commencement of the attack a final victory was accomplished;

and the terrified fugitives dispersed as suddenly as they had appeared, many throwing themselves into the water and diving to avoid the shots that were fired after them. The loss on the part of the natives was supposed not to be greater than upon the former occasion, but its results were longer and more fearfully remembered. Three men belonging to the colony, serving at the guns on the eastern post were wounded, Gardiner and Crook dangerously, Tines mortally; the Agent received three bullets through his clothes, but providentially escaped without any bodily hurt.

There was at this time but little surgical knowledge, less skill, and no instruments at the settlement. Its dispensary was liberally furnished with James's powders and febrifuges; but for broken bones, and extracting pieces of pot-metal or copper ship-bolts from shattered limbs, there had been no provision whatever. A dull penknife or razor were substituted for lancets; and for probes there was nothing to be had but pieces of priming wire; the sufferings of those compelled to carry in their cankering wounds the corroding metal, were indescribably afflicting; and served to exemplify, most completely, the cruelty of placing men subject to the casualties of war, beyond the reach of surgical assistance.

A movement on the following night, supposed to indicate hostility, induced the officer, on duty at the western post, to open a pretty brisk fire of musketry, with several discharges from the large guns. This, however, proved a most fortunate circumstance, for it was not only the cause of bringing immediate relief to the settlement, but was finally productive of the most beneficial results.

The English colonial schooner, Prince Regent, laden with military stores, having as passengers Captain Laing of the Royal African Light Infantry, and a prize crew commanded by Midshipman Gordon, belonging to H.B.M. sloop of war, Driver, six days from Sierra Leone, bound for Cape Coast, was at the time in the offing (a little past the Cape). So unusual a circumstance as cannonading at midnight could not fail to attract notice, and the vessel lay to till morning, when a Krooman carried on board intelligence of the situation of the settlement, and was immediately despatched on shore with offers of assistance.

On the following day the officers landed, and kindly undertook to mediate on behalf of the colonists. An interview with the native Chiefs was without much difficulty procured, their warriors having dispersed, and themselves being overwhelmed with vexation and shame. After a little show of affected reluctance, they were easily induced to sign an instrument by which they became bound to observe an unlimited truce, and to refer all their future differences with the settlers to the arbitration of the Governor of Sierra Leone. It is scarcely necessary to remark that having no real grievances to submit, they never had recourse to this provisionary reference; from which time the colony has been considered invincible to native force, and consequently has been permitted to prosecute its plans in the utmost tranquillity, uninterrupted even by the semblance of war.

The death of the amiable and lamented Gordon, with eight out of eleven generous seamen, who volunteered their services to remain on the settlement to guarantee the truce settled by Captain Laing, was the first event that occurred to interrupt the general joy that prevailed after the consummation of peace; these gallant fellows all fell victims to the climate, within four weeks after the departure of the Prince Regent, on the 4th of December.

On the 8th of the same month, the colonists received fresh assistance through the friendly offices of Captain Wesley and his officers, whose vessel, a large privateer schooner, under Columbian colours, came to an anchor off the town. By the aid of mechanics, obtained from this vessel, the settlement was put into a superior state of defence, while the sufferings of the wounded were alleviated by the assiduous attentions of a skilful surgeon. After conferring upon the settlers countless obligations during a term of four weeks, Captain Wesley's vessel sailed, bearing with it the sincerest wishes of a grateful people.

The Agent's health, which had promised improvement, sunk into a state of hopeless debility, and by the 16th of December, medicines utterly failed to produce any beneficial effect. It was at this period that a remedy of the most singular nature was presented to him by a French charlatan, who, accidentally touching at the Cape, offered his services; a drowning wretch it is said will catch at a straw, and from despair rather than hope the Agent submitted to his adviser, and consented to try the effects of his prescription. A potion, was accordingly prepared, of which one ingredient was *a spoonful of calomel*! Having administered this, the Frenchman proceeded on his voyage, leaving the patient to abide the consequences of his docility. Such, however, was the weakness of his system, that he could neither throw it off, nor take it into circulation for five days. The crude poison was then voided, and a distressing salivation ensued, in the course of which all other morbid symptoms disappeared: by the middle of February, he was restored to health and the active duties of his station. Two out of the number of captive children had been delivered up for a small gratuity; five still remained, for whose release an extravagant ransom was demanded, terms steadily rejected by the colonists. It speaks well, however, for the humanity of the natives, that their first object had been to place these young prisoners in the care of experienced nurses. These protectresses so entirely won the affection of their charges, that when the chiefs determined eventually to restore them unransomed to their parents, they were obliged to be taken from their nurses by main force.

The long illness of the Agent, had relaxed the principle of industry and order, which he had been so anxious to establish; and on his recovery he found that it required all his influence to rouse the colonists into those exertions, which were necessary to secure their comfort, and the safety of their stores, during the rainy season. The huts were still without floors, and except the storehouse there was but one shingled roof, so that through the thatch of nearly all, the rain could easily penetrate in continued streams.

The store of provisions was now consumed, and still remained unreplenished by any shipment from America, while the neglect of effective financial arrangement on the part of the Colonization Society at home, rendered it difficult for the Agent to make purchases from occasional vessels, and he had already a larger pecuniary responsibility, than as an individual he could justify either to himself or others; the productions of the country had been rendered available, but the few disposable goods which the settlers possessed were now all exhausted in their purchases.

Matters had arrived at this extremity, when, on the 12th of March, the welcome intelligence of the arrival on the coast of the U.S. ship Cyane, R.T. Spence, Esq. was announced, by a Krooman from Sierra Leone. By the judicious and indefatigable exertions of that officer, the hulk of the dismantled and long-condemned schooner Augusta, was again floated, and metamorphosed into a seaworthy and useful vessel, on board which Captain Spence placed a crew and a quantity of stores for the new settlement, under the command of Lieut. Dashiell. Not satisfied with these important services, he rendered the Agent's house habitable, and caused the Martello tower to be completed, chiefly by the labour of his own crew, before the 20th of April; and it is to be deeply regretted that the sickness which had begun to make fearful inroads in the crew of his ship, during her stay at the Cape, terminated in the death of no less than forty persons, soon after her return to America.

Dr. Dix, the surgeon of the Cyane, became the earliest victim of a too generous zeal for the advancement of the colony. The tears of gratitude fell upon his grave, which was closed over his remains by the hands of a sorrowing community. The case of the amiable Seton is still more worthy of memorial, in him the blossoms of youth had just ripened into the graceful bloom of manhood, giving to a person naturally prepossessing, the higher ornament of a benevolent disposition, and accomplished mind. He perceived that his services would be invaluable to the colony, and he became the voluntary companion of the solitary Agent. His conciliating manners, and judicious counsels, completed the conquest of public approbation, and rendered his decease (which took place on board the Oswego, five days after he had re-embarked for the United States), a subject of unmitigated grief to the whole colony.

The arrival of the above-mentioned vessel, bringing an accession of sixty-six emigrants from the middle states of America, with ample stores and a physician, terminated the difficulties of the colonists, and since that period, the settlement has continued rapidly improving in all those resources necessary to the comforts of peace; as well as in those means of defence which serve, at once, to repel, and even defy the incursions of war.

From this period the affairs of the colony have rapidly improved. In a short time after peace was restored, sixty-one new emigrants, and a supply of stores, under the charge of Dr. Ayres, augmented the resources of the colonists; but that gentleman was obliged, in consequence of the state of his health, to resign, at the close of 1823, the superintendance of the interests of the colony to Mr. Ashmun, who continued, until the period of his death, to act as principal Colonial Agent to the Society. To Mr. Ashmun's admirable management of the affairs of the colony, much of its contentment and security may be attributed. He purchased from its natural owners, all the territory he occupied; and as not an acre was taken without an equivalent, the natives were well pleased to cultivate an intercourse that was at once so profitable and desirable. In 1825, a number of fresh emigrants arrived, whose pursuits were of an agricultural nature, and as they desired to go into the jungle at once, and commence operations, a negotiation was opened with the neighbouring tribes for the purchase of land. The ground selected was a tract of about twenty miles, varying from one to three miles in breadth, lying on the navigable part of the St. Paul's river. The advantages of this accession of territory, consisted in the opportunity it afforded the settlers of dwelling on their plantations, instead of being compelled to live in the town, at an inconvenient distance from them; in the fertility of the soil, which was sufficiently rich to enable the emigrant to support himself and his family, a short time after his arrival; in making the agricultural settlement more available and compact; and in securing the trade of the St. Paul's river, which was an object of great importance. Subsequently to that period, other additions have been made to the possessions of the colonists; and, at present, the colony extends nearly 150 miles along the coast, and a considerable distance into the interior. The government of the colony commands eight trading stations, established on the purchased land for the convenience of, and intercourse with, the natives, from Cape Mount to Trade Town; and the prospects and advantages of the colonists, are every day improving.

The laws by which a colony so prosperous and happy is governed, must suggest a subject of deep concern to every man who is interested in any project, that has for its end the promotion of the well being of any section of his fellow-creatures. In this little colony, which has succeeded so effectually in securing the confidence and attachment of the natives, the utmost vigilance appears to have been exercised from the commencement, to prevent any dangerous precedents from being established, that might afterwards be cited for the defence of customs injurious to the interests of the settlers. One of the first principles adopted, even before the regulations by which the colonists were governed assumed the tangible shape of law, was that all persons born in the colony, or residing in it, should be free, and enjoy all the rights and privileges of citizenship known to the United States of America, which was taken as the model of the Liberian Constitution in all respects, except that anomaly, the institution of slavery. It must always continue to be a matter of surprise and regret, that a country which expended so much blood on the purchase of its independence, should sanction within its boundary the existence of slavery as a legal right. The ermine is said to die if a single stain fall on its spotless skin, and one would suppose that the giant republic of the new world would be equally susceptible throughout her mighty frame of the taint of slavery; but, perhaps, there is a fine moral in the fact, to shew us that the works of man, even in his most elevated inspirations, must of necessity be imperfect. The wisdom and power of the Godhead alone can produce perfection.

The colonists of Liberia resolved to avoid the error of the parent country. They began by banishing the very name of slave, and they have persisted in their resolution to keep themselves free. Under the provisions of their constitution, the Colonization Society is empowered to make such regulations as may appear requisite for the government of the colony, until it shall withdraw its superintendence, and leave the colonists to govern themselves; the common law, as it is in force in the United States, is applied to the jurisdiction of Liberia. In 1824 a regular plan for the civil government of the colony was drawn up, and a digest of laws framed, which have been approved of, and are now in full operation. By this plan, the Agent is invested with sovereign power, subject only to the decision of the colonial board; municipal and judicial officers are appointed; the choice of certain offices is vested in the colonists, subject to the approval of the Agent; and standing committees of agriculture, of public works, of colonial militia, and of health are appointed, whose duties are clearly defined and rigidly enforced.

The criminal code is singularly mild: the highest degree of punishment being expulsion from the colony, which is a very beautiful exemplification of the sense of honour and integrity that the colonists entertain, when, for the most flagrant violations of civil rights and good order, they deem it a sufficient disgrace and infliction to cast out the guilty person from all further communion, the property of the exile being given to his heir; or, in lack of an heir, reverting to the general stock.

The remarkable success which crowned the efforts of the settlers in Liberia, has subsequently led to the consideration of more extensive plans for the establishment of colonies for liberated slaves. Of course, in proportion as the circle of manumission is enlarged, the provision for the future welfare of the emancipated blacks must he increased:—with a double view, therefore, not only to prepare adequate settlements for their reception, but by the exercise of an active liberality to encourage the spirit of freedom which was found difficult of accomplishment at first, but which ultimately yielded to the energies of the opponents of the slave trade in America. Many attempts had been made in the United States to abolish, or at all events diminish the practice of slavery, bat in vain; for it appears, however startling and apocryphal the statement may seem, that the English Government, during the period that they exercised sovereignty in the Union, always refused to sanction the abrogation of slavery. Even so far back as 1698, the mother country rejected a proposition made by the assembly of Pennsylvania, to levy a duty of 10 per cent. per head on the importation of slaves; which was intended to operate as a prohibition. Indeed, one of the proximate causes of the Declaration of Independence (July 1776) was the unrestricted introduction of slaves. Soon after the American war had terminated, it was suggested as an appropriate measure, in fulfilment of views which had been so long defeated by the influence of English authority, to establish a colony on the coast of Africa, but the continued pursuit of the degrading traffic by almost all the powers of Europe, prevented the benevolent projectors from carrying their design into effect. Twenty years afterwards, the plan was revived, and the most strenuous exertions were made in the different States to organize a body of opinion, which should finally triumph over the self-interests and reluctant morality of the slave-owners. At this period, one of the difficulties which the philanthropic abolitionists experienced was the want of a suitable refuge for such slaves as they might be enabled to liberate. The legislature of Virginia, which contains nearly one-third of the black population of the Union, pledged itself to release all its slaves, if Congress would undertake to provide an adequate asylum for them. President Jefferson negotiated in vain for a territory in Africa, and the Brazils. The legislature of Virginia again renewed its pledge, and as much of the bigotry of former times had now been obliterated by the diffusion of enlightened principles, the renewal of the proposition was followed by the best results. General Mercer, familiarly designated as the Wilberforce of America, opened a correspondence with the principal advocates of emancipation, which ultimately produced the formation of the American Colonization Society, on the first of January, 1817. The labours of the Society were greatly facilitated by the laws of the Union, which left to each State the uncontrolled power of legislating for itself on the subject of slavery. The members of the Society had therefore merely to address themselves to the humanity and understanding of the slaveowners, in order finally to attain their purpose. The progress of moral truth, however slow, is always certain, and the issue of those proceedings has been such as the excellence of their object might have led us to anticipate. Several of the States have already signified their willingness to forego all the pernicious advantages of slavery. And the number of slaves offered gratuitously by owners in different parts of America, vastly exceed the present means of the Society to provide for them in Africa. The legislature of Maryland appreciate so highly the utility and importance of the settlement of Liberia, that they have voted in the first instance a considerable sum, to be appropriated annually to its support, and have subsequently, within the last six months, voted two hundred thousand dollars for the purpose of assisting in the formation of another settlement on the same principles.

It is, therefore, sufficiently evident, that what is now required to complete the united objects of manumission and colonization, is, not so much the consent of the slave-owners, as the power of carrying the design into operation. Mr. Elliot Cresson, of Philadelphia, an active and enthusiastic supporter of the cause, visited England in 1832, for the purpose of drawing attention to the subject, and of appealing to the well-known generosity of a country that has uniformly taken the lead in advancing the interests of civilization. A Society was formed, under the patronage of H.R.H. the Duke of Sussex, with the view of extending colonization in Africa, on the same system which has proved so successful in the case of Liberia. The subject, unfortunately, did not excite the attention which might have been anticipated, partly, I fear, because it was ill-timed, and was considered by the general body of Abolitionists, as a diversion tending to distract the public mind from the great question of emancipation, which was then undergoing anxious discussion; and partly, because it was considered by some, as a palliative likely to prolong the existence of slavery, in the same ratio as it diminished its evils. The selection of so unseasonable a moment for introducing the subject to the public, was influenced by the necessity Mr. Cresson was under of returning to the United States, but previously to his departure, the objections to the efforts of the Society were fully answered, and the important fact of the independence of each State, in reference to slavery, was stated in ample detail. From those statements it appeared, that the law of slavery, in some cases, prohibits—not only the emancipation; but the education of slaves, in order to render their bondage still more hopeless and oppressive: but that the efforts of the Society were gradually abating the rigour of those cruel restrictions. The Society has hitherto endeavoured, as far as its powers would permit, to extend the principle of colonization, by removing, invariably, with their own consent, such slaves as have the good fortune to obtain their freedom, to a spot where they were not only free from competition with the white population, but where their education, imperfect as it might have been, rendered them the superior instead of the inferior class: thus silently promoting the blessings of Christianity and civilization amongst the native tribes. Mr. Cresson, during his residence in England, distributed several illustrative documents, sanctioned by names of distinguished persons in the United States, and to which I am indebted for some of these particulars. From these documents, were there even no other evidence, it may be fairly inferred, that Liberia affords uncontrovertible proof of the practicability of establishing colonies on the African coast, composed of persons of the African race, nearly, if not wholly, freed from the control of the whites; that the expense of establishing such a colony is moderate, not having exceeded, in the case in point, 4000l. per annum; that it is greatly favoured by the natives, with whom the colonists are rapidly extending their commercial and friendly relations to their mutual benefit; that it has not only placed a large number of manumitted slaves in a prosperous situation, but led to the emancipation of many, who must otherwise have still continued in bondage; and, finally, that it has completely put an end to the slave-trade in the immediate neighbourhood of the settlement, where that nefarious traffic was hitherto most extensively prosecuted. It is to be deplored, that although Great Britain has recently made a noble effort to abolish slavery in her own dominions, there are other countries which still sanction a usage so degrading to our age and religion. But a very short time since, several vessels were captured, the united cargoes of which amounted to a thousand slaves, and when we refer to the large proportion which the liberated Africans bear to the rest of the population in Sierra Leone, equal to about three-fourths of the whole, and consider the heavy expense at which this country endeavours to fulfil the serious responsibility it has taken upon itself in the liberation of these unfortunate captives, I am persuaded that all the particulars which can be collected respecting Liberia, will be deemed worthy of the most serious attention. My readers, therefore, will not, I trust, think that I devote too much space to the subject, if I close my rapid sketch of the progress and fortunes of this settlement, with the latest information respecting it, which has been received in Europe. It is of a very recent date, and is from the pen of Dr. Mechlin, the Governor of Liberia:—

"The colony is daily adding strength and respectability to its character, and if even now all patronage were withdrawn, the colonists are fully capable of sustaining and defending themselves from any assaults of the natives, and regulating their own concerns in such a manner as to secure the prosperity of the colony. A court, courthouse, and trial by jury, are established. At this moment, since the departure of Governor Mechlin, and until the new Governor arrives out, there are none other than blacks among the inhabitants of Liberia.

"The slaves who were captured and brought into St. Augustine, and Key West, after remaining in the United States from six to twelve months, were sent to Liberia, a quantity of land being granted to them there. They have gone on to cultivate it in a manner equal, if not superior, to that of the colonists. They have been able to accomplish thus much from what experience they gained while in this country. These people arrived at Liberia naked; they have clothed themselves from the avails of their labour, and, what is rather singular, they have gone into the town to seek out for themselves wives, esteeming themselves too far advanced in civilization and refinement to form connexions among the natives, although they might obtain from among them much more comely persons than they are enabled to find among the very meanest of the colonists, from whom they are obliged to select. This fact alone shows, that but a small degree of civilization infused into this people, tends to the elevation of their character.

"The colonists of Monrovia are said to be much more inclined to trade than to cultivate the earth. The English and the French vessels which come there, have engrossed almost the whole trade of the colony, the Americans not being able to compete with them. Many of the natives come into the town, and are employed as labourers by the colonists. The colonists also receive some of the children of the natives into their families, and send them to school. At different times the natives have made three or four attacks on the settlements, but have always been repelled with spirit; for the last year the natives have been very quiet and friendly. The colonists can bring into the field, if necessary, about 500 troops, which are considered a match for ten times the number of natives. Many tribes of these natives hold slaves, which are treated with much cruelty, and it is doubtful if even their masters are so well off or so happy as the slaves in our southern states. They are much less civilized and more ignorant.

"The people there called Kroomen, reside in the country. They come down to the sea-shore and pitch their tents, and launch their canoes, and, sailing all along the coast, they become pilots to the traders; and these are the men with whom the Spaniards trade for slaves. These

Kroomen keep no slaves themselves, neither do they allow any of their own tribe to be sold as slaves; and they become of so much importance to the slave-dealers on the coast, acting as a sort of brokers, negotiating among the tribes for slaves, that they themselves, knowing their own consequence, do not hesitate to board a slave-vessel, andthere is no instance of their ever being kidnapped."

The history of this little colony, which I have endeavoured to sketch from the information furnished by Mr. Ashmun, appears to me to afford matter for serious reflection. The principle involved in colonization is, I am aware, liable to some objections, and I am not indifferent to the arguments to which it has given occasion. But the strength of truth and reason seems to be altogether in its favour. The dogmas of Malthus maybe right or wrong, the statistical propositions of Mr. Sadler, and the philosophical deductions he derives from them may be right or wrong: with these querulous rhetoricians, I have nothing to do. But one thing is certain, that while the fertile earth, in any of its endless divisions, affords the means of sustenance, no human being ought to be suffered to want, because the notion of emigration does not square with certain opinions of a despotic school. That some countries are overpopulated in reference to the resources of their superficies is, I take it for granted, a fact above impeachment. That there is room enough on the surface of the earth for all the population it contains, is another truth which very few persons will be hardy enough to contest. The principles of Providence in the economy of space appear, therefore, to be that the superabundant population of one place, shall seek in the uncultivated and scantily peopled regions of other countries, for those means of existence which are denied to them by the pressure of the demand on the soil at home. The immutable law of benevolence, drawn from the institutes of Christianity, ordains the earth for the sustenance of man. But that law is perverted by those who resist emigration under the circumstances to which I have alluded. What is to become of the surplus population, if it be not allowed a space wherein to fertilize the virgin soil, and supply its wants? If its own land denies it the means of life, must it die, that some philosopher may triumph in his doctrines?

It is very true that colonization frequently terminates disastrously, and that instances might be cited, in which emigrants have suffered terrible privations, and have even fallen beneath the insalubrity of unaccustomed climates. But these cases merely prove the necessity of adopting sufficiently precautionary measures, before the emigrant commits himself to a venture, upon which the happiness and interests of himself and his family altogether depend. If a man rashly goes out uncovered, and exposed, into a storm, he will surely run a chance of catching an illness: so too, if a man penetrate to the tropics, and carry with him the habits of England or France, he will certainly peril his life, for these habits are unsuitable to places where a vertical sun pours down its scorching rays upon the body. Every climate requires especial modes of conduct for physical constitution. Brandy and water might be a very good beverage, and even a medicinal protective at the North Pole, but it would be ruinous if taken in excess at Sierra Leone. It is because emigrants do not sufficiently study the situation to which they bend their steps, that they so often complain of failure. We have seen in the first expedition from the United States, that the project terminated fatally for nearly all the colonists; but why? Because they went to a low marshy island, at the commencement of the rainy season, when disease in its worst horrors was just setting in. How could they expect to escape a contagion, which they actually seemed to court?

If the example of the colony of Liberia were to be followed, if wholesome laws were laid down to regulate the movements of emigrants, and proper precautions taken, by which all the advantages of position might be seized, and the disadvantages avoided, I have very little doubt that colonization would ultimately prove a valuable safety-valve for society. The idle and wretched, who have no hopes or friends at home, might always be thus beneficially drafted off to infant states, where they could be made to labour, and where their recovered habits could be rendered subservient to the common good. At home they hang on the necks of the industrious; there they might be converted to useful members of the great community, improving the means of the social body, instead of deteriorating its morals, and wasting its resources.

CHAP. VI.

The Kroo Country—Religion of the Kroo and Fish men—Emigration of the Natives—Sketch of their habits and customs—Purchase of wives— The Krooman's *ne plus ultra*—Migratory propensities—Rogueries exposed—Adoption of English Names—Cape Palmas—Dexterity of the Fishmen—Fish towns—The Fetish—Arrival at Cape Coast—Land with the Governor—Captain Hutchison—Cape Coast mode of taking an airing—Ashantee Chiefs—Diurnal occupations—School for Native Girls—Domestication of Females—Colonel Lumley—Captain Ricketts— Neglect of Portuguese fortresses—A native Doctor

Monday, Oct. 8th, 1827.—Light airs and variable, with frequent heavy showers. Land in sight, bearing N.E. At noon calm and very hot. Lat. 5°. 32'. N. lon. 10°. 17'. W. Cape Palmas E.S.E. 168 miles. Hoisted in the pinnance, which we had been towing all the way from Sierra Leone, in consequence of the crowded state of the ship.

Tuesday, 9th.—At noon, lat. 4°. 55'. N. lon. 9°. 17'. W. Cape Palmas S. 76°. E. 83 miles. At one a canoe came off to the ship, at this time we saw a remarkable rock, called the Swallow, or Kroo rock, which is detached from the main land, about two miles and a half from the entrance of the river Waffen. There is a safe channel for vessels inside of this rock, with seven fathoms water, and a muddy bottom. Nearly twenty leagues to the westward of the Waffen is the river Cestus,[20] in which river, Captain Spence, an old African trader, has had a timber establishment some years.

Being now off the Kroo country, I think it desirable to introduce a short description of it, and its inhabitants.

The Kroo country is situated on that part of the coast of Africa called the Grain Coast, the chief towns of which are Settra Kroo, Little Kroo, Kroo Barru, Kroo Settra, and King Will's town. It does not appear that it extends any distance inland. The manners of the natives are sufficiently curious to merit some description. They are pagans, and place much faith in charms, auguries, and oracles. The most celebrated place for oracles is near the banks of the river Cavally, a little to the westward of Cape Palmas, and this spot is in as great repute amongst them, and the surrounding tribes (particularly those along the coast, even so far down as Cape Lahou), as ever that of Delphos was among the ancient Greeks, and so far as we can learn, imposes with equal success on the credulity and superstition of the poor ignorant natives.

The Kroomen, that is, the Kroo and Fish men, for they all come under the general denomination of Kroomen in Sierra Leone, are almost the only people on the coast who voluntarily emigrate, to seek for labour out of their own

---

[20] Nine miles to the westward of the mouth of this river, is the rock Cestus, where there is a settlement of about seventy Fishmen, who have run away from their own country, to avoid the penalty of the law. They are principally from Niffon, Baddon, and Pickaninny Cess.

country. They come to Sierra Leone, to work in any capacity in which they can obtain employment, until they are possessed of sufficient property to enable them to purchase several wives. The object they propose to themselves in this increase of their domestic establishments, differs in some respects from the indulgences of the east. The Kroomen compel their women to perform all the field-work, as well as the necessary domestic duties, in conformity with the usages of savage life, and when they can purchase a sufficient number of wives to fulfil all these employments, they pass the remainder of their days in ease and indolence. Before they are able to accomplish this object, they are obliged to make several visits to Sierra Leone, as they do not like to be absent more than two or three years at a time from their own country. The average duration of this voluntary banishment is perhaps about eighteen months. A sketch of the progress of the Kroomen from their first visit to Sierra Leone, to the final consummation of their wishes, in the attainment of their Paradise of idleness, will fully illustrate the peculiar character of a tribe, one of whose usages is that of seeking abroad during the vigorous years of life, the means of dwelling with ease and comfort in old age at home.

When they have arrived at healthy boyhood, they first come to Sierra Leone in the capacity of apprentices to the old hands, who are considered as headmen or masters: these headmen, according to their influence, or station in their own country, have a proportionate number of apprentices attached to them, fluctuating from five to twenty, to teach them what they call "White man's fashion." The profit of the labour of the youths is always received by the headmen, who returns them a small portion of it. When an apprentice goes back to his own country, after his first trip, he is considered to have passed through the period of initiation, and when next he visits Sierra Leone, he comes upon his own account. The amount of the gains of this visit (a great part of which consists of what they have been able to steal) is delivered up to the elders of his family, who select and purchase a wife for him. A short time is now spent in marriage festivities with the respective relatives of the parties, and then a fresh venture to Sierra Leone is undertaken, on which occasion he leaves his wife with her relations. The proceeds of the third visit are dedicated to the building of a hut, and the purchase of another wife. But he does not remain long at home, before he prepares to set out again for the purpose of making fresh accessions to his wealth, so that he may increase his household up to the desired point where his own personal labour will be rendered unnecessary to his support. In this way he continues to visit Sierra Leone, accumulate property, and purchase wives, the general number of which varies from six to ten, until he has secured the requisite domestic establishment, when he "*sits down*" (as they call it) for the remainder of his life, in what he considers affluence and happiness. The process of wife-buying is remarkably curious. For the first wife they pay two bullocks, two brass kettles, one piece of blue baft, and one iron bar; but the terms upon which they obtain the rest, depends entirely upon the agreement they make with the parents of the brides. A convenient condition is attached to the marriage articles, which secures the husband against any risk of being disappointed by the bargain. If, after marriage, he discovers in the lady any imperfection, or qualities that falsify the account given of her previously by her parents, he is at liberty to turn her away in disgrace, and the rejected bride is for ever after looked upon as an abandoned character. In a very ancient history of Ireland, it is stated, that a practice formerly prevailed in that country, of permitting the bride elect to live with her intended husband twelve months before marriage; and if, at the end of that time, the gentleman was not satisfied with the lady's character and disposition, he was allowed to send her back to her parents, taking upon himself the charge of their offspring, in case they should have any. The gallantry of that people, however, appears not to hare visited the female with any odium in consequence: she was regarded by her friends with the same respect and tenderness as before. The Kroomen cohabit with their wives in succession, passing two days in rotation with each.

Of course, it does not fall to the lot of every Krooman who goes to Sierra Leone, to secure such luxuries for the decline of life, many of them being too imprudent to take sufficient care of their earnings.

The Kroomen sometimes come to Sierra Leone in their own canoes, which are comparatively small for such a voyage, but they manage them with skill, taking the precaution to keep close in with the land, and go on shore every night. They are also conveyed in vessels that trade on the coast, which they prefer, for the sake of economy, as they get their provisions for assisting in navigating the vessel. On returning to their country, however, they cheerfully pay 15s. a-head for their passage, in any vessel they can procure; and, at these times, their luggage, including the fruits of their plunder as well as their earnings, makes no inconsiderable appearance in the ship. When they can afford to return home in these larger vessels, they prefer them, on many accounts, to their canoes, which are not only inconveniently small, but expose their goods to the wet, and always liable to be attacked and plundered by the Fishmen, who are more expert on the water. They are also subject to great danger from some runaway blacks, who infest the coast near the rock Cestus, going out in canoes, and watching their opportunities for plundering any boat or vessel that they are able to overpower.

When the Kroomen leave their own country for Sierra Leone, they do not bring any thing with them, except their gregories (various charms), some native medicines, consisting merely of a few herbs, and a little box containing certificates of character from the different persons with whom they have served. These certificates they prize highly, as forming introductions to future employment; however, but very few of them could be possessed of such testimonials if their masters were better acquainted with their conduct. I have been informed by some persons who have visited the Kroo country, that they have seen in the huts of the natives, silver forks and spoons, knives and forks, table-cloths, towels, &c. &c., things which they never bought, but which they had, no doubt, stolen from their employers. The articles that they generally purchase for themselves are shawls, handkerchiefs, blue baft, and other cloths for wearing round their waist, fine beaver hats, muskets, ammunition, knives, common spoons, and various fancy articles for their women.

It was my intention to have visited their country, had not the Eden proceeded so soon to Fernando Po, but as I was very anxious to be present at the first operations in the formation of our establishment on that island, I reluctantly abandoned my design. Any person would be quite safe in the Kroo country, who would place himself under the guidance of one of their respectable headmen, and Englishmen in particular might visit the interior of their country under great advantages, as the people are well acquainted with them in consequence of the trade which is carried on in ivory, at their own towns on the coast, as well as the intercourse which is constantly kept up with Sierra Leone. There have occasionally been upwards of 2000 of these people at one time in Freetown; but, shortly before our arrival, an order in council was issued to restrict the resident Kroomen to 600, for the purpose of throwing open the labour market to the free blacks, as well as to prevent in some measure the drain of profit which the Kroomen caused by their frequent immigration and departure. Notwithstanding a great proportion of what they earned was expended on articles of British manufacture, which they took away with them, still a material injury was sustained by their constant robberies, which more than counterbalanced the benefit of their expenditure. Independently of this political motive for restricting their numbers, it was useful as a measure of social protection. They resided by themselves in a suburb of the town, apart from the rest of the inhabitants, and used to emerge at night from their close retreats, and commit the most daring burglaries. The stolen property was carefully secreted in their own quarter, where they had a much better opportunity of concealing it than if they dwelt promiscuously in the town at large. They frequently stole calves, pigs and poultry, always adopting the precaution of immediately dressing them, and burning the hides or feathers, as well as any of the offal, that might probably lead to detection. In consequence of these practices their moral character was very low at Freetown, but as they were active, muscular, and intelligent, they obtained a decided preference as servants and labourers. Some of them were also usually employed as sailors in nearly all vessels that remain on the coast. One very remarkable trait in these people is the bond of close union that keeps them together, and preserves an interest in common throughout the whole fraternity. If one of them should commit a crime, it is a very rare occurrence to find another informing, or bearing witness against him; and they carry this principle of combination so far, that they will rather suffer for the offender than denounce him. If the authorities attempt to elicit the facts by a course of examination, they only obtain subterfuges and prevarications, and seek in vain by threats or promises to shake the constancy of the witnesses. The headmen manage their rogueries with so much ingenuity that charges can very seldom be proved against them. They send out their apprentices, under particular instructions, to commit robberies, and, like the Spartan youths, they consider the most expert thief to be the cleverest fellow: should any of these young men be caught, they are left to get out of the scrape in the best manner they are able, for unless it be to swear falsely to an alibi, or some other evasion of truth, their masters never appear in the affair afterwards.

The native denomination of a Krooman is Kroo, and that of a Fishman Krepo, and they have distinguishing marks for their respective countries tattooed on their face.

From the difficulty which exists in ascertaining their own names, they always add some English word as a personal designation. The selection of the word is quite a matter of chance, and it is of no consequence whether it belong to a person, place, or thing. For instance, if you ask one of them what his name is, he will probably say, "My name is Soda Water, Massa," another will tell you that his name is "Bottle Rum," or "Bottle o' Beer," and others, "King Will, Jack Freeman, Tom Freeman," &c. &c. Freeman being one of the most common and favourite names amongst them.

On Wednesday, October 10th.—we were off Cape Palmas, bearing N.E. twenty-one miles, where a number of canoes came alongside with a few trifling articles for sale, but their object was evidently more to beg than barter. The article chiefly in demand amongst them was tobacco. On taking their leave, one of the men got into his canoe by leaping overboard while the ship was going very fast, and the boat paddling hard to keep up with her. He swam to the canoe, and rolled himself over the gunwale in a horizontal position, the people in the boat leaning over the opposite side to prevent it from upsetting. These men may truly be called Fishmen, for they appear almost as independent in the water as the fish who inhabit it; they think nothing of having their canoes upset on the wide ocean, for they can easily recover its former position, and get the water out of it when they resume their places. I was informed they will also attack a shark in the water without hesitation, and they are very expert in catching almost every description of fish. The Kroomen stand no chance with them on the water, and when they happen to encounter each other in their canoes, the first thing the Fishmen try to do is to upset the Krooman's canoe, after which they are quite at their mercy. They arc also much better seamen, as well as boatmen, yet notwithstanding this difference of character, they are in appearance the same people as the Kroomen, and a stranger would not know the difference. Formerly the Fishmen were without the distinguishing mark down the forehead, which is now commonly adopted. Their country, as I have before remarked, is in the vicinity of Cape Palmas, and their principal towns are Bafoo, Wapee, Batoo, Little Cess, Grand Cess, Garaway, Cape Town, Cavally, Tabor, and Bassa. They are much more numerous than the Kroomen, but neither Kroomen nor Fishmen have a united government; for they have frequent wars amongst themselves; Fishtown against Fishtown, and Krootown against Krootown, but they both possess one great and generous characteristic, that of never selling each other for slaves on any pretence. This, in a country where the slave-trade is so universal, may be noted as a very extraordinary and remarkable feature in their character.

When any person dies in the Kroo, or Fish countries, unless the deceased may have expressed a wish to the contrary, his friends apply to the Fetish-men to know how he came by his death, when they invariably fix on some obnoxious character, either man or woman, as having been the cause. This person is then compelled to drink what they call saucy-water, the infusion of the bark of a tree, well known for its deleterious qualities. Of this preparation they are obliged to take three heavy draughts of about a quart each. On the effect of this depends the supposed guilt, or innocence of the accused. If it remains on his stomach he is considered to be guilty of the alleged crime, and he consequently dies; but, if evomition takes place no evil consequence attends it, and he is declared to be innocent. Where it fails to produce the latter effect, the people hunt him about the town as they would a mad dog, until he is at the point of death, which generally takes place a few hours after he has drank the prescribed potion.

Saturday, 13th.—At noon. Cape Three Points E. 1/2 N. 7 miles.

Five leagues to the westward of Cape Three Points, is Axim, where the Dutch have a fort; and about one league further to the westward is the mouth of the river Ancobra. Six leagues to the eastward of Cape Three Points, is Dix Cove, where we had a fort occupied by a small detachment of the Royal African Corps. At half past eight in the evening, we anchored for the night in 15 fathoms water, for fear of running past Cape Coast roads before daylight, the currents being very irregular; and, early on the following morning, we proceeded on our voyage. At 9 o'clock we were abreast of the Dutch fortress of Elmina, which is 7 miles to the westward of Cape Coast Castle, off which place we came to an anchor about 10 o'clock, in 9 fathoms water. We found the African steam-boat, and the Diadem transport, waiting our arrival; there was also an English merchant brig in the roads, but we heard nothing of our schooner. At noon saluted his Honour the Lieut.-Governor, on his leaving the ship, taking his secretary and myself with him in the canoe, which was a fine boat, pulling 17 paddles: we were seated on chairs, fixed to a platform in the forepart of the boat. The castle saluted the Lieut.-Governor on landing, and the shore was lined with natives to receive him. The surf not being very high, we were enabled to land without a wetting, which is rarely the case. On entering the castle, I was introduced to the officers of the garrison, and to Capt. Hutchison, a merchant of this place, who is well-known for his eminent services in this country. The first thing that brought him into particular notice was being associated with Messrs. James and Bowdich, in their mission to the King of Ashantee, in 1817. He was left at Coomassie, the capital of that kingdom, as the accredited British agent, after the departure of the mission, on their return to Cape Coast. The King of Ashantee was pleased with his remaining, for it not only shewed the confidence he had in him, but it was a proof of the sincerity of our intentions, by thus leaving him as a pledge for the fulfilment of our part of the treaty that had just been negotiated; and the forfeiture of his life would, no doubt, have been the consequence, if the King had even suspected any breach of faith on our part. In this situation he remained several months, without the society of any white man, among savages, who think no more of the life of a human being, than a vicious boy does of a dog or cat. Some time after his return from this mission, Capt. Hutchison was called upon to serve in a military capacity against the very nation where all his efforts had been directed to preserve a pacific disposition: and we here find him no less distinguishing himself in the field of proud honour, with his sword in his hand, than he had done in his diplomatic character; for, notwithstanding he had an important command assigned to him, he was personally engaged in almost every battle, in one of which (at Affatoo) he was severely wounded in both arms, and before these wounds were healed, he was called upon to take command of the centre hill on the lines at Cape Coast, when it was attacked by the Ashantees, and all the nations that the powerful king of that country was in alliance with.

I took a ride with Capt. Hutchison before dinner, in his carriage, which was a gig, with a head to it, on four wheels, drawn by as many men; but, if these fellows could have been placed behind us, as they were in the canoe, it would have been desirable, for their muscular exertions produced an effluvia, which was any thing but agreeable. Objectionable, however, as this style of travelling may appear, it was certainly better than being carried about in a sedan-chair, or a palanquin, excepting for travelling at night, or any great distance.

My countrymen will, perhaps, think it very cruel to see men substituted for horses, but when they are informed, that it is undertaken voluntarily on their part, and even eagerly solicited by them, for the reward attendant thereon, there will be no reason for complaint. As a proof of their not feeling the employment derogatory, the following observations will be sufficient to convince the most sceptical:—when a gentleman, who has not a sufficient number of persons on his establishment to employ in this way, wants to take an airing in his carriage, he has only to mention it to his servants, and the house will soon be surrounded with volunteers, soliciting to be selected for the service. There are two reasons why the vehicles at Cape Coast are drawn by men instead of horses, the principal one being that horses are very dear, and do not live long in the climate; the second, that, even if they had a sufficient supply of horses, they could not find a drive of four miles in any one direction, without making a road expressly for the occasion. The short one that they already have, requires constant attention to keep it clear, the vegetation being remarkably rapid and luxuriant.

Captain Hutchison obligingly invited me to take up my quarters with him, but as Colonel Lumley also desired me to consider myself as his guest during my stay at Cape Coast, I divided my time between the Colonel and his officers at the Castle, and Captain Hutchison with the principal merchants of the place. Dined with the Lieutenant-Governor at the officers mess at the castle.

Tuesday, 16th.—Immediately after breakfast I accompanied the Governor and Captain Ricketts to visit a native school, which is composed of 100 boys, some of whom were very intelligent, and wrote and read English remarkably well.

I was present to-day when the Governor gave audience to twenty Ashantee chiefs, who were introduced by the King of the Fantees, or Cape Coast nation, accompanied by a number of his carboceers, or great men, who acted as interpreters to the Ashantees. These twenty chiefs were part of a mission, composed of one hundred and twenty sent by the King of Ashantee to the commandant at Cape Coast Castle, but as the Lieutenant-Governor of Sierra Leone happened to be there at the time, it was thought to be more complimentary that he should give them an audience. They came rather as petitioners than as equals, their object being to sue for a peace, offering to deposit a certain quantity of gold in Cape Coast Castle, as a security for their strict observance of the treaty. After the meeting, I had some conversation with the King of the Fantees, and several of his carboceers, all of whom spoke English.

Wednesday, 17th.—I will just give an outline of my diurnal occupations, which were pretty much the same during my short stay at Cape Coast. My first visit every morning was to Captain Hutchison about 7 o'clock, when I was sure to find him at breakfast. I remained with him about a couple of hours, which time was passed very agreeably in conversation, excepting occasional interruptions by a visit from one of the carboceers, who called on matters of business, or to get him to settle some disputes among their people, for he had so much the confidence of the natives, that both their great men and the common people, preferred referring to him to settle their quarrels than to their own authorities. At 9 o'clock I always repaired to the castle to breakfast with the Governor, and Captain Ricketts, the commandant, after which I used to pass my time among the different merchants, who had all called on me on my first arrival, and given me a general invitation to their houses. About noon I usually found a party assembled at Captain Hutchison's to *relish* with him, as it is significantly called, which in fact was an early dinner, as was the custom of the place. At 4 o'clock they took a ride in the manner before described, or called on each other, and at 6 they took their tea with meat, &c.

This evening I accompanied Colonel Lumley and the officers at the castle, to the merchants club-room, where some played cards, while others passed the time in conversation, billiards, &c. In the intermediate hours during the day I called on various persons, and visited different parts of the town, to glean what information I could. The Horatio, schooner, tender to the Eden, arrived this evening.

Thursday, Oct. 18th.—Passed through the market this morning, which is always held at an early hour, where the articles for sale consist principally of fruits and vegetables. The sales here are conducted by barter, the merchants generally exchanging tobacco and other goods for the articles they want to purchase.

I visited to-day an English school for native girls (21 in number) the expense of which is defrayed by the Government. These children were not all black, for there were a few very pretty Mulattoes amongst them. A custom that must appear strange and immoral to my own countrymen, but which is not held so at Cape Coast, prevails, in reference to these girls, when their education has been completed. Although none of them are regularly affianced, some of them are taken from the school into the household of resident English gentlemen, where they perform all the domestic duties in an anomalous capacity, combining all the responsibilities of the married state, without its legal bond. A previous engagement, and clear understanding is entered into with the parents of the girls, to the mutual satisfaction of all parties, and their offspring is afterwards provided for according to circumstances. These young women usually receive the elements of a good education, and constitute the only female society which an Englishman can enjoy here, as the climate is so debilitating to English ladies that they cannot reside in the place for any length of time. This, indeed, is the only excuse that can be offered for a custom, which it must be granted does not admit of an apology beyond the mere necessity of the case. The girls are excellent managers in domestic concerns, and good and careful nurses, qualities that are exceedingly valuable in such a situation.

Friday, 19th.—Being on the point of taking leave of my friends at Cape Coast, I cannot better occupy a few pages than with some general retrospective observations.

Colonel Lumley, Lieutenant-Governor of Sierra Leone claims my first attention. I had the good fortune to make his acquaintance at the seat of government, and during the whole time I had the pleasure of knowing him, I always found him to be actuated by a most zealous devotion to the many important duties which his situation imposed upon him. Nor was his high character as a public officer more praiseworthy, than his estimable qualities us a man. I shall always look back with pride and satisfaction to the period of our intimacy, which was clouded only with the apprehensions I entertained of the fate that awaited him. Perhaps the prophetic forebodings with which he was impressed might have led me to such gloomy anticipations; for he often observed to me, he felt convinced that if he should ever be attacked by the fever, it would prove fatal, as it unfortunately did, not very long after I left the colony: and I was informed he caught it from a young friend whom he was kindly attending, and who fell a victim to the disease.

With Captain Ricketts, the commandant of the fortress, I also had the pleasure of enjoying an intimate acquaintance. Captain Ricketts has served many years on this coast, and was engaged with the Ashantees at the battle of Essamacow, where Sir Charles McCarthy lost his life. On that occasion he had a most miraculous escape, both in, and after the battle, particularly on his return to the coast, where he was obliged to follow the course of rivers, traverse the jungle and forests alone, to evade the murderous Ashantees. He subsequently became commandant of Cape Coast Castle, in which capacity he acquired so much influence with the natives as to succeed in prevailing on them to build a market-place, to lay out several new lines of streets, and otherwise improve the town; but above all, to induce them, after a great deal of persuasion, and perseverance, to take down all the houses adjoining, and in the immediate vicinity of the castle walls, a measure which must have greatly interfered with their religious prejudices, as they were obliged to remove the remains of their relatives, who are always buried under the apartments they inhabit, and to carry them to their new habitations to be deposited in a similar manner. He had also succeeded with the King and carboceers in getting them to cut away all the jungle from the suburbs of the town, for three or four miles distant, and in fact his influence was so great, and the positive utility of the works he designed so obvious, that the natives of Cape Coast almost adored him. The castle, which is a fine building, was kept in the best order under the superintendence of this active and useful officer.

It is astonishing that the Portuguese, who have been so enterprising, and expended so much money on their early discoveries in the erection of fortresses, many of which may still be considered good modern fortifications, should now allow most of their foreign possessions to go to decay, and even to fall into ruins. Look at the once celebrated city of Goa on the Malabar coast, dwindled into insignificance, and proverbially called a city of priests and beggars. What is the cause of this decadence? Is it a just visitation for the unjust means they practised to acquire those possessions? All for the thirst of gold! Or is it that the active spirit of the Portuguese ceases with the acquisition of novelties, and that they are destitute of those persevering qualities which improve and foster the possessions that are originally obtained by enthusiasm and energy?

We had frequent heavy showers during our stay at Cape Coast, although this was not the regular rainy season, for these showers were what are called the after-rains, which last about a fortnight.

When the weather clears up after very heavy rains, many of the poor people, principally old women and children, take up the mud from the gutters, and wash it well in calabashes, when they generally find a few grains of gold for their pains. This is also the case after a very heavy surf has subsided which, during the violence of the storm, generally throws up a great quantity of black mud on the shore.

There is a strange exhibition to be witnessed every morning on the sea-shore, which, however, I shall forbear to describe.

There is a singular old man, upwards of 60 years of age, at Cape Coast Castle, who is well known by the name of Dr. Saguah, and who acts in the capacity of a native doctor. This person excites a great deal of attention, not only by the peculiarity of his manners, but by the circumstances through which he has reached a station of some consideration. He was originally a slave to the African Company at Cape Coast, and having been accidentally placed in the house of the medical establishment, he learned to compound medicines. In the duties which he performed in this capacity he rendered himself very useful, and continued at the pestle and mortar until Sir Charles McCarthy's arrival, when the African Company was dissolved, all their slaves liberated, and the new charter proclaimed, (for Sierra Leone and Cape Coast) on March 29, 1822. Having received his freedom, he now assumed a position of some importance, and was retained on the medical establishment as dispenser, with a small salary. His excellent conduct and judgment in the discharge of his new office procured him the general respect and confidence of Europeans, and his reputation, when I was at Cape Coast, stood so high that he was frequently consulted on the diseases of the climate in preference to medical gentlemen from Europe. He is in the habit of making daily visits to all the European residents, whether they require his services or not, and they generally invite him to take some refreshment, handing him at the same time the keys of their celeret or cupboard, that he may help himself to spirits, or wine. He sometimes avails himself of their offer, chiefly for the sake of gratifying his vanity, by shewing to the servants the confidence that is reposed in him; for no other native, perhaps, except himself, would be entrusted with the keys of any place where wine and spirits are kept. Trade was very dull during my stay at Cape Coast, and had been so for some time; the merchants, however, looked forward to its revival, in consequence of the prospects of peace with the Ashantee people, who were very desirous to terminate hostilities, for the sake of being enabled to resume their commercial intercourse with the English, and other Europeans on the coast. During the war it was believed that they had accumulated a great quantity of gold and ivory, which are the principal articles they barter for goods of European manufacture, and for which they had no sale while hostilities lasted, except in some few instances, where individuals risked the hazard of embarking in smuggling transactions.

Captain Hutchison (whom I have before mentioned, as being left at the Ashantee capital after the departure of the mission), when the troops returned to the coast, subsequent to the Ashantee war was appointed commandant of the Fortress of Annamaboe, a post which he resigned for a time, in consequence of some difference of opinion with Colonel Lumley, acting Governor of Sierra Leone, when he was at Cape Coast; however, he was afterwards induced to resume the command of the fort, where he has a mercantile establishment, as well as at Cape Coast. His opportunities of acquiring popularity have been very favourable, for he has held several high posts at one and the same time, namely:—

Commissioner of Requests,
Commandant of Annamaboe,
One of H.M. Justices of the Peace for the Gold Coast,
Colonial Secretary of Cape Coast, and
Captain of the Royal Gold Coast Militia.

And I have the satisfaction of adding my personal testimony of his worth, having found him a most intelligent, hospitable, and friendly man. In addition to all the kind offices he had rendered me during my short residence at Cape Coast, he presented me with a hoop basket-worked ring, richly chased, made of virgin gold from the Ashantee country, and also an Ashantee stool, which is described by Bowdich to be made out of a solid piece of wood, called zesso, which is very light, white, soft, and bearing a high polish. In addition to the soft nature of the wood, it is said to be well soaked in water to make it still softer, previous to its undergoing the process of carving.

From its being the custom among the Ashantees for their great men to be seated on stools, some of them take much pride and pains in having them highly carved or ornamented. The pattern is generally the same, being a very low concave seat; the only difference is the manner of ornamenting them. Bowdich relates, that in one of the grand processions at Coomassie, the stools of the great men were carried on the heads of favourites, and he observes that they were laboriously carved, with two bells attached to each. He also describes the King's stool as being entirely cased with gold. The word stool also signifies a high place of office in the King's council, to which his captains are occasionally raised for any distinguished act of bravery; but this promotion is attended by a heavy fee to the King's household, being no less than eight ounces of gold. When a rich man dies, the person that succeeds to his fortune is said to succeed to his stool. I will conclude the subject of stools with an observation relating to cushions, which is, that no subject can sit in public with a cushion on his stool, unless it has been presented to him by the King, or one of his four principal captains.

CHAP. VII.

Recollections of the Ashantee War—Battle of Essamacow—Accession of Osay Aquatoo to the Throne—Battle of Affatoo—Investment of Cape Coast—Flight of the Ashantees—Martial Law proclaimed—Battle of Dodowah—Ashantee Mode of Fighting—Death of Captain Hutchison

I cannot sufficiently express my sense of the uniform kindness I experienced from the residents at this station. My excellent friend, Capt. Hutchison, lodged me in a good stone house, which was entirely appropriated to my own use, and I had also apartments allotted to me at the castle, so that I passed my time as agreeably as I could possibly desire. The interesting conversations in which I had the good fortune to participate, afforded me a variety of curious and valuable particulars respecting the natives; and, when it is remembered that the gentlemen from whom I derived those anecdotes and descriptions, had mingled personally in the scenes to which they referred, they acquire an enhanced value, from so unequivocal a proof of their authenticity. Many incidents, connected with the Ashantee war, were related to me with all the fire and energy which the soldier exhibits when he enumerates the dangers he has escaped, and the victories in which he has shared; I wish I could transfer to my pages the spirit which inspired my informants; but I must leave the imagination of the reader to supply the strong feelings of personal interest involved in the details, contenting myself with a plain recital of a few short reminiscences.

The battle of Essamacow, which is registered in the Gold Coast Almanack, with the significant prefix of "fatal," was fought on the 21st of January, 1824. Hostilities commenced about two o'clock in the afternoon, when both parties opened a brisk fire across a small river, that separated their forces. Our troops consisted of only a few regulars, a small body of militia, and some irregular native allies, the whole commanded in person by his Excellency Sir Charles McCarthy, Governor of Sierra Leone.

The regulars and militia alone were armed with bayonets, so that, in the event of close collision, in which, unfortunately, this conflict terminated, we were at a fearful disadvantage, contending against a foe so much superior in numbers, and so expert in the use of their hand-arms. The firing across the river continued for four hours, but at six o'clock in the evening, the English were compelled to cease in consequence of having exhausted all their remaining ammunition. The Ashantees, perceiving the difficulty in which our troops were placed, resolved to turn the opportunity to immediate account, and, uttering discordant yells, rushed into the river, and advanced *en masse* upon our forces. Sir Charles McCarthy saw that there was but one means of resistance left, and received the tumultuous enemy at the point of the bayonet. For some time, the steadiness and courage of the English prevailed over the barbarian rage of the multitudes that threw themselves upon their "serried ranks," and the Ashantees fell in rapid succession; but it soon became evident that the strictest discipline of such an inferior body, could not withstand the increasing crowds that poured upon them: the English soldiers, finding themselves so hemmed in that their muskets became inconvenient to them, for want of space to exercise their arms with freedom, relieved themselves from the encumbrance by unfixing their bayonets, and casting their muskets away. With this awkward weapon they continued the engagement against an enemy armed with long knives, in the use of which every Ashantee is singularly skilful. All the advantages of European knowledge and cooperation, were at an end. It now became a terrific scene of slaughter, in which physical power had the inevitable superiority. Opposed to such infuriated masses, the coolness of the English was of no avail. They fell quickly before the knives of the Ashantees, exhausted from the loss of blood, and covered with numberless wounds. Happily their sufferings were of short duration, for the enemy, in the fulfilment of a barbarous usage, cut off their heads as they fell, as trophies of their own personal prowess.

Sir Charles McCarthy saw that the day was lost, and that it would be but an inglorious sacrifice of his own staff, and the few soldiers that yet remained, to continue on the field. He, therefore, prepared to retire; but this resolution—which, in the breast of so brave an officer, was slow to find a place—was taken too late. A large body of the enemy had already advanced upon his rear, and intercepted his retreat. All hope, even of escape, was now cut off. The victory of the Ashantees was complete: and nothing but conjecture is left as to the cruel sufferings which were inflicted upon our gallant countrymen and allies before they surrendered their spirits to their Creator on that fatal day.

Two officers only escaped—Brigade-Major Ricketts and Lieut. Erskine. Almost all the principal Europeans were slaughtered, and only one, Mr. Williams, is known to have survived: he was sent to the court of Ashantee. The most melancholy feature in this affair is, that the officer who had charge of the ammunition, neglected to keep the troops properly provided with powder, for had the supply been sufficiently prompt, it is believed that the Ashantees never could have succeeded in their advance movement, or, indeed, that they never would have attempted it, so great was our superiority over them in loading and firing. It is to be feared, that great blame is attached to the management in this part of the arrangement for the necessities of the battle, for when Major Ricketts opened the three last kegs supplied to the troops for ammunition, he found, to his consternation, that they were filled with macaroni! although, when the Ashantees plundered our camp the day after the battle, they discovered ten kegs of ball-cartridges, amongst a great quantity of valuable booty. But, however lamentable this negligence was, it should be suffered to pass into oblivion. The officer upon whom it is charged, perished with his brave companions; and, like them, he is placed for judgment before a higher tribunal: it is, therefore, unnecessary, as it would be cruel, to pain his friends and relatives by registering his name, to mark a military error, which might have been caused by the unexampled confusion of the scene in which he was called upon to act so responsible a part.

Shortly after this disastrous event, the late King of Ashantee, Osay Tootoo Quamina, died. He just lived long enough to receive the intelligence of a triumph which inspired the Ashantees with the most extravagant hopes, and led them to prosecute the war with sanguinary violence. Osay Aquatoo (the Orange[21]), the brother of the deceased king, had no sooner succeeded to the vacant throne, than he resolved to follow up the advantages of the war with vigour. He believed that the death of an officer of such estimation as Sir Charles McCarthy, must have thrown the ranks of the British soldiers into confusion and despair, and, taking it for granted, that a military demonstration, on his part, would be sufficient to complete the successes which had opened so successfully under his predecessor, he departed from his capital to take the command of the army, which was then advancing on Cape Coast. On this occasion, agreeably to the superstitious usage of the natives, the head of the late king was carried into the files of the Ashantees, as a charm to protect them in the battle, and an incentive to the performance of valorous deeds. When the King had made some progress towards the encampment, he sent a sarcastic message to the Commander-in-chief, who was then at Affatoo, within ten miles of Cape Coast, which abundantly shewed the confidence by which he was animated. His message was to the effect, that he had learned, in Coomassie, [22] that all the white men had been killed in the late action, and demanding to be informed, what he, the Commander, and all his young men were about, that they had not taken the Castle.—"Stop!"—was the *naïve* reply of the General to the messenger—"Stop till Friday, when the white men are going to attack us: then you can carry back to the King the news of what you see, and of what the young men have to do." Friday came in due course, and the army of the Ashantees went forward to redeem the pledge of their exulting General. This was the battle of Affatoo, which took place on the 21st of May, 1824. The result was disastrous to the cause of the King. The natives were completely routed and driven from the scene of action, without the loss of a single officer on our side, and with but one wounded (Capt. Hutchison), who commanded the Annamaboe militia, and who was shot through both arms, while he was leading his men to the charge.

The Anglo-Fantee army, immediately after the battle of Affatoo, fell back on Cape Coast Castle, as had been previously arranged by Colonel Sutherland, who had arrived from Sierra Leone just before the battle. This movement of that portion of our troops, enabled Major Chisholm, who possessed the entire confidence of all the soldiers, to take the command in the field. The King of Ashantee, now joined the army, which he headed in person, and concentrating all his forces, he advanced towards Cape Coast Castle with the intention of blockading the town. On the 10th of June, 1824, he pitched his gorgeous

[21] From the colour of his skin.

[22] From "Coom," to kill, and "assie," under, meaning under the large Banian, or Indian fig-tree, that stands in the market-place, opposite to the palace.

pavilion, [23] sparkling with its rich colours and costly embroidery in the effulgent sunlight, on a height to the northward of the town; in the valley between which and the back of the town lay the ground where the important issue was to be contested.

For a whole month the belligerent parties lay in sight of each other, mutually watching their opportunities to attempt a decisive movement. Several skirmishes took place from day to day, but without making much impression on either side; and during this interval of suspense, in which our troops were exposed to the rays of a vertical sun, and in continual expectation of a hidden and treacherous attack from a barbarous horde, greatly superior in numbers, and with whom "revenge is virtue," ascending volumes of smoke wreathing up into the air, and blackening the bright expanse of heaven, marked the terrific conflagrations that were constantly taking place in the surrounding country.

At length the eventful day arrived on the 11th of July, 1824. In order to understand the peculiar perils which our army had to encounter, it is necessary to observe that Cape Coast Castle stands near the sea, and that the town is built on the west side of it, at a short distance from the beach. Upon three conical hills that arise close to the back of the town, and run nearly parallel with the coast, our troops were stationed. The right hill was occupied by Major Chisholm's division, the left by Major Purden's, and the centre by Captain Hutchison's; while the subordinate officers commanded the passes between the valley and the town, which were four in number, two beyond the hills, and two between them. These passes were choked up with a dense jungle. The whole army was commanded by Colonel Sutherland, assisted by Sir John Phillirnore, and most of the officers, seamen, and marines, of H.M.S. Thetis.

At noon the enemy pushed forward in immense numbers, and with ferocious valour towards the passes, with the design of forcing them. Their attention was particularly directed to the right wing, as the town was considered to be most accessible on that side. Their savage cries, their heedless desperation, and tumultuous onset, were well calculated to unnerve the bravery of troops accustomed to discipline and a more honourable species of warfare, but our soldiers met the Ashantees with an unmoved front: the resistance was as courageous as the attack was fierce; and the first approach of the enemy was repulsed with steadiness. It was at this crisis that Lieutenant Swanzy fell, covered with wounds at the head of his detachment. To this fine young man, whose gallantry was conspicuous in the action, might be applied with truth the celebrated words of the poet,

"The young, the beautiful, the brave!"

The conflict raged with great fury, and the indomitable self-possession of our soldiers at last threw the Ashantees into confusion. Their wild exultations

---

[23] This was a very splendid tent that had been presented to him some years before by the Dutch Governor, General Daendals.

gave way to universal despair, a panic seized upon their irregular masses, which now filled the valley in a state of fearful commotion, and exhibited a terrific picture of savage desperation. Perceiving the incertitude of his army, the King descended from the hill for the purpose of animating the troops by his presence. The royal *cortége*, as it swept down the height, and mixed with the heaving crowds below, was singularly imposing. The King advanced with a gaudy umbrella held over his head, followed by a glittering and diversified train, consisting of his numerous wives and eunuchs celebrating his praises and his deeds in barbarous lyrics, while others amongst his retinue were employed in waving brilliant feathers and fans, and the tails of elephants and horses over the head of the monarch, keeping regular time with the inspiring war-song, to which all his guards contributed in an uproarious chorus. The King exhibited great personal courage and perseverance; again and again he rallied his disconcerted troops, who were seen flying about in all directions in the utmost disorder. In this way the conflict was prolonged until darkness fell upon the scene and terminated the battle. On the cessation of hostilities, the Ashantees retired, with the intention, as the British soldiers believed, of renewing the fight with the return of daylight. Major Chisholm, taking advantage of the circumstance, removed into the fort for the night, and discovered for the first time, that the stock of ammunition, particularly the musket balls, was nearly exhausted. Rapid measures were adopted for repairing this disaster; all the leaden and pewter vessels in the town were immediately put in requisition, melted down during the night, and cast into ounce balls. Yet even this additional supply would have been of little avail, had the enemy renewed the attack on the following day. But when the dawn returned, the Ashantees were seen in the distance, encamped in stillness, and without exhibiting any disposition to encounter our soldiers again, and as evening began to fall, preparations were visible of an intention to retire from the field, and in a few hours afterwards, the King of Ashantee, despairing of success, retreated with his army under cover of the night.

From this period a cessation of arms followed; but the Ashantees becoming turbulent again, martial law was proclaimed on the 6th of June, 1826. Affairs were in this position, when the battle of Dodowah was fought on August 7, 1826, between the English, assisted by the native allies, and the Ashantees, with their allies, commanded in person by the king, commonly known by the designation of the Tiger-King.

The ground on which the battle was fought is an extensive plain, the surface of which is occasionally interspersed with clumps of trees and brushwood. It is distant from Accra, N.E. about seven or eight leagues, and lies four miles S. of a village called Dodowah, from which it takes its name. The day on which it took place being considered by the Ashantees as favourable to enterprises, was on that account anticipated by us, so that we were enabled to prepare for the action in time. About eight o'clock in the morning, our scouts brought intelligence that the enemy were already in motion, and the English drums immediately spoke with their fine martial music to our troops, who formed their lines with promptitude, stretching about four miles from E. to W. The variety of costumes, and flags of different nations, exhibited by the European lines, including the native allies, presented a very picturesque and imposing appearance, and invested the scene with a peculiar arid inspiring interest. For several days previous to the battle, a dispute was maintained between the King of Akimboo, the King of Dunkara, and the Queen of Akim, [24] as to who should have the honour of attacking the King of Ashantee's own band. This point, however, was finally settled by an arrangement which satisfied all parties; it was decided that the King of Akimboo should take the extreme right, while the King of Dunkara and the Queen of Akim should occupy the extreme left. Their zealous aspirations, notwithstanding their ardour, were disappointed after all, for the King of Ashantee hearing that the white men filled the central position of the European lines, chose that point for his own attack, on account of the great honour which he hoped to acquire by meeting the English in person.

The officers and gentlemen engaged in the battle were Lieut.-colonel Edward Purden, commanding the whole. Captains Kingston and Rogers, and Lieutenant Calder, of the Royal African Corps; Dr. Young, of the staff; Mr. Henry Richter, merchant, Danish Accra, with his own men, about 120; Mr. I.W. Hanson, merchant, British Accra, with his men, amounting nearly to a similar force; Mr. J. Jackson, merchant, Cape Coast, with Mr. Bannerman's men (Mr. Bannerman being in England in bad health), amounting also to about an equal strength; and Captain Hutchison, Annamaboe, with the Cape Coast artificers, part of the town's people (volunteers), assisted by Bynie, a native chief, whose people, including the above mentioned from Cape Coast, amounted to about 150. These formed the centre, and were drawn up in lines, with the Royal African Corps as a reserve.

---

[24] This extraordinary woman, who displayed unexampled energy throughout the whole of this war, was about five feet three inches in height, and was distinguished by an almost infantine character of face, and a voice low and soft as the tones of a flute. It was thought that she habituated herself to that style of speaking to conceal her really masculine nature, and to interest her audience. Her voice, notwithstanding its sweet inflections, was broken, or "cracked," as singers term it, a circumstance occasioned, perhaps, by the constant use she made of it, for she was not a little remarkable for that volubility which a rude jest attributes to her sex in general. She was a very successful beggar, too, amongst the rest of her accomplishments, for munition and strong drink. Just before the battle of Dodowah commenced, she passed along the ranks, encouraging her people with an appropriate harangue, and waving at the same time a gold-hilted sword in one hand, and an elephant's tail (the emblem of royalty), in the other, with a necklace, well adapted for the occasion, composed of a string of musket halls. This heroine said to some of our countrymen, who called on her the day before the battle, "Osay has driven me from my country because he thought me weak, but he is mistaken; for, although I have the form of a woman, I have the heart of a man!" an observation which her extraordinary prowess in the fight fully justified. She was to be seen every where in the heat of the battle, encouraging and exciting her troops; wherever the greatest danger was, there, too, was the energetic Queen of Akim. Her conduct reminds us of Queen Bess at Tilbury Fort, and perhaps still more of Boadicea herself.

The attack commenced from right to left about half past 9 o'clock. Several of the natives, unaccustomed, probably, to the regularity of European movements, came to the troops in the centre, and reproached them in coarse and offensive language with cowardice, for not opening their fire, which circumstance being communicated to the commanding officer he ordered them instantly to advance. They accordingly moved forward about 400 yards, when a heavy well directed fire took place on our side. From this point the English troops continued steadily to proceed, the enemy slowly and sulkily giving way as they advanced. No prisoners were made, for as they fell they were put to death. Even in this summary cruelty there was a species of mercy, as many were ripped up, and their hearts torn from the vital region, in order that the blood might be poured out on the ground as an offering to the triumph of the English arms. The fighting in many instances was of the most barbarous and ferocious description. In some cases, single men marked their particular adversaries and dragged them from the ranks; and thus, combating in pairs, they wrestled and cut each other, until the knife of the more fortunate gladiator entered the vital part of his antagonist and terminated the revolting contest. The enemy was pressed so hard by our troops, that a distinguished Captain of the Ashantees, either from despair, or to end his misery the more speedily, blew himself up. A cry now arose that the Ashantees were advancing between the centre and the right wing of the army: the alarm was caused by a panic amongst the party from Danish Accra, the native troops in that quarter having, with their Carboceer at their head, retreated early in the action, it being, as they afterwards explained, "against their Fetish to fight on a Monday," and thus created in the remainder of the body apprehensions of weakness. This cowardly conduct of the Danes compelled the centre to fall back, and abandon all the advantages their valour had obtained, a movement which immediately exposed them to a galling fire from the enemy, who now rushed onwards in immense numbers to crush the retiring troops. At this important crisis of the battle, Colonel Purden advanced with the reserve, who brought rockets with them, a few of which thrown amongst the enemy spread the most appalling confusion. The hissing sounds of these novel messengers of death; the train of fire; the explosion; with the ghastly wounds inflicted by the bursting of the rockets; led them to suppose that this terrible instrument could be nothing less than thunder and lightning.

While these proceedings were going forward in the centre, another party of Ashantees attacked the left wing of King Chebbo (of Dunkara), the Winnebahs[25] having fled at the first fire, and never paused until they reached Accra. King Chebbo, however, was in advance with a handful of his people, driving back his opponents, and a few rounds of grape fired over the heads of our troops soon relieved his party from their assailants. On the right wing, the

---

[25] These are the same people who murdered Governor Meredith about fourteen years before. For that crime, the English blew up their fort. They have always acted basely in battle, and are notorious for gluttony, cruelty, and cowardice. The Ashantees said that if they went to Winnebah, they could catch the people like swine.

battle was never doubtful throughout the day. The King of Akimboo swept all before him, penetrated to the King of Ashantee's camp, took them in flank, and shewed his rapid and victorious progress by a column of smoke that extended to the very heart of the enemy's lines.

The example of the Ashantee Captain, who blew himself up to escape from the hand of his adversaries, was followed by several other Ashantees in command. The sight of these suicides on the field of death was terrible: the explosion of the gunpowder, the shouts and groans of the combatants, the discordant noises produced by the rude instruments of the barbarian soldiery, the general *melée* of the raging battle, and the confusion that arose in consequence of the grass having caught the flames from the firing and the exploding powder, presented a scene which, with a little aid from the imagination, might have been easily translated by a poet or a painter into a vivid picture of the infernal regions.

The effects of the rockets and grape-shot, produced so extensive an alarm amongst the enemy, that they fled in all directions, and were at last completely routed. The Danish flag now advanced from the rear, and it was soon seen that the Fetish of the recreants, although it had forbidden them to fight on a Monday, had not made any provision against the commission of acts of spoliation, for these people were the very first to plunder the Ashantee camp, and then to run off with the booty, as fast as they had fled from the field of battle.

The Ashantees lost in this engagement the whole of their camp baggage, including a great quantity of gold. Towards the evening a number of prisoners were made, for our allies, tired of slaughter, contented themselves with making as many prisoners as they could for slaves. They were supposed altogether to have lost 5000 men, amongst whom were most of the principal chiefs, and the King himself was wounded. One of his wives (to whom Mr. Bannerman introduced me at Accra) and a female child were taken prisoners. Our loss was comparatively trifling, not amounting to more than 800 killed, and 1600 wounded. Colonel Purden received a contusion on the higher part of his right leg, from a spent shot, and Mr. Richter received a shot through one of his thighs. Amongst the deaths, there were three native chiefs, who commanded in our lines.

Soon after the battle, some of the Annamaboe people brought several heads of Ashantees whom they had slain to Captain Hutchison, as a proof of their personal courage, and individual prowess. Some of these heads were recognised by Captain Hutchison as belonging to natives who had been known to him. Amongst the spoils one head was found by the Aquapim chief, which excited curiosity, by the care with which it was enclosed in wrappers, and Captain Hutchison desired that the covering should be removed. On taking off the first wrapper, they found the second to be a fine parchment, inscribed with Arabic characters; beneath this was a final envelope of tiger's skin, the well known emblem of royalty among the Ashantees. The evident pains which had been taken in the preservation of this head, satisfied all the by-standers that it was the head of Sir Charles McCarthy, to which it was generally understood regal honours had been paid by the natives. The gratification which this discovery gave to our countrymen may be easily conceived, and they lost no time in sending the head to England, together with the first account of the battle of Dodowah. The head, however, had scarcely been forwarded to its destination, when some prisoners who had been taken in the action, made the disagreeable disclosure that the head belonged, not to Sir Charles McCarthy, but to the late King, Osay Tootoo Quamina, and that it had been taken into the battle in conformity with the prevailing usage of the people. The effects of this information though painful were ludicrous enough. The head of the Ashantee King had found its way to England as an accredited relique of the lamented Sir Charles McCarthy, and was the first remains of an Ashantee that had ever, perhaps, received the solemn rite of Christian burial; while, on the other hand, the head of Sir Charles McCarthy, had been deposited with all the rude pomp of their heathen ceremonials in a Pagan cemetery. However disappointed the friends and countrymen of Sir Charles McCarthy must feel at the discovery of this strange interchange of reliques, the Ashantees are still more mortified at a circumstance which has robbed their royal catacombs of one of its mementos, and broken the line of death's heads by which the chronology of the throne is perpetuated. They are quite ashamed of the occurrence, and greatly annoyed whenever it is alluded to; more particularly as the Fantees, their immediate enemies, take every opportunity of reproaching them with a loss which they consider to be a disgrace.

Connected with this subject is the Ashantee mode of fighting, a description of which will serve to illustrate the previous details. In the first place, we must suppose them to be encamped, with the intention of advancing to attack their enemy. They commence their operations by cutting a number of footpaths for a single person only to make his way through the bush; these paths are cut parallel, equi-distant, and just within hearing. By these numerous paths they all advance in Indian file, until they arrive in front of the enemy, when they form in line, as well as circumstances will admit. Their arms and accoutrements consist of a musket without a bayonet, the lock of which is covered with a piece of leopard's or some other skin to protect it from the weather, a pouch tied round their waist containing the powder, in about twenty or thirty small boxes of light wood, each having a single charge; a small bag of loose powder hanging down on the left side; and in addition to this a keg or barrel of powder is carried for each party to replenish from when required. Their shot is langrage, composed of pieces of iron, lead, ironstone (broken in small pieces), &c. &c., and is carried loosely in a bag. The last of these materials is most generally used, as it is procured with facility, being found lying in great quantities on the surface of the earth. They load their muskets with a large charge of both powder and shot. In their buckskin belts they carry from six to twenty knives of various lengths, together with a cutlass or bill-hook, the former for cutting off heads, and the latter for clearing their way through the underwood. On arriving near the enemy, they cut a path transversely in front of those before mentioned, in which path they form their line, within twenty or thirty paces of the enemy, having a little brushwood in front for their protection. They then immediately commence firing through the intermediate bush. So soon as one of either party observes an opponent fall, he rushes forward and seizes him by the throat, when with great dexterity he separates the head from the body by means of one of his knives, and runs off with it to lay it at the feet of his captain. After the action is over, the captain collects all the heads that he has received, puts them into bowls, and causes them to be presented to the chief of the army.

I cannot take leave of this subject, or of the scenes to which it relates, without reverting to the name of Captain Hutchison, a sharer in the dangers and the glories of the war, and one to whom I am indebted for many valuable particulars, and for an anxious and steady friendship, upon which I shall always look back with satisfaction and gratitude. Very lately—indeed while these memoirs have been in preparation for the press—the painful intelligence of his death has reached me. I had been favoured by a visit from him since his return to England, after an absence of seventeen years in Africa, and anticipated shortly to have had that gratification renewed, looking forward to our meeting with something like the anticipations of a veteran, who hopes, in the society of some ancient and well-beloved comrade, "to fight his battles o'er again!" But these pleasurable dreams of life are not at our own disposal, and we must submit to the will of that Power in whose hands are the agencies of all the elements, of which man is but a perishable compound. My acquaintance with Captain Hutchison commenced under circumstances which cannot easily be obliterated from my memory, and ripened into friendship almost unconsciously. I speak of him as I knew him, and even my partiality, heightened by my regret, cannot much exaggerate his merits. He was a brave officer, and an intelligent gentleman. His mind was practical, prompt, and energetic; and he united to the qualities of a strict disciplinarian, all the kind feelings that embellish the character of social benevolence. Peace to his ashes, and honour to his name!

CHAP. VIII.

Embarkation—Departure for Accra—Land Route—Accra Roads-Visit to Danish Accra—Dilapidations of the Fortresses at Dutch and English Accra—Captive Queen—Mr. Thomas Park—Cause of his Death unknown—Departure for Fernando Po—First view of the Island—Anchor in Maidstone Bay—Early History of the Settlement—Captain Owen's Expedition—Visited by the Inhabitants—Site for the Settlement determined—Author's Mission to the King of Baracouta—Visit of the King—Native Costume—Ecstacy of the Natives—Distribution of Presents—Second Visit to the King—His Majesty's evasive Conduct—Renewed Interviews—A Native Thief—Intended Punishment—Cutthroat, a Native Chief—Visit to King-Cove—Purchase of land

Friday, Oct. 19.—When on the point of embarking with Mr. Galler, the purser of the Eden, we took some refreshment at Mr. Castle's, a commissariat officer, whom I had the pleasure of unexpectedly meeting again at New South Wales, and who is one of the few survivors, after serving some years at Sierra Leone and Cape Coast. Embarking, as well as landing, at this place, is a matter of some moment, the passengers and a part of the crew being obliged to get into the boat before they launch her from the beach; for the surf is occasionally so heavy as to become exceedingly perilous. Canoes are frequently upset in the attempt to get off in bad weather, and the purser of a man-of-war was drowned in this manner a few years before; but the natives, who are like fish in the water, are indifferent to the danger; all they care about is to keep the boat from being stove, and to save her appointments. There was a small lodge of rocks about one hundred yards from the shore, that would answer for the foundation of a breakwater, which it is calculated might be effected at the cost of from three to five hundred pounds, and which certainly would be most desirable for affording protection, and facility to boats, both on landing and leaving the shore.

Saturday, Oct. 20th.—At eight this morning we left Cape Coast Roads with a fine breeze, for Accra, a distance of sixty miles by sea, and eighty-five by land. A sketch, of the land route may not be uninteresting. Four miles eastward of Cape Coast is Moree, and the Dutch Fort Nassau; six miles from Moree is Annamaboc, the most complete fortification in the country; five miles from thence Cormantine, the first fort possessed by the English, and built by them about the middle of the seventeenth century. It was taken afterwards by the Dutch, and being stormed, was almost destroyed by the Ashantee army, before it attacked Annamaboe; the position is very commanding. Tantumquerry, a small English fort, is about eighteen English miles from Cormantine (crossing the small river Amissa, an hour's walk inland from which is Mankasim, the capital of the Braffoe district of Fantee), the natives call the town Tuam; eight miles from Tantumquerry is the town of Afram, where there is a Dutch fort, and a small river; eight miles from Afram is Simpah or Winnebah. The people of Simpah are Fantees, but their language is called Affoottoo. They are in the district of

Agoona. About nine miles from Simpah is the Dutch fort Berracoe; the natives call the town Leniah. Attah, of Akim, laid a contribution on this fort in March 1811. About twenty-seven miles from Berracoe is Accra or Inkran, once subject to Aquamboo, which people, according to Isert, formerly drove them to Popo.

We had only the Horatio schooner in company, the African steam-vessel, and Diadem transport, having sailed the preceding evening for Fernando Po.

Sunday, 21st.—At eleven o'clock this forenoon, we anchored in Accra Roads, where we found His Majesty's ship Esk, Captain Purchass, who came on board to wait on Captain Owen. I had the pleasure of accompanying this gentleman on his return, first to his ship and then to the shore, in a very fine canoe of the country, belonging to Mr. Bannerman, who is the only English merchant at Accra. This canoe was fifty feet in length, pulling seventeen paddles, and Mr. B. has had it raised two feet in the fore part (where the passengers were seated on chairs), expressly to protect him from the sea in his occasional voyages to and from Cape Coast Castle.

We found the beach equally bad for landing as at Cape Coast. Some of the officers of the Eden and Esk, as well as myself, dined with Mr. Bannerman, and I slept at the house of Captain Fry, who was commandant of the English fort here, which is in a most ruinous state, and instead of being *fort*, I should say it was *foible*.

Monday, 22nd.—After breakfast, a party of us in two gigs, drawn by four blacks each, went to Danish Accra, a distance of two miles, and a very good road. The Danish Governor and all the officers received us very politely, and invited us to remain and pass the day with them. The fortress was very clean, and every way apparently in good order. What is called Danish Accra is merely the fortress, which is the case with Dutch and English Accra, [26] for there are no Europeans living in private houses, except Captain Fry and Mr. Bannerman. The fortress of Dutch Accra is even in a more ruinous state than that of the English, and is entirely deserted. There is a native town, of course, and in it are to be found jewellers, who make ornaments of every fashion, out of the purest gold, brought from the interior. The gold is four pounds per ounce, and they charge an additional pound for converting it into necklaces, bracelets, or any other ornaments, of whatever pattern you may fancy.

Mr. Bannerman invited us to visit one of the King of Ashantee's favourite wives, who had been made prisoner during the war, with her daughter and grand-daughter, whom Mr. B. had accommodated with part of his house, where his own two sisters were living, distant about a quarter of a mile from the house of business where he resided. They were apprized of our visit, and were dressed accordingly to receive us. Mr. Bannerman is himself a gentleman of colour, and a man of education; he resided a long time in England, and is a sensible, mild, and gentlemanlike man. He supplies all our men of war, on the African station, when they call at Accra, with bullocks, vegetables, &c. &c.

---

[26] Accra is a European corruption of the word Inkran which means an ant.

Mr. Thomas Park, who left England, as one of the Midshipmen of the Sybille, but with three years leave of absence from his ship so soon as she arrived on the coast, ordered by the Admiralty for the express purpose of travelling in Africa, with the avowed intention of endeavouring to discover the course, and source of the Niger, was landed at Accra some time since from that ship, and passed a short time there in studying some of the languages of the countries through which he meant to travel. He left Accra to proceed on his journey into the interior on the 29th of September, 1827, and arrived at Mampong in Aquapim on the 2nd of October; this he left on the 5th for Acropong, the chief town of Aquapim, and on the 10th left Acropong, for Aquambo, a town at the head of the Volta river, where he arrived on the 16th of October. I heard that he had been kindly treated, so far as he had penetrated, but at the last mentioned place, he took a fancy to climb a particular tree, which the natives entreated him to desist from, saying that it was Fetished, [27] however, he persisted and accomplished his wish. A few days after this he was taken ill, and as every one knows, he did not survive to tell his own story: perhaps the precise cause of his death will ever remain in doubt. This gentleman was a son of the celebrated Mungo Park, than whom no man was better calculated for such an enterprise, and whose loss is perhaps more to be regretted than that of any other African traveller; but I lament to say that from the moment I heard of his son, an inexperienced young man, undertaking an enterprise of such magnitude, as that of penetrating alone into the interior of an unknown country, to solve a problem in the pursuit of which so many distinguished travellers had failed and fallen, I confess I never supposed he would live to return: in fact, the project appeared to me, what is emphatically expressed in the old proverb, "a wild-goose chase." For where men of maturer judgment and greater experience found that they could not contend against the superstitions, prejudices, and artifices of

---

[27] The word Fetish is derived, I believe, from the Portuguese word Fatisa, or Phatisa, which means "a charm." It is used on all occasions by the natives, when they are asked any question which they do not understand, or which they do not wish to understand, particularly if it relate to their religion. Thus the sacrifice, the rocks, and the sacred groves where they imagine their deities dwell, are all called Fetish: also, their priests, or priestesses, when they are going through any antic ceremonies, are said to be making Fetish, and are consequently called Fetish men or Fetish women. Some have regarded the Fetish as an object of worship to the natives of Africa; it ought, however, more properly to be considered only as a *charm*, to which a superstitious and reverential feeling is paid; in which an implicit confidence is reposed. Whether it be intended to exercise a public or a private function, it consists of some body, either animate or inanimate, selected according to fancy, as a dog, cat, tiger, snake, an egg, the bone of a bird, a piece of wood, a feather, or any other substance: this is rendered sacred or endowed with its supposed virtues by peculiar ceremonies, and afterwards honoured with a species of worship, vows of abstinence from particular or occasional pleasures, and other services; in return, the party to which it belongs looks up to it for protection and assistance on all occasions—if successful, he attributes it to its intervention; if unlucky, to its displeasure.

those cunning savages, how was it to be expected that a youth of nineteen could possibly succeed?

I have heard, that his desire for travelling in Africa, arose from a romantic notion, that had entered his head when a boy, of seeking for his father in the interior of that country, to ascertain whether he was alive and in slavery, or had lost his life by sickness, or violence. This filial enthusiasm continued to haunt him until a short time before he left England, when he abandoned the fond hope of recovering his father, whose death was confirmed by a variety of coincident circumstances, but still he resolved to persevere in his long-cherished scheme of visiting the interior of Africa. Impelled, perhaps, by the name he inherited, and a latent passion to emulate the deeds of his father, on the same field of action, he embarked in this hazardous and unfortunate enterprise. But mark the difference of character and qualifications. The father, a man of mature judgment, whose experience in the world gave him considerable advantages; was also of an age and temperament that rendered him less liable to the endemic diseases of such a climate, [28] while his patience, perseverance, and medical skill, enabled him to surmount difficulties which a younger man, by his rashness, would only increase. The son, a young sailor, just entering life, full of enthusiastic ardour, and, perhaps, of confidence, from the information he had collected from books, little thinking that theoretical knowledge is of no avail in comparison with the practical study of human nature, particularly amongst savage tribes, which time and experience alone can give, was, of all persons, the worst qualified for such an undertaking. He possessed no knowledge whatever of the country, or the people, and had not a single individual to hold council with, amongst a variety of savage nations, where he would, occasionally, meet with some of the most cunning and intriguing people in the world. I, of course, allude to the Arabs; who alone possess any influence, or can be supposed to be secure amongst the Africans of the interior, cut off, as they are, from all European nations on the coast:—the Mahommedan religion is the only one that is generally known, and the only written one amongst these people, the rest being mere superstitious forms and customs: which, however, do not vary, in any great degree, in the whole country. The Arabs are very jealous of the ascendancy they possess over the various nations of the continent of Africa, and studiously endeavour to prevent strangers from traversing the interior, from the fear of losing the influence they have acquired over this poor, ignorant, and superstitious people.

It appears singular, that there should have been no rain at Accra, where their crops were failing for the want of it, although it rained every day at Cape Coast. There were several heaps of shells on the beach at Accra, principally consisting of the common cowrie, and the large muscle. They had been collected for the

[28] In my opinion, no man under thirty years of age, should think of travelling in an unhealthy country; before that age, the constitution is more liable to the infection of the endemic diseases of a hot climate than afterwards. Perhaps, between forty and fifty would be the best age—"ceteris paribus."

purpose of undergoing the process of calcination. In the absence of limestone, they are used as a substitute, and are considered to produce a finer and stronger lime.

About sun-set we embarked in the same large canoe from which I landed, and immediately after our arrival on board, the Eden got under weigh, when we shaped our course for our ultimate destination, the Island of Fernando Po, a distance of 530 miles, bearing about E. by S. 1/4 S. while H.M.S. Esk, left Accra roads for Cape Coast.

Friday, 26th.—After a four days' passage across the Gulf of Guinea, at seven o'clock this morning, we saw the island of Fernando Po, bearing S.E. This island can be seen from a considerable distance, being distinguished by some very high peaks. At four in the afternoon, the wind fell away nearly to a calm, when we found ourselves close in with the land, and a current carrying us still closer; however, fortunately, a light breeze sprung up, when we were glad to stand off for the night. On the following morning (*Saturday, 27th*) we made towards the land, sailing along the coast, which presented the most picturesque, scenery that could well be imagined, until we anchored in Maidstone Bay, at half past three in the afternoon, 12 fathoms water—black mud.

The island of Fernando Po, situated off the western coast of Africa, in the Gulf or Bight of Biafra, between 3°. and 4°. N. latitude, and 8°. and 9°. E. longitude, is about one hundred and twenty miles in circumference. It is generally believed to have been discovered in the year 1471, by a Portuguese navigator, who gave it the name of Ilha Formosa, or the Beautiful Isle, afterwards changed for that of its discoverer, which it now retains. The Portuguese first established a settlement upon it which they, however, abandoned, and subsequently transferred the right of possession to Spain, receiving in exchange the Island of Trinidad, off the coast of Brazil.

In the year 1764, a new settlement was founded by Spain, which, after a lapse of eighteen years, was also abandoned, for causes which have not been satisfactorily explained, although it is generally believed that a series of misunderstandings with the natives took place, which principally produced that result. [29]

---

[29] The following extract from the letter-book of the late African Company, throws considerable light upon this subject:

'Cape Coast Castle, 30th January, 1783.

'Captain Lawson, who has been lately at the islands of Princes and St. Thomas, says that the Governor, who was inimical to the English, is returned to Portugal; he hired to the Spaniards at Fernando Po, one hundred soldiers to make reprisals on the English, in consequence of Captain Ragan having endeavoured to cut out of the island a Spanish packet, which was there in March and April last. Captain West of his Majesty's ship *Champion*, cruized off Fernando Po, two days in July last, in order to fall in with a frigate of thirty guns, and a sloop of fourteen, but, being both in the harbour, they would not

Since this period the island has been left to its native inhabitants, excepting that various European, and particularly English vessels, have occasionally touched at it for the purpose of procuring water and yams; the latter of which it grows the finest in the world, and which the natives were accustomed to barter for pieces of iron.

At length, a variety of considerations determined the British Government to attempt a new settlement on this island; these it may be proper briefly to state.

In the first place, the convenient situation of the island, at the distance of only twenty miles from the main-land of Africa, and in the immediate neighbourhood of the mouths of the many large rivers which pour their waters into the Gulf of Biafra, appeared to afford a most eligible point for checking the slave-trade, of which this position may be considered the very centre.

Secondly, it, was imagined,—and the consideration reflects the highest honour on the humanity of our Government,—that the adoption of the measure would tend materially to diminish the sufferings of the miserable objects of human traffic—the unfortunate slaves—who too frequently sank under the confinement and disease incidental to a protracted voyage to Sierra Leone, before their liberation could be legally accomplished.

In the third place, it was hoped that the greater salubrity of the new colony would lead to the eventual abandonment of the settlements of Sierra Leone and Cape Coast Castle, the direful effects of whose climates upon European life have long been proverbial. The Insular position of Fernando Po, and the nature of its climate and localities, appeared to offer an earnest that it would not abound with those, destructive malaria which have proved, on the neighbouring continent, so fatal to our brave countrymen.

I might also advert to the facilities which the situation of Fernando Po, at the estuaries of so many great rivers, together with its insularity, holds out for extending and protecting our commercial relations with Central Africa, and

---

come out. These two vessels remained in St. Thomas's in October last, where they had carried 200 troops, the only remains of 3000 that had originally been sent to Fernando Po, where the Spaniards had made a settlement, and landed a great quantity of brass cannon, and all kinds of military stores; but the natives were so disgusted with the Spanish Government, that they poisoned the water, which caused a great mortality and obliged the survivors to go away. However, previous to their departure, they dismounted and buried the cannon and all the stores; and, after they were gone, the natives demolished all the fortification, and threw the stones into the sea. A few Portuguese natives of St. Thomas's who for misdemeanors had been sold to the Spaniards by the Portuguese Government, are now remaining in the island ready to shew where the cannon and stores are buried; and, from what Captain Lawson has heard, the natives seem to wish that the English would come and settle among them, promising to render us every assistance in their power in erecting a settlement there. The importance of the trade carried on to Leeward having already been represented to you, I shall not add on the subject.'

probably extending the blessings of civilization amongst its inhabitants; these, however, although important, were minor considerations with the British Government.

To carry the proposed object into effect, an expedition was fitted oat in the early part of the summer of 1827, under the command of Captain William Fitzwilliam Owen, of His Majesty's ship *Eden*, who received the appointment of superintendent of the colony, and than whom no one could be better adapted to fulfil the important duties which were to devolve upon him; Captain Harrison, a highly meritorious and indefatigable officer, received the chief civil appointment under him. A number of appropriate artificers, with an abundant supply of the requisite stores, including several framed wooden houses ready for immediate erection, were embarked in a transport; and it was arranged that a body of troops, with an additional number of workmen and labourers from Sierra Leone, should be attached to the expedition on its arrival at that settlement.

On first approaching the island, its mountains were shrouded from view by heavy clouds and a hazy atmosphere; which, however, gradually dispersed as we neared the shore, and revealed to the eyes of my companions a magnificent display of mountain scenery, closely studded with large trees, and thick with underwood, whose luxuriant foliage of various tints and hues, blending with the scarcely ruffled bosom of the ocean, and the retiring clouds, making the sky each moment become more lucid and transparent, formed such a variegated picture of natural beauty, that we unanimously hailed it as the land of promise.

It was not long before the scene began to assume an aspect of animation, the immediate consequence of our arrival; for, in less than half an hour after we anchored, a number of canoes, with several natives in each, who had already been trafficking with the Diadem, [30] approached us for the purpose of bartering the productions of their island, namely, yams, fowls, palm-wine in calabashes, fish, some boxes made of split cane, monkey and snake skins, with other trifling articles; for pieces of iron hoop, a few inches long, which we afterwards found they made into two-edged knives, by beating them between stones, until they succeeded, in shaping the blade to their purpose, when they fitted it into a wooden handle, from four to six inches in length. In the first instance, however, they evinced considerable doubt and timidity, as they did riot venture to come alongside, but kept the stern of their canoes directed towards us, to be ready to paddle away on the first show of hostility, while a man remained in the forepart to carry on the barter. We in vain attempted to induce them to come on board, for, pointing in reply to their Fetish, they gave us to understand that this was either prohibited or imprudent. It was easy to perceive that the natives were fine-looking, active, middle-sized men, with an agreeable and animated expression of countenance. The natural colour of their skin was not ascertainable, the whole body being painted, or rather daubed over with a composition of clay, or ochre, mixed up with palm-oil. The prevailing colour was red, which seems to belong more exclusively to the lower classes: some few,

---

[30] The Diadem arrived in the bay a few hours before us.

however, had used a yellow, and others a grey pigment, probably as a mark of distinction, and which we afterwards found appropriated to the kings, or chief men. The faces were much seamed or scarified, while other parts of the body, and particularly the abdomen, were more or less tattooed. It is curious to remark, among the African savages, the variety of delineations on their skin, tattooed in lines, figures, or tropes, by way of ornament, fashion, or distinction, in nation and rank, which, perhaps, cannot be better described than in the words of the poet:—

Prince Giolo and his royal sisters,
Scarr'd with ten thousand comely blisters,
The marks remaining on the skin,
To tell the quality within:
Distinguish'd flashes deck the great,
As each excels in birth or state;
His oylet-holes are more and ampler;
The king's own body was a sampler.

Their weapons were wooden well-barbed spears, with their points hardened by fire, each individual being provided with three or four. We afterwards, however, found that these were not the only means of defence, as they are possessed of slings, in the use of which they acquire no inconsiderable expertness. The canoes appeared to be from 15 to 30 feet in length, and each capable of carrying from three to twelve persons; these were provided with sails made of a kind of split rattan matting, of an oblong square form, the longer side placed perpendicularly, and some of them had a staff erected in the bow, with a bunch of feathers at the top of it.

When our muskets were fired at sunset, the whole immediately shoved off, being evidently much alarmed at the report; and most of them, hoisting their sails, endeavoured to reach the shore with all possible celerity.

Sunday, October 28.—Notwithstanding it rained heavily this morning, a great number of the natives came off to us at an early hour for the purpose of renewing their barter, to exchange their articles for pieces of iron, a metal which they appear to hold in the highest estimation, and which became the almost exclusive medium of our traffic with them. This metal they wisely prefer, nay, almost worship, for its usefulness; knives, hatchets, and iron-hoop, rank first in their good opinion, scissors and razors holding a secondary place; for they deem six inches in length of old iron-hoop, a quantity which would purchase half-a-dozen yams, varying from six to twelve pounds each in weight, far more valuable than the best razor you can present them with; in short, the *ferri sacra fames* may here be well substituted for the *auri fames* of more civilized nations. We may safely aver, that in our intercourse with these people, we have the 'love of iron' the chief exciting principle of their more generous, as well as malignant passions,—an opinion which many subsequent anecdotes in this narrative will prove.

The natives had to-day gained an evident accession of confidence, as some of them ventured on board, not, however, without many symptoms of timidity. A boy of twelve years old allowed himself to be conducted over the ship, and was shewn a variety of articles, of course entirely novel to him. With these he was, as may be supposed, exceedingly astonished, but more particularly with a looking-glass, and by the ringing of a small bell.

In the course of the day, Captain Owen landed at various points for the purpose of investigating the localities of the neighbourhood, and with a view of selecting the most eligible situation for our intended establishment. Lieutenant Robinson also went on shore to take sights for comparing the chronometers. Several natives approached the latter gentleman, offering him yams in barter, but were careful not to come too near, so long as his men remained armed with muskets. As it was evident from their signs that they wished these to be laid aside, Lieutenant Robinson, in order to inspire them with confidence, directed his party to ground arms, while he and Mr. Jeffery advanced towards them. Satisfied with this demonstration, their whole anxiety now appeared to be, how to dispose of their yams, which they professed, by signs, and with affectation of fatigue, to have brought from a great distance. They were not a little disappointed that our party, being unprovided with the necessary medium for payment, hoop-iron, were unable to effect the purchase.

Monday, Oct. 29.—The natives, who have visited us in great numbers to-day, are evidently increasing their stock of confidence, and, indeed, beginning to be, not a little troublesome, as we have no small difficulty in preventing them from coming on board. At seven o'clock in the morning we changed our anchorage to the opposite side of the bay, near the Adelaide islets, and close to Point William. A party went on shore for wood and water, in the procuring of which they were assisted by the natives.

Tuesday, Oct. 30.—Captain Owen, having now thoroughly investigated the vicinity of this place, determined upon the site of our future settlement. For this purpose, Maidstone Bay, in consequence of its capacity, (being about four miles and a half from Cape Bullen, its north-western limit, to Point William); the excellency of its anchorage, and the smoothness of its water, offered peculiar advantages; to which may be added, its reception of the waters of the Baracouta river, with other smaller streams, and the abundance of its fine fish of various kinds, including two or three species of turtle. On the south-eastern side, adjoining to coves which have received the respective names of Clarence and Cockburn Coves, two necks of land project into the bay, the one named Point Adelaide, with two small islands off it, bearing the same name; the other Point William. It was on the latter, constituting a kind of peninsula, projecting nearly six hundred yards into the sea, that Captain Owen decided upon fixing the infant settlement, which is probably destined to become the future emporium of the commerce, as well as the centre of civilization of this part of the globe,— giving it, out of compliment to His Royal Highness the Lord High Admiral, the name of Clarence. Besides the above named peninsula, the new settlement comprises other adjoining lands, which were afterwards respectively known by the appellations of Bushy Park, Longfield, Paradise, and New-lands, with some which have not yet received any name,—the whole constituting an elevated plain, lying between one and two hundred feet above the level of the sea, and at present thickly covered with timber and jungle. In Clarence Cove, there is an excellent spring of water issuing from a cliff, about sixty-six yards above low water-mark, well calculated to supply the exigencies of the settlement, and which it is intended to conduct, by means of shoots, down to the beach.

The above situation having been finally decided upon, Captain Owen determined to lose no time in commencing operations, and, in the course of the day, notwithstanding it proved rainy, a party of a hundred Kroomen and other black labourers, were landed, under the command of Mr. Vidal, the senior lieutenant, and immediately began to clear a road through the jungle, to the spot selected for the new town.

Accompanied by Mr. Morrison, I also went ashore at Baracouta, for the purpose of inviting the supposed king of the island, but who, we have since reason to believe, is only the chief of a tribe. His Majesty would have accepted our invitation, had not his attendants offered a strong opposition: all we could gain was a promise that he would visit us early on the following morning. Our interpreter was a black soldier of the Royal African Corps, named Anderson, who professed to have some acquaintance with the language of the islanders. We found afterwards, however, that his Fernandian vocabulary was scarcely more copious than a sensible parrot might acquire in a month: his knowledge of the English, at all events, was so exceedingly defective, as to make another interpreter necessary, to explain what he meant to express, in our language. This man was left to pass the night at the royal residence, in order that he might avail himself of opportunities to inspire his Majesty with confidence, and be ready to accompany him on his visit in the morning.

Wednesday, Oct. 31.—The steam-vessel (*African*) arrived to-day, and brought in two vessels under Brazilian colours, which Lieutenant Badgeley had boarded and detained, under strong suspicion of their being engaged in the slave-trade.

At nine o'clock, the King of Baracouta, accompanied by his brother and five or six other chiefs, came on board according to promise, and without betraying any symptoms of timidity. The party were immediately conducted to the captain's cabin, and entertained with wine and biscuit, which they appeared to partake of with considerable relish. His Majesty, however, had not come unprovided, his canoe having been stored with some calabashes of palm-wine, which he sent for and distributed freely. We partook of this wholesome beverage, but some of the natives mixed it with Madeira. I must not omit to mention that, whether as a point of etiquette, or intended as an expression of gratitude for the attentions they were receiving, the King, and his Chiefs, were particularly desirous of rubbing their long beards against those of our party who happened to be possessed of a similar ornament. Amongst other circumstances which gave them satisfaction, they were highly gratified by sitting on our chairs; and we have since learned, that, in their own residences, they are in the habit of using logs of wood for this purpose, a custom differing from many of the African nations.

A description of their dress, which was in the most fanciful savage taste, cannot fail to be interesting. In the first place, the body was completely smeared over with the kind of paint I have before described: His Majesty's colour, like that which distinguishes the imperial family of China, being yellow, while the livery of his attendants was dark red. The hair of the head was dressed in long small curls hanging down behind, and which, instead of hair powder and pomatum, were well stiffened with ochre and oil: in front, similar curls dividing from the forehead, hung down on each side below the ears, somewhat in the style of Vandyke's female portraits of the age of Charles I. The forehead was generally round, sufficiently elevated to give phrenological indications of a fair portion of intellect, and, perhaps, unusually well displayed by a custom which prevails of having the hair shorn in front an inch beyond the line of its natural growth, so as, in conjunction with the peculiar disposition of curls before described, to leave the part fully exposed. In some instances, seven or eight strings of beads, in imitation of the natural curls, were adjusted with much care over the forepart of the head, and conducted separately behind the ears, the end of each string reaching down to the shoulders. This singularly ornamental head-dress was surmounted by a flatfish low-crowned hat, with a narrow brim, the whole shape not a little resembling that of Mambrino's helmet; the frame-work, constructed of loosely wove split rattan, was covered over and ornamented with leaves, the bones of monkeys and other animals, and a few white, and occasionally red, feathers; the latter of which appeared to have been dyed in the blood of some animal. This hat was secured to the head by a skewer, which passed through the crown, and penetrated a tuft of hair collected above the vertex. The neck, arms, body above the hips, and the legs below the knee, were encircled by ornamental bands, in the form of bracelets, which were, for the most part, composed of strings of beads, or the vertebrae of small snakes; to the girdle, which thus surrounded the body, was appended, hanging down in front, the only article of covering which they can be said to wear, consisting of the skin of some animal, and which, in many instances, was decorated with a bunch of herbage. His Majesty, however, as a mark of distinction, wore also a similar covering behind.

After having been entertained in the cabin, we conducted the party along the main-deck, and shewed them our horses, oxen, pigs, &c., with the whole of which they were highly gratified, especially with the cow, whose tail was a source of ineffable delight to them, each of them handling it in succession, plucking out its hairs, and shaking it with every indication of astonishment. The band was directed to play for their amusement, and delighted them to such a degree, that they could not restrain themselves from running into the midst of it. The King's brother was so enraptured, that he capered about with excess of joy, making the most uncouth gestures in accordance with the music.

"So play'd Orpheus, and so danced the brutes."

Our more difficult task was yet to be encountered—the distribution of presents. His yellow Majesty was in the first place complimented with the whole of an iron hoop straightened out for the occasion, and also with half a dozen fishing-hooks; to his brother we gave half the quantity: while the minor chiefs received about a foot in length each. Some squabbling occurred during this arrangement, which was, at length, happily concluded, pretty much to the satisfaction of the whole party, and they left the ship in apparent good humour, evidently highly gratified with their visit.

Thursday, Nov. 1.—A heavy fall of rain disappointed us in an arrangement to visit the chiefs on shore.

Friday, Nov. 2.—Notwithstanding it continued to rain heavily at intervals, I went on shore in company with Messrs. Galler and Morrison, for the purpose of arranging with the King for the establishment of a market. On landing, we were surrounded by a number of natives, who treated us with more kindness than on our preceding visit, not forgetting, however, both male and female, from the youngest to the oldest, to importune us incessantly for iron; it was almost dangerous to take particular notice of any individual, for they immediately assumed it as an indication of a disposition to make them a present, and began to double their importunities. Not finding the King or his chiefs on the beach, we sent to announce our arrival, yet we had to wait two hours before they condescended to appear. During this time, Mr. Galler amused himself with shooting monkeys; which appeared to afford some interest and amusement to the natives, who assisted in pointing out *the game*, and laughed heartily whenever he missed his aim.

At length the King arrived, and we explained as well as we could the object of our visit, to which he listened with great attention, appearing to comprehend, so as finally to accede to our wishes. He then proposed, in order to preserve a mutual good understanding, that, in the event of any breach of faith on the part of their people, we should immediately communicate the same to the chiefs, who would take care to have the delinquent properly punished; while, on the other hand, if any of our people were guilty of improper conduct towards them, they would represent it to our chief. This proposal, after a deliberate discussion, was agreed to on both, sides, the contract confirmed by drinking palm-wine, and a mutual exchange of presents, as follows, we tendered an axe to the King, and he returned the compliment by presenting us with a fowl.

We now proposed to accompany his Majesty back to his village. With this he appeared perfectly acquiescent, taking me by the hand, and leading me forward, as if he were conducting me to the point proposed; but we soon found that his real intention was to lead us to our boats. We still, however, imagined that this was only with the view of taking us some nearer way home; but when we wished him to enter the boat, with the intention of coasting it to another part of the shore, he positively declined, giving us to understand that his house was not good enough to receive us, and that it contained nothing in the shape of refreshments sufficient to do honour to the visit. We were, however, predetermined, and, as our interpreter was acquainted with the way, proceeded with Captain Smith and Mr. Jeffery, in addition to our former party. When we arrived, we were ready to admit that his Majesty had some reason not to be over-anxious for our company: for neither was the road, nor the accommodations of his hut, calculated either for a visit of pleasure or ceremony; in many parts the path was not only slippery, but interrupted by roots of trees and pools of water; added to which, it lay through a thick jungle, which swarmed with myriads of ants. His Majesty's hut was a mere thatched roof, the eaves of which nearly reached to the ground, supported by posts, and with only one end protected from the weather; the chief articles of furniture were logs of wood, as substitutes for stools, and an inclined plane of wood, five feet in length, to serve the purpose of a bed, the pillow of which was a round bar, three or four inches in diameter, supported at the proper height by two brackets. The king's brother, who had arrived first, received us with much good humour, but regretted that he had nothing to entertain us with. In a short time, however, a calabash of stale palm-wine was handed in, which, having first tasted, according to the African custom, with a view of proving that it contained no poison, he presented to us. After resting a short time, we returned to our boats.

In order to prosecute the formation of the now colony with the greatest energy, every hand which could possibly be spared, was sent on shore. A better approach to Point William, the acclivity being more gentle, was discovered this morning, and a large party immediately employed in clearing away the timber and brushwood, for the purpose of making a broad road through it.

Saturday, Nov. 3.—The Eden was moved nearer to Point William and the Adelaide Islands, for the greater convenience of landing the working parties, stores, &c. The steam-vessel and her prizes also left their anchorage in the bay, and moved into Clarence Cove. Not a single canoe was visible on the water, and very few natives on the shore; we were informed by our interpreter, that they were occupied with the funeral of a chief, but suspect that the different tribes were assembled in council to discuss the subject of our arrival, and our evident intention to form a settlement among them.

Nov. 4.—Some native chiefs were much delighted with sitting in our chairs; but, when the Captain presented them with a few knives, small looking-glasses, and other trinkets, their delight was raised to rapture, expressed by clapping their hands and singing certain short sentences in a high tone of voice, at the same time bowing their heads, as if to indicate their readiness to admit our superiority. We were afterwards informed, that these songs were in our praise, and implied the following meaning:—"Truly you are come to do us good." We entertained them with palm-wine, Madeira, biscuit, fish, and yams; we found, however, on this, as on all other occasions, that these unsophisticated people preferred their native viands to our European delicacies. They appeared much interested with the three European females we had on board; but, whether they had sufficient taste to prefer them to their native beauties, I shall not pretend to determine. After remaining two hours on board, they took their leave, and returned to the shore.

Monday, November 5.—Anderson, who had been absent two days, returned this morning in a large canoe of seventeen paddles, accompanied by the same party of chiefs who had visited us yesterday, with, however, an addition of the king's son. Before coming alongside, they pulled round the ship, singing most loudly and merrily. Though Captain Owen was on shore, they were taken into the cabin, and entertained until his return, after which he gave a present to each of them. Notwithstanding this liberality, the principal chief fixed his covetous eye upon an axe, and expressed a most eager desire to become possessed of it. Captain Owen, however, notwithstanding his wish to conciliate the natives as much as possible, did not think proper to gratify his cupidity; but he promised, that it should be presented to the King at the next interview with him. In the afternoon, a tornado arose and drove most of the canoes away; the chiefs, however, remained on board until it was over, and then left us under an arrangement that the Captain should pay a visit to the King on the following Wednesday.

Tuesday, Nov. 6.—We had a wet morning, succeeded by a fine day. Many canoes, full of natives, came alongside. About noon, a native was discovered, by the master-at-arms, to have stolen an axe, which he had secreted in a piece of canvas that he had picked up and tied round his waist in the manner of an apron. On taking it from him, he made a desperate attempt to escape, by running down the ship's side into a canoe, from whence he made his way over several others, with a view of reaching his own, but he was arrested in his progress. A warm discussion now arose among the chiefs present, as to the punishment he ought to be subjected to, having been taken *flagrante delicto*, under their own eyes. Captain Owen, to evidence his high displeasure at the transaction, cut the matter short, by ordering them all out of the ship. This gave rise to another commotion and discussion, the result of which was, that the culprit was assailed on all sides by his countrymen with their paddles; even a boy in the same canoe inflicted several blows, and he was finally severely injured about the head and body, when, with the blood streaming from various parts, he was compelled to leap into the sea, in order to wash it away, before they would allow him to re-enter his own boat. His punishment, however, did not terminate with the above discipline; for as he assisted in paddling his canoe ashore, his countrymen followed him with every denunciation of vengeance. On landing in the neighbourhood of our market, he was seized, conducted a short distance from the beach, and surrounded by an immense crowd of the natives. Mr. Jeffery, who happened to be near the spot, penetrated into the midst of them, with a view of ascertaining the nature of the affair, when, to his surprise, he was immediately laid hold of, and tied hand to hand with the bleeding prisoner. It may be imagined that this proceeding excited considerable alarm in Mr. Jeffery, who was led to infer that the wounds of the prisoner had been inflicted by our people, and that the natives were about to retaliate upon himself. A soldier, who was passing at the moment, lost no time in giving an alarm at the camp, when Capt. Harrison came with a party of soldiers to the assistance of our comrade; but Mr. Jeffery had, by this time, contrived to disengage his hand; and, our people appearing, the natives desisted from farther attempts upon him. It turned out that their object in offering this apparent violence, was merely to secure an evidence on our side of the final punishment of their countryman, which they now proceeded to carry into effect in the following extraordinary manner:—the poor wretch was, in the first place, tied hand and foot with his back to a tree, after which a discussion took place, between the chiefs and a man, whom we conceived to be a priest. This being finished, one of the chiefs, who, in consequence of the prominent part he played in this dramatic scene, was ever after known among us by the honourable name of Cut-throat, very coolly stepped up to the prisoner, the whole of the natives at the same time falling on their knees, and was proceeding with great deliberation to cut his throat, when Captain Harrison and Mr. Jeffery hastened forward, and prevented the perpetration of the act by holding back his arm, and making signs that our chief was coming. Fortunately, Capt. Owen was actually coming on shore at this juncture, and, having passed to the centre of the assembly, by means of signs succeeded in explaining that it was not his wish to have the man so severely punished. He then took him by the hand, led him through the crowd, and thus liberated him from the sanguinary vengeance of his own countrymen. During the whole of this trying occasion, the prisoner neither shrunk from the numerous and severe blows inflicted upon him in the earlier part of it; nor, in the latter part, did he indicate the slightest symptom of fear. This is one of the many traits we met with of either the great fortitude or little sensibility of these islanders.

We were much surprised at finding a Demi-John in the woods at the back of our encampment; it certainly indicates that we are not the first Europeans who have visited this spot.

Wednesday, November 7.—Anderson, accompanied by two chiefs, came on board at 9 A.M. to say, that the King was on the beach, waiting for our boat to fetch him off. At eleven, the Captain, accompanied by several of his officers, myself, the band, and a party of marines, with a variety of presents, went in three boats for the purpose of paying our intended visit to his Majesty. We landed at a small cove, three miles to the eastward of the ship, since known by the name of King-Cove, and were conducted by the chiefs to a small open place in the woods, at the distance of about a hundred yards from the rocky shore, where the natives had placed a number of stones in the water in such manner as to leave a channel for only one canoe to land at a time. When the Captain was seated, a small ram, and several calabashes of palm-wine, were brought forward. After waiting an hour, the King arrived, when the Captain, rising to receive him, ordered a red cloak to be thrown over his shoulders, and a velvet cap to be put on his head; as his Majesty wore his native hat, ornamented with a pair of ram's horns on the fore part of it, it became necessary to place the velvet one above it, and secure it in its position by means of a bone skewer, which, piercing both at the same time, fastened them effectually to the tuft of hair on the top of the head. The sight of our presents, but more particularly the quantity of iron, excited so uncontrollably the feelings of the royal party, that the good order previously observed, could now no longer be maintained; we were pressed upon on all sides, and with such an inconceivable clatter and confusion of tongues, that the bellowing of cattle would have been comparatively musical to our ears; however, to do them justice, notwithstanding this horrid din, they did not make the least attempt upon our persons or property. It was noticed that the King himself gave away several small pieces of iron to certain individuals, probably an act of policy, which, by leading others to expect a similar token of royal favour, would restrain them from attempting to help themselves, and thus diminish the quantum of his own presents. During this scene of confusion, we retired to the beach and entered our boats, the crowd following us to the shore, and many even into the water. On this occasion, we calculated that there could not have been less than two thousand natives assembled, including many women, but they were kept apart from the men. Mr. Galler spoke to some of them; but they were excessively timid, although the men endeavoured to encourage familiarity by placing some of the younger women's hands into his. One peculiarity was remarked on the present occasion, that many of the natives had lost one of their hands, and some both, indeed we found this so common in the island, that there was no doubt of the deprivation of this part of the body being resorted to as a punishment. Before returning to the ship, I went with Messrs. Galler and Jeffery to visit the works at Clarence, when we were informed that the men employed in clearing the jungle, had discovered the Indian-rubber tree, and one or two other indigenous plants which had not been previously noticed.

Thursday, November 8th.—The importance of our acquiring a knowledge of the language of the natives of this island, must be obvious. In order to promote this object. Captain Owen selected an active and intelligent young man of the name of Elwood, who volunteered to reside for a week at a village in the interior of the island; and he left the ship this morning in pursuance of the plan. The Captain this day fixed upon a spot for the site of a house intended for his own residence: he also gave the name of Paradise to a portion of ground which had been cleared to form a garden for the use of the colony, and changed the appellation of Glover's Stairs for that of Jacob's Ladder. This consists of a flight of 150 steps, leading from the beach to the acclivity on which Clarence is situated that had been constructed, since our arrival, by Mr. Glover, and his body of English artificers.

Friday, 9.—During the night there had been much thunder and lightning, succeeded, in the morning, by heavy rains, which went off at eleven o'clock, and recommenced at two, accompanied by strong gusts of wind; at four, it cleared up again: scarcely a canoe or native was to be seen throughout the day.

Saturday, 10.—The weather is to-day extremely fine, and yet very few canoes or natives have been seen: and none have approached the ship. We apprehend that something has occurred to displease them—a suspicion afterwards confirmed. In the afternoon, at the time I happened to be on shore, a deputation of seven chiefs came to Mr. Jeffery, at Newmarket, with a complaint that our Kroomen had been cutting down the palm-trees for the leaves to thatch their huts with; and, also, that they were much annoyed by the frequent firing of muskets. In reply to the latter complaint, Mr. Jeffery explained to them, that the firing proceeded only from the attempts of our officers to shoot monkeys; to confirm which statement, the purser very opportunely came up at the instant with a large monkey and a small deer, which he had just shot. They did not, however, appear properly satisfied; for they shook their heads, and intimated that, if we persevered in cutting down the palms, it would not only deprive them of the advantages of that valuable tree, but, by diminishing the quantity of wood, extend the system of firing musketry farther into the interior of the country. At length, with a view of settling all grievances, and convincing them we had no intention of inflicting any injury, we took them a short distance beyond the points our men were occupied in clearing, and, placing a quantity of iron on the ground, gave them, by signs, to understand, that we would give them all that iron for the land contained within that boundary. The nature of this treaty for purchase, they appeared to understand well, and signified their assent by placing sticks, at equal distances from each other, in the line proposed. Mr. Jeffery, at the same time, marking a tree as an evidence of the agreement on our side. The quantity of land of which we had thus made a *bonâ fide* purchase, was equal to about a square mile in extent. The treaty was afterwards more fully ratified, and the property involved formally taken possession of by a public act, which will be duly noticed. Both parties being now satisfied, we returned to Newmarket, the natives accompanying us, and, sitting down in a row together, farther confirmed the bargain by plentiful libations of palm-wine.

Sunday, 11.—At half-past one divine service was performed by Captain Owen, when four of the natives attended, and behaved with great decorum; they also made signals to their companions in the canoes to avoid all noises which might disturb us.

Monday, 12.—A numerous deputation of chiefs, gaily dressed, came to our camp at Clarence, to conclude a definitive arrangement respecting the land we had purchased on Saturday. Captain Owen accompanied them to the boundary line, and marked an additional number of trees, to define the limits with more accuracy. He also promised them additional payments: after which he took four of the principal chiefs on board, drank palm-wine with them, and made them a variety of presents. Confidence was now fully restored, and great numbers of both sexes visited us before the day terminated.

Tuesday, 13.—We have additional proofs of the return of confidence on the part of the natives: a man and a boy insisted on remaining on board to sleep, probably induced by the anticipation of a present. There never were more harmless, inoffensive, or tractable people: for, when most troublesome, they may be led in any direction you choose, by taking hold of the hand, or even of a finger.

CHAP. IX.

Native Simplicity—Resources of the Blind—Royal Village—Gathering of
Natives—Native Priests—Royal Feast—Inhospitable Treatment—
Uncomfortable Quarters—Vocabulary of the Native Language—Beauty
of the Female Character—Women of Fernando Po—Anecdotes—Aspect
of the Country—Productions—Preparations for the Settlement—
Discovery of a Theft—Mimic War Customs—Native Chiefs—Female on
Board—Monkey for Dinner—Flogging a Prisoner—Accident to a Sailor—
A Voyage of Survey round the Island—River named after the Author—
Geographical and Meteorological Observations—Insubordination—A
Man Overboard—Deserter taken—Death of the Interpreter—Method of
Fishing—Visitors from St. Thomas—Ceremony of taking Possession of
Fernando Po—Interview with a Native Chief—Celebration Dinner—
Indirect Roguery—Chief and his Wife—Hospital near Point William—
The Guana—Mistake at Sea—Suggestions on the Slave-Trade—Fishing
Stakes—Schooner on a Mud-flat

Thursday, Nov. 15.—Soon after landing this morning, I fell in with a party of
natives, with whom I shook hands, as usual, when a young female, whom I had
frequently met in the market-place, with her parents, perceiving that I did not
immediately recognize her as an old acquaintance, with the most natural
simplicity, placed my hand on her bosom, in the presence of her relations and
countrymen, who all laughed heartily, and appeared to enjoy my astonishment
very much. If, however, any of us had ventured upon such a liberty of our own
accord, the men would have been highly indignant, for they were extremely
jealous of their women, and did not like us to shew them any marked attention,
by purchasing their articles first, or making them a present in preference to
themselves:—such a distinction, in contradiction to the usages of civilized
society, being considered derogatory by these savage lords of the creation.

Matthew Elwood, the young man who had been sent into the interior,
returned to-day, and I am afraid without having derived much advantage from
his journey. I expect, however, an opportunity of adverting more fully to its
results at a future time. A quantity of bricks were landed for the purpose of
constructing a forge. The natives soon found out that they possessed the
property of sharpening their knives, and began to shew a very eager desire to
become possessed of them.

Friday, 16.—The natives have crowded upon us in such numbers, that we
have taken up the stakes which enclosed the market, with the intention of
holding it in future without the boundary line. Several unpleasant occurrences
have taken place, partly the fault of our own people, who have been criminal
enough to sell their tools, and partly of the natives, who have been eager to
purchase them. The following are, perhaps, the average terms on which our
barter has been conducted: an axe would purchase a sheep, or a goat; and three

or four inches of iron hoop, from two to four fowls, from eight to twelve yams, or two or three calabashes of palm-wine, each containing about one gallon.

Saturday, 17.—The number and confidence of the natives continued to increase, as well as the annoyance we experience from their importunities;—it had been found necessary to protect the market by a guard of soldiers. On returning from the market to-day, near the border of Hay river, a party were daring enough to snatch the sentinel's bayonet from out of its scabbard, and throw it into the river. The soldier, however, succeeded in recovering it, and, to deter them from proceeding to greater lengths, fired his musket over their heads. This alarmed them so excessively, that away they scampered like a flock of sheep, without daring to cast a look behind; indeed, such is their terror of fire-arms, that it is only with the greatest difficulty that they can be persuaded to touch a musket.

Monday, Nov. 19.—The young man, named Matthew Elwood, who had so recently returned from his visit in the interior, where he had been sent by Capt. Owen, with a view of acquiring some knowledge of their language, volunteered to repeat it, accompanied by another young man, and they had now been two days at the same village a few miles distant from the settlement, where the King resided. Anxious to lose no opportunity of obtaining information respecting the manners and customs of this singular people, I determined on joining the party, and fixed upon the present day for my journey. I have ever, throughout life, but perhaps more particularly since the loss of my sight, felt an intense interest in entering into association with human nature, and observing human character in its more primitive forms: this propensity I have previously had opportunities of enjoying, in some of the countries most remote from European knowledge, amidst the wilds of Tartary and the deserts of Siberia; and I can refer to the indulgence of it many of my more pleasurable sensations. I know that the world declaims against the absurdity of an individual, circumstanced like myself, professing to derive either pleasure or information from such sources, and maintains that travelling by the fireside would better suit those circumstances, and convey an equally gratifying interest. I answer confidently that this is not the case, and that I believe the intensity of my enjoyments under the system I have adopted, equals, if not surpasses, what other travellers experience who journey with their eyes open. It is true, I ascertain nothing *visibly*; but, thank God! I possess most exquisitely the other senses, which it has pleased Providence to leave me endowed with; and I have reason to believe that my deficiency of sight is to a considerable degree compensated, by a greater abundance of the power of imagination which presents me with facility to form *ideal pictures* from the description of others, which, as far as my experience goes, I have reason to believe constitute fair and correct representations of the objects they were originally derived from. It must be recollected that I have formerly enjoyed the power of vision; and, although my colourings may occasionally be too weak or too vivid, it is fair to infer that the recollections of my former experience are sufficient to prevent me from running into gross inaccuracies or incongruities. Place me, as some have suggested, in the situation of the man in the farce, and carry me in a limited circle around the same point, under the assurance that I was travelling to distant and ever-changing scenes, and support the stratagem by every circumstance calculated to give it the fullest effect; it would never impose upon me: for the tact which nature and experience have given me, and the inconceivable acuteness of perception I derive from it, would immediately detect inconsistencies scarcely appreciable by others, and at once overturn and expose the deception which was being practised.

At 3 o'clock in the afternoon I left the Eden for King Cove, at which place we found a few natives, who assembled on our landing. Anderson, the interpreter, had been appointed to conduct me, but Mr. Jeffery kindly accompanied me for the first half mile, in expectation of leaving me in the care of a chief of our acquaintance. However, before we had proceeded far, the assemblage of natives had become so great, and their importunities to purchase palm-wine and other commodities so annoying, that I was glad when he returned, under the expectation that his separation from me would prove, as it did, a diversion which, by drawing off a considerable part of the natives, would permit me to continue my journey with less interruption. I now advanced with Anderson as fast as the paths would admit, being anxious to arrive at our point of destination that evening; my companion, however, was desirous of passing the night at the hut of a chief in the neighbourhood of the beach, and endeavoured to dissuade me from prosecuting our journey this evening. I have already spoken of the qualifications of this man as an interpreter, and have now to observe, that he possessed others, which made him a useful medium of communication with the natives: for instance, he was a good-tempered fellow, could laugh heartily whenever they laughed, eat and drink whatever was placed before him, however repugnant to an European stomach; and, being somewhat of their own colour, i.e. not many shades darker, they were inclined to be particularly partial to him.

Our path was at first tolerably good, and lay through a level country, but, when we had proceeded about half way, became hilly, rugged, and slippery, particularly after passing the second of two streams which intercepted our road. A number of the natives, principally women, continued to follow, passing evidently a variety of jokes upon us, and laughing heartily at every false step I happened to make. Before we reached the end of our journey, the number had increased to many hundreds, who shouted, and halloed incessantly at the novelty of our appearance, similar to a European rabble, when following any extraordinary sight. To relieve Anderson, who had the luggage, I took hold, for a short time, of the arm of a native, who conducted me well, until we became surrounded by a crowd of his countrymen, and then, whether he felt compelled to answer their queries, or was proud of his charge, or anxious to exhibit the high confidence reposed in him, I found him a very troublesome guide; for he was constantly turning his head over my shoulder, and speaking or hallooing to those who were behind him.

At length we arrived at the royal village, where Elwood and his companion came to receive us at the hut that His Majesty had appointed for our accommodation. It was so late, that my countrymen were surprised to see us; and, the King having retired, we were obliged to relinquish the honour of an interview until morning. I therefore took tea, and was happy in lying down for repose, after my fatiguing journey. It was not without much concern I learned from Elwood, that, during the present visit, neither he nor his companion had met with the hospitable treatment or attention which they had expected; on the contrary, they had been compelled, immediately after their arrival, to expose the contents of their bags, and actually obliged to surrender up to the King one-half of the little stock of iron with which they had provided themselves for the purpose of barter. The consequence was, that, after paying three pieces to the natives who had conveyed their luggage, another for a couple of fowls, and presenting a fifth to Canning, (a chief who had been Elwood's principal friend on his former visit, and to whom he had given this distinguished name,) to secure his good services,—they had only one remaining for their future resources; and it was by no means satisfactory to be thrown upon the casual generosity of the natives. It is true, they had with them some salt beef and biscuit, and it was understood, when they quitted the ship, that Captain Owen had engaged to compensate the King for their protection and entertainment.

Tuesday, 20.—At daybreak we were visited by Canning, and several other chiefs, who brought with them a large yam, and some palm-wine intended for our breakfast. We were from time to time, in reply to our inquiries, assured that the King was coming; we waited, however, two hours in vain expectation, and at length sent Anderson to inquire into the cause of delay, when we were informed that His Majesty was busily occupied at his toilet, or, in other words, having his head dressed, in order, as I suppose, to enable him to appear with more dignity on this important occasion. About 8 o'clock he made his entrée, accompanied by several of his chiefs. At first his manner was somewhat reserved, but, after a short conversation, which held out to him the prospect of receiving presents, confirmed by the actual gift of two large knives from myself, he became highly animated, loquacious, and agreeable. He now ordered a plentiful supply of palm-wine, which he caused to pass freely round; and, after staying with us about an hour, returned to his own residence, from whence he shortly after sent us half a dozen yams.

There was a native priest resident in our hut, probably placed there to observe our conduct, and who, for the whole morning, had been occupied in smearing himself with coloured clay. We noticed that this man, during our visit, performed every morning a few religious ceremonies, and repeated prayers, in which the natives appeared to join. After the King's departure, he began to exercise some of the more mysterious functions of his office. I know not what the occasion was, but the ceremony consisted in frequent repetitions of certain short sentences, in which the individual on whom he was operating occasionally joined; and, in the intervals between these sentences, he shook a bundle of rods over the head of the latter, making, at the same time, a noise which resembled the squeaking of a pig.

I am enabled to communicate but little respecting the religious sentiments of this people. The duties of the priests appear to be more surgical than clerical; of which opinion the following are illustrations: A female applied to one of the priests with an inflammatory tumour on the hand; after making an incision into the tumour, and squeezing it in a manner which made his patient grin with pain, he blew and spat upon the part. Upon another person, who had an abcess of the eye, with an accumulation of some white matter in it, he performed the following delicate operation: having first applied his mouth to the part, he began to suck it with great eagerness and perseverance, after which he ejected from his mouth a chalky-looking substance, which he appeared to have extracted from the diseased structure: this process he repeated several times, with a similar result. These were, at least, substantial duties.

Our priest had a sacred corner in the hut, with a particular seat which none else presumed to occupy; the former, a receptacle for dirt, the latter, formed of a large stone, with four smaller ones, which served for legs or supporters.

I endeavoured in vain to gain any satisfactory account of their funeral ceremonies; no indications of graves have been seen by our people, and the probability is, as is not unfrequently the custom in Africa, that they bury their dead under the earthen floor of their huts. I know not whether this opinion will be deemed as confirmed or not by the fact, that, in returning from a walk, this afternoon, we passed a closed hut, with five hats hanging in front of it, the owner of which, we were informed, had died shortly before our arrival.

Our friend Canning supplied us with a fowl for dinner, and, when it was dressed, appeared perfectly ready to assist us in disposing of it.

The following is, probably, the general mode which these people adopt of hunting or catching wild animals, of which we had the fortune this day to meet with a specimen: A goat, which was very wild, had been secured to a rail, when, taking fright at the approach of my companions, it contrived, by floundering, to break loose from its confinement. The King, and some of his chiefs, who were at hand, immediately ran for some long grass nets, rolled upon poles, and which were about four feet wide. These they expeditiously unfolded, and then encircling the goat, very skilfully and speedily recaptured him. They have, however, other methods of taking wild animals; on enclosing yam plantations with stakes seven feet high, they place traps at the sides of the fence.

Wednesday, 21.—We returned His Majesty's visit this morning at eight o'clock. He received us on the outside of his hut, and seated me on a stone at his right hand, but immediately after a few words had been exchanged, he made signs to us to return to our own residence; where on our arrival, we found he had sent a sheep, with a view of giving us a sumptuous feast. His Majesty, accompanied by his chiefs, soon after joined us, and they immediately proceeded to the operation of killing the sheep, which was conducted in the following manner: The animal having been first hung up by the hind legs, its throat was cut, care being taken, in effecting this, not to wound the windpipe. The blood, as it flowed, was caught in a calabash, and then given to the priest, probably to be reserved for some religious ceremony. The next process was to skin the animal, in doing which the operator commenced with a fore leg, then the corresponding hind one, then the other fore leg, and so on; he then proceeded to the abdomen, and afterwards completed the operation in the usual manner. The gall-bag and bladder were now extracted and thrown away; after which the whole of the remaining viscera were removed and placed aside for subsequent use. A large portion of the flesh from one of the shoulders was now presented to the King, who cut it into the form of a long string, beginning at the outside, and proceeding to the centre. This he wound round a stick, and held over a blazing fire, until half broiled; and, then dividing it into a number of small pieces, distributed them to the party around him, doing myself the honour of presenting me with the first piece. The remainder of the animal was, in the next place, taken within our hut, where the stomach and intestines, without any other preparation than imperfectly squeezing out their contents, were warmed over the fire, and then, in nearly a raw state, divided among the natives, who ate them with great relish, the King receiving his portion with the rest. His Majesty now presented our party with a leg, shoulder, breast, and small saddle, and afterwards divided what remained among his chiefs, reserving the head for himself, which, after being well scorched, he ordered to be taken to his hut.

A more curious part of this singular feast remains to be described. On opening the animal, it was found to be with young, when the uterus, containing two lambs, each about six inches long, was, as a particular mark of favour or respect, placed in my hands: but, not appreciating the gift so highly as probably had been expected, I immediately laid it aside. After the departure of the King, it was a second time brought to me, and I now contrived, by shaking my head, and other demonstrations, to make them comprehend that I did not intend to make use of it, and that it was entirely at their service. This was, without doubt, very agreeable intelligence; for, having pricked the sac, to allow the liquor to drain away, and laid it for a short time before the fire, the whole was divided into portions, and eaten up apparently with avidity and delight.

The above meal was purely carnivorous, for neither yams nor palm-wine were introduced as accompaniments; in the afternoon, however, his Majesty made us another short visit, and sent a quantity of wine. We offered the natives salt to their meat, but they refused it with every sign of disgust, and even wanted to throw away our little store of this, to us, so necessary a condiment. They also shewed an equal dislike to tobacco; and, when one of our party made preparations for smoking a cigar, the priest held out his rod as if in prohibition, while others endeavoured to prevent him from lighting it. Canning, indeed, who had witnessed more frequently the practice of smoking on board, shewed less aversion.

Though we were at a considerable distance from the settlement, we could hear the reports of the morning and evening gun; for the first two or three days, the natives appeared, or pretended to be, much alarmed at this, as they hallooed for some time after. They would frequently come up to us, levelling a stick like a musket, and accompany the action with bang! bang! We had reason to consider them much afraid of every species of fire-arms, and I cannot but think it would be good policy to keep this apprehension alive, rather than to endeavour to remove it by attempts to explain the principles of their action, and to familiarise them with the effects. In this respect, I deem the general practice of our voyagers and travellers to be decidedly faulty, since the superior advantages which fire-arms give, may be said to constitute our chief compensation for deficiency of numbers, and thus enable us to preserve that vast pre-eminence which we possess over the uncivilised inhabitants of newly-discovered countries. If the policy of our Government requires an intercourse with savage nations, both prudence and humanity justify our retaining the means of commanding that intercourse, by the superiority of our modes of defence; for, in the event of hostile collision, the numbers of the savages, possessed as they are, individually, of physical strength and bodily activity, at least equal to our own, could scarcely fail to be overwhelming. This also agrees with Vaillant's opinion, for he remarks, that, "when you travel among savages, you ought never to employ your arms, or shew the use of them, except to render them a service, either by procuring them game, or destroying such ferocious animals as are obnoxious to them."—*Vaillant*, vol. ii. p. 127.

About ten o'clock this evening, a great noise from persons talking commenced in the village, accompanied, at times, by loud hallooing, and a clattering of a kind of rattle-boxes, which many of the natives wear around the neck, and which somewhat resembles the upper half of the leathern-case of a spirituous-liquor bottle, within which is appended a clapper made generally of a sheep's jawbone. This noise, the meaning of which I could not comprehend, continued, with little interruption, throughout the night.

Thursday, Nov. 22.—Soon after breakfast, the King sent for us to his hut, and regaled us with palm-wine, poured out by the fair hand of a young female, whom my companions pronounced the most beautiful they had seen in this island, and whom we supposed to be his Majesty's favourite wife. On this occasion, he took the opportunity of reminding us of the presents he expected to receive from Captain Owen, and directed some of his chiefs to shew us those which he intended to offer in return, consisting of sheep, fowls, &c. &c. We were then conducted to our hut, and given to understand, by signs, that it was his Majesty's pleasure we should forthwith pack up our luggage, and return to our settlement. We thought, however, it would be more pleasant to take an early dinner first, and with this intention commenced the preparation of a kind of Irish stew, consisting of mutton and yams: being defective in the latter article, we requested a further supply; but this did not please our hosts, and it was intimated that we should find plenty at the end of our journey. We still, however, urged our wishes, when, at length, they brought us a couple of pieces. We could not avoid expressing dissatisfaction at this scanty supply, when they began to assume a very savage and sulky appearance; even our friend Canning arose with a menacing countenance, and laying hold of his spears, threatened to compel our immediate departure. It would have been imprudent to continue to irritate them at this juncture, and at best have only exposed our own weakness: we therefore thought we should most preserve our dignity, and, at the same time, retain a just ground of complaint of their want of hospitality, by giving way to their wishes, yet not without evident signs of our high dissatisfaction. I believe they had, subsequently, reason to repent of their conduct, as Capt. Owen afterwards treated them with apparent coldness, and probably abridged his intended presents: not but that they were amply remunerated, although the measure of it fell short of their own expectations. We took our dinner deliberately, notwithstanding this urgency, and then commenced our journey, accompanied by Canning and another chief; besides an old man, who had resided in the hut with us, carrying our luggage. We were soon joined by the persons who carried the presents intended for Captain Owen. We also met the King, but he, instead of accompanying us, as we had expected, went off immediately to his own residence, bearing on his shoulders a quantity of wood, for the use, as we supposed, of the royal household; we shook hands with his Majesty on taking our final leave.

As on the journey up the country, we had, on our return, great numbers of idle people following us, either from motives of curiosity or interest, and teazing us to give them palm-wine, iron, &c. The road, in various places, was extremely rugged and narrow, with steep declivities from the sides to the centre, and very slippery from the rain that had fallen in the morning. We again crossed two streams, the chief of which, although broad and rapid, was not sufficiently deep to be dignified with the title of a river. Towards evening, we arrived at King Cove, where, proceeding to the beach, we washed the clay from our trowsers, and then went to our quarters for the night.

The hut in which we took up our residence, consisted of a wooden roof, thatched with palm-leaves, and supported on stancheons of wood; the leaves, on all sides, approaching within two or three feet of the ground, indeed so low, that it made it very inconvenient to get in or out; for, unless great caution was observed, there was considerable risk of getting wounded by the prickles on the leaves of the palm-tree. Previously to its becoming dark, we were invited to drink palm-wine on the outside of our hut; and, afterwards retiring within, our native companions employed themselves busily enough in roasting and eating their yams, while we enjoyed the refreshing beverage of tea. We then lay down for the night; but, alas! not to sleep; for, although our hut was not very large, it contained about twenty persons of different sexes and ages, who were, of course, pretty closely stowed: and from its not being closed at the sides, with much thunder and lightning taking place, accompanied by high wind and heavy rain, which continued throughout the greater part of the night, the latter beat in under the roof, and also drove the smoke of three fires towards us, until we were nearly suffocated. It will be conceived, that our situation was not the most enviable; those near the outside were exposed to the pitiless storm; while they who occupied the centre, where we had spread our hammocks, were necessarily oppressed with heat and smoke. About two o'clock, some of the natives, finding it impossible to sleep, got up and amused themselves until daylight in conversation, and roasting yams on the fire.

Friday, 23.—At day-break, the whole of the natives rose and commenced their yam feast, succeeded by plentiful supplies of palm-wine. As the heavy winds and rain shewed no appearance of abating, we began to doubt whether we should get on board to-day; however, about eight o'clock, it moderated, and before noon, the weather was sufficiently favourable to induce us to make the attempt. Having taken our seats in the canoes, together with the chiefs who accompanied us, a party of the natives urged them over the surf, and away we paddled for the ship, which we reached in less than a couple of hours. Before getting on board, however, we were treated with a specimen of eager covetousness and want of decorum in our late friends; for, instead of waiting to allow us to get up first, or offering to assist us, no sooner did the canoe touch the ship, which she happened to do under the main-chains, than away they all started with their presents, leaving us to bring the boat to the gangway, and get out as well as we could; they even gave up all care for the safety of the canoe; the consequence of which was, that *they left us adrift in it*, and the commanding officer was obliged to send a boat to bring her alongside again.

Saturday, 24.—Having now spent some days in what may be termed the domestic privacy of the island, it will be inferred that I have become more intimately acquainted with the character of its inhabitants, who may justly be considered as constituting one of the most extraordinary races of savages at this time in existence. I shall, therefore, avail myself of this opportunity of developing farther than has yet been done in the preceding pages, whatever occurred to me as being most interesting in their manners, habits, customs, and peculiarities. This I shall follow up with some details respecting the natural history and productions of the island; which, however imperfectly they may be treated, will probably be deemed worthy of attention as subjects of scientific research. In these descriptions, I must, however, plead strongly for the indulgence of my readers, as many serious obstacles have opposed themselves to the inquiry after satisfactory information; among which, none have been more uncompromising than those experienced in acquiring a knowledge of the language; for, although we have been in constant communication with the natives, at present so little progress has been made, that our attempts in this respect may be said to have almost entirely proved abortive. We have, indeed, some reason to believe that the natives are desirous of throwing impediments in our way, since, notwithstanding they evince much quickness in catching words of our language, repeating the orders issued by the officers, and are also possessed of considerable power of mimicry, they shew little inclination to communicate their own terms or names. It has not unfrequently happened, that when, according to the usual custom of persons who are not conversant with each other's language, we touched, significantly, any thing which we were desirous of knowing, they used different words in reply, as if with the intention of confusing us; and, again, when we believed that we had ascertained the right name from one source, on inquiring from others, a very different word was given; so that we eventually remained in doubt as to the proper one. The few small vocabularies we have succeeded in collecting, seem to prove that there are distinct dialects, or idioms, among the different tribes. This is particularly exemplified in the case of the numerals; for not only are different words used to express the same number, but peculiar modes of counting are made use of—for instance, one tribe, after counting five in the usual way, proceeds to ten and twenty; while another, after going on progressively to ten, starts at once to twenty. The language itself is, generally speaking, harmonious, most of the words terminating in vowels, as will be perceived from the subjoined vocabulary, which is as correct as circumstances would admit of our obtaining.

The mode Captain Owen adopted of gaining an insight into the Fernandian language was, perhaps, the best that could have been devised: viz. the sending a person to reside with the natives in the interior, as has been before stated; but the result proved very unsatisfactory; for he added little to what we had previously acquired. Another mode adopted was, the promise of a reward to that individual who might gain the earliest and best knowledge of the subject.

A VOCABULARY OF THE NATIVE LANGUAGE OF FERNANDO PO.

Etwee, head.
Isilla, hair of the head.
Lotto, ear.
Booyah, mouth.
Nokko, eye.
Lopappo, eye-lashes.
Kokalako, chief, or head man.
Mohoonka, chief's wife.
Icancunee, little one.
Ebeo, boy.
Ternapo, mother.
Murugudu, eye-brows.
Vompo and Mompo, nose.
Bello and *Wello*, tooth.
Ezaddoo, beard.
Lobabbo, tongue.
Lobok, arm.
Dialla, hand.
Aboobooso, wrist.
Anné, finger.
Jpapo, thigh.
Eddo, and *Etoko*, knee.
Lopola, leg.
Inkakase, ancle.
Dekotto, foot.
Deballe, female bosom.
Babilla, belly.
Djakkee, navel.

Bopa.

Motto.

Djeecha.

Eppoo buttocks.

Elleboo, trinket of wood, in form of a bell.

Motoocko, belt of shells and pebbles.

Dpibbo, bracelet.

Longebo, armlet.

Touno, black shell bracelet.

Ebebbo, snake skin collar.

Loppollo, vertebrae of a snake.

Eboote, hat.

Mu-u, bulls, or cattle.

Me-he, sheep, or goats, or their flesh.

Kohoko, fowls, or their meat.

Tonatchetolo, tattoo, or marked.

Empoo, dog's jaw.

Tokko, round shell ornament like a button.

Epehaunah, purse, sheep's scrotum.

Looka, man.

Daka, woman.

Labole, ship.

Labolechee, or *Epoode*, boat.

Wattoo, canoe.

Ikahaddee, long reed, in the stern of canoes.

Kalsokoola, sail.

Nossapo, mast.

Inkappa, paddle.

Bonokee, fishing.

Itokka, sun.

Tolo, moon.

Bockao, eggs.

Boka, water.

Mooheelya, bar of iron.

Pooripoodee, cloves.

Sokolaee, Chili pepper.

Epeepee, tomatos.

Etoka, potatoe.

Saly, yams.

Beentok, or *Lilo*, cocoa tops.

Topy, or *Nakko*, palm-wine.

Loma, to drink.

Looba, or *Bata*, give.

Taleppa, take it away.

Omitta, to hold.

Vallee anger.
Atehee, done, no more, finish, end.
Anjoo, come here.
Sheerskalle, fine, pretty.
Boola, or *Lilla*, or *Illee*, one.
Epa, or *Taba*, two.
Buelly, or *Twelly*, three.
Betoh, or *Totoh*, five.
Beho, ten.
Bo, fifteen.
Eeckee, twenty.
Olaito, thirty.

It would be superfluous to repeat the descriptions which have already, on various occasions, been given of the persons, dress, and characters of the male inhabitants of this island. The reader will have inferred, that they are generally a harmless and inoffensive race of savages: it may be added, that they are probably the most dirty people existing under the face of the sun; for, with the exception of occasional immersions in the sea, when occupied in the affairs of business, we have never known them to wash themselves. The only systematic method they appear to adopt of cleansing, as well as of dress, is to give themselves a new coating of clay and palm-oil, whenever the previous one happens to be injured. Some few individuals, indeed, appear to renew this covering as a matter of fashion; particularly one dandy chief, who frequently changed the colour of his skin, and, in consequence, became familiarly known to us by the name of Chameleon; and what is singular, this man, like our European dandies, was in the habit of scenting himself.

The transition from the male to the female sex, through the intermediate species of Macaroni, is easy, if not natural; and I shall indulge my own particular feelings and partialities in entering upon that part of my observations which relates more exclusively to the fairer and softer portion of this aboriginal people. The infinite modifications of person, mind, and manners, exhibited by the sex in the different grades of society throughout the world, whether formed by the influences of climate, government, or education, present a most interesting subject to the speculative observer of human nature: and to one who, from early life, both by profession and inclination, a traveller, has wandered under every temperature of our eastern hemisphere, who has studied and admired the sex under every variety of character, no wonder that the contemplation of woman, as nature left her, inartificial, unsophisticated, simple, barbarous, and unadorned, should seem fraught with peculiar interest. Are there any who imagine that my loss of eye-sight must necessarily deny me the enjoyment of such contemplations? How much more do I pity the mental darkness which could give rise to such an error, than they can pity my personal calamity! The feelings and sympathies which pervade my breast, when in the presence of an amiable and interesting female, are such as never could have been suggested by *viewing* a mere surface of coloured clay, however shaped into beauty, or however animated by feeling and expression. The intelligence still allowed me by a beneficent Providence, is amply sufficient to apprise me of the existence of the more real—the diviner beauties of the soul; and herein are enjoyments in which I am proud to indulge. A soft and sweet voice, for instance, affords me a two-fold gratification;—it is a vehicle of delight, as operating on the appropriate nerves, and, at the same time, it suggests ideas of *visible* beauty, which, I admit, may, by force of imagination, be carried beyond *reality*. But, supposing I am deceived, are my feelings the less intense?—and, in what consists my existence, but in those feelings? Is it otherwise with those who *see*? If it be, I envy them not. But are those who think themselves happier, in this respect, than I am, sure, that the possession of a more exquisite sense than any they enjoy, does not, sometimes at least, compensate, or more than compensate, the curtailments to which the ordinary senses, and particularly the one of eye-sight, is liable?—and if they should think so, let them not, at least, deny me the resources I possess. I shall not, however, persist further in a description of that situation, those circumstances and those consolations, which the all-feeling comprehension of the poet hath so justly caught in one of its diviner moods of inspiration:—

And yet he neither drooped nor pined,
Nor had a melancholy mind;
For God took pity on the boy,
And was his friend—and gave him joy
  Of which we nothing know.

The personal appearance of the females of Fernando Po, is by no means attractive, unless (de gustibus non est disputandum) a very ordinary face, with much of the contour of the baboon, be deemed so. Add to this the ornaments of scarification and tattooing, adopted by the sex to a greater extent than by the men: and the imagination will at once be sensible how much divinity attaches to Fernandian beauty. Like the men, the women plaster the body all over with clay and palm-oil, and also in a similar manner wear the hair long, and in curls or ringlets, well stiffened with the above composition. The children of both sexes, or those who have not obtained the age of puberty, have the hair cut short, and are not permitted to use any artificial covering to the body. One trait is, perhaps, peculiar to the women of this country, and may be regarded by some as an indication of their good sense—that they have no taste for baubles, or, at all events, do not appear to desire them more than the men. With respect to articles of clothing, they are equally exempt from such incumbrances as the other sex:—

Happy the climate where the beau
Wears the same suit for use and show,
And at a small expense your wife,
If once well pink'd, is clothed for life.

Their lords and masters contrive to keep them in great subjection, and accustom them to carry their burdens; they evince also a considerable degree of jealousy, and shew evident marks of displeasure, whenever strangers pay attentions to them. As, however, this is equally the case whether the lady be young or old, it is not improbable that it may, in some measure, arise from their considering it too great a condescension on their parts to notice persons whom they deem so inferior. They rarely brought them to the ship, and for some time did not allow them to appear at market. If we are to credit our people, some of the young women are great jilts, and very expert in wheedling them out of iron and other property, under pretence of admitting them into their favour, and then running away, with a laugh at their credulity.

Mr. Jeffery witnessed the following ludicrous occurrence. He went one day, for the purpose of barter, to a part of the shore eastward of Hay river, where the surf was too great to allow his boat to remain on the beach, and he was, therefore, compelled to lie off in deep water; this, however, did not prevent the natives from carrying on their traffic. Some young women, in particular, came off to the boat, bringing a calabash of palm-wine in each hand, and treading the water so soon as they were out of their depth. These they contrived to deliver safe, without the wine becoming in the slightest degree impregnated with the briny wave. One of these females, having been taken into the boat, began to ingratiate herself into the favour of an honest tar, who, nothing loath, seated her near him, with his arm around her neck. At this juncture, the boat beginning to move, she made a sudden plunge over the side, and nearly carried the astonished seaman into the water; in short, he only escaped a good ducking by laying fast hold of the seat. The lady now, in an instant, dived under the boat, and, reappearing at some distance on the opposite side, swam, laughing, to the shore, evidently much amused at Jack's surprise and disappointment.

This was not the only instance Mr. Jeffery met with of the superior talents of the fair sex, in swimming and diving. On one occasion, having thrown into the sea a few small pieces of iron which had been rejected in barter, a number of natives of both sexes dashed after them, with a view to their recovery, when it was evident that the females were the more active and successful.

To elucidate more fully the character of the native women, I shall conclude my account of them with the details of an occurrence which possesses enough of the romantic to be capable of exciting, in the hands of a better painter than I am, an interest in the bosoms of such of my fair readers as may delight in tales of love and jealousy, with their sequel of rage and revenge. A female, about twenty-five years of age, who resided at a village in the neighbourhood of our settlement, had been guilty of an offence, probably infidelity to her husband, which subjected her to the dreadful penalty of having her hands cut off. Hoping to avert this punishment, she adopted the resolution, accompanied by her child, a fine and engaging boy of two years old, of entering our lines, and throwing herself on our protection. Captain Harrison received her favourably, and, for additional safety, sent her on board the Eden, where she remained several days before any inquiry was made respecting her. Although evidently of much firmness and decision of character, her personal appearance was by no means attractive, the face being greatly seamed with scars, and the abdomen tattooed all over. Captain Owen directed her to be placed under the care of our European females, who, either from envy or the force of habit, not approving the Eve-like dress in which she came on board, immediately clothed her in blue cotton garments. The poor child of nature, unused to such incumbrance, which probably, in her opinion, served only to irritate the skin, and prevent the contact of the refreshing atmosphere, felt any thing but easy, or gratified with this addition to her circumstances, and availed herself, at first, of every opportunity to lay it aside; but our unrelenting countrywomen were equally zealous in persisting to replace it. At length, she either became more accustomed to it, or aware of the necessity of compliance with the wishes of her new friends; this effort was, however, not unaccompanied by some ludicrous occurrences: for instance, whenever her tormentors were out of sight, she lost no time in tucking the grievance up round the waist, and dropping it below the shoulders from above, thus leaving her limbs, and the general surface, as free as nature intended them to be. On being taken on shore some days after, and placed under the protection of the wife of a seaman who had charge of the guns and ordnance stores, she had become sufficiently reconciled to her new dress to wear it with less apparent inconvenience; she was, indeed, once caught tripping, having one evening taken an opportunity of throwing it off, when finding herself light and free, like a bird on the wing, she ran into the jungle, where she frisked about and enjoyed herself for some time; after which she returned to the seaman's hut, and resumed her dress.

When this woman had been with us about a week, her husband came to Captain Harrison, bearing with him a present of two calabashes of palm-wine, and a couple of fowls, intimating his wish to have the child restored to him. With regard to his wife, he at this time shewed no anxiety to recover her; he afterwards, however, returned with a deputation of chiefs, and expressed his wish to have both of them restored to him. This being represented to Captain Owen, in order to convince them that she was under no restraint, he conducted her to the boundary line, and, pointing first to her countrymen, and then to our settlement, gave her to understand that she was at liberty to make her choice. One of the chiefs now advanced, and taking her by the hand, evinced his intention of leading her away, but Captain Owen would not permit this without her free consent; and, that his presence might be no restraint, left her to walk with her husband on the outside of the boundary line, attended by a sailor armed with a musket. They had not walked many paces, before five natives started from the bush and attempted to carry her off by force, when she immediately ran towards the sailor, and putting her hand on his musket, intimated her wish that he would fire at them. He did so, and they all immediately scampered away as fast as they could, leaving her to return with the sailor to his hut. Foiled in this attempt, the husband soon after came again and induced her to permit him to stay the night with her, and to take away the child in the morning, under the promise of bringing it back next day; a promise which he failed to perform, and which rendered the lady so indignant, that, although he afterwards came to visit her himself, bringing some fowls and palm-wine as a peace-offering, she persisted in rejecting all compromise. This produced a violent quarrel, which ended in their parting in high wrath, the husband threatening to return in the night and inflict some dreadful vengeance upon her for it, but he did not dare to carry his threats into execution.

I regret that my circumstances do not permit me to investigate the general aspect and natural history of this island, as it abounds with many interesting subjects which would well repay the trouble of inquiry. It is to be hoped that Government will ere long send out some intelligent naturalist for the purpose. The general appearance of the island is rocky and volcanic; on the north-eastern extremity, where our settlement is situated, one mountain, named Clarence Peak, rises to the elevation of 10,655 feet above the level of the sea, the easiest ascent to which is from its eastern side, being only interrupted by a few valleys of no great depth, while the western side exhibits a series of chasms and precipices, the sides of which from the sea appear almost perpendicular. The southern part of the island, although the least populous, is very picturesquely mountainous, being broken into several peaks, each supposed to be from one to three thousand feet in elevation, with numerous streams and beautiful cataracts descending in various parts and directions. In consequence of the hilly nature of the country admitting of no lodgment of water, we have reason to believe that few marshes exist throughout the island, a circumstance which must contribute greatly to its salubrity.

The soil of that part of the country with which we are best acquainted, is of a red argillaceous nature, generally forming a stratum of nine or ten feet in thickness, lying over one of sandstone, in which are imbedded fragments of lava; the latter stratum, at Point William, appears to decline to the east, at an angle of ten or twelve degrees.

The whole of the island is most luxuriantly wooded, even to within three or four hundred feet of its highest peaks, while some cleared spots, particularly in the north-east part, which is the most populous and cultivated, affords evidences of its great fertility. There is an immense variety of timber, comprising some of the finest trees in the world. I have already mentioned the Indian-rubber tree as indigenous here. The island also produces a species of black pepper, and we have reason to believe that cloves and nutmegs are to be met with. Yams are cultivated in abundance; they are remarkably fine and large, and constitute the principal food of the natives. Of this root they prepare a food called foo-foo, made by beating a quantity of well boiled ones together for a long time in a wooden mortar, which forms it into a highly tenacious mass, somewhat similar to bird-lime, but this mode of preparing them is not peculiar to Fernando Po, for it is commonly practised among the African nations. There is also a variety of other edible plants, particularly the eddoe, which is well known in the West Indies, and whose leaves, when young, form a good substitute for spinach. It is in general use when yams are out of season. A few plantains have also been brought to us. Wild fruits, not generally known, are found here; but there do not appear to be any oranges, lemons, limes, pine-apples, bananas, sour-sop, or sugar-canes, which are peculiar to such climates.

The following is the mode adopted for procuring the sap of the palm-tree, commonly known by the name of palm-wine: the lower branches of the tree having been cut off near the trunk, the sap exudes abundantly from the extremity of the divided part, and is received in calabashes appended thereto, which are secured from the aggressions of insects by enclosing the mouth of the vessel with the end of the branch, by leaves, and secured with wooden pins. The natives are remarkably expert in ascending the tree for the purpose of attaching and removing the calabashes; to assist them, they make use of a hoop sufficiently large to encircle the trunk, and allow, also, the body to move freely within it. This the individual moves upwards or downwards whenever he wants to change the position of his feet, according as he wishes to ascend or descend.

The juice, when procured, is, in the first instance, sweet, and not unlike cyder, but rapidly undergoes a process of fermentation, by which, in the course of two or three hours, it acquires a slightly vinous flavour: in both those states I found it a very pleasant beverage. If procured in the morning, [31] by the afternoon it becomes slightly acid, and, on the following morning, perfectly sour: sufficient alcohol is, however, formed to produce considerable exhilarating effect, when taken in even moderate quantity; but, when drank inordinately, it stupefies and intoxicates. The natives, notwithstanding they are fond of it, much to their credit, rarely abuse this bountiful gift of nature, and, in this respect, are well deserving of imitation by more civilized people.

The preparation of the palm-oil is conducted an follows:—A circular and slightly concave hole, about a yard in diameter and a foot deep, is made in the ground and paved with small stones. In this hole the palm-nuts are beaten into a pulp, and the oil afterwards extracted. It is then preserved and brought to market in native boxes, each containing from a quart to a gallon.

The island abounds with monkeys, which are eaten by the natives, many are of considerable size, some having been killed above 50 lb. weight. Several species have been noticed, particularly one with long, shaggy, jet-black hair; another with short silver-grey hair; and a third auburn, inclining to gold, with the hair of an intermediate length; so that it might be said we have gold and silver monkeys. The Kroomen, who are very partial to their flesh, hunt them successfully with sticks and stones. If any one makes them a present of a monkey, after feasting on the carcase, they thankfully return the skin, well dried.

The only domestic animal on the island is a dog of a peculiar cur species, very diminutive, and of a red and white colour; these we have reason to believe the natives eat, and they use the under jaw for a clapper to their rattles.

There is a great variety of fish; and also two species of turtle: viz. the green, and hawksbill; the former good for eating, and the latter only desirable for its shell.

---

[31] The calabashes are taken down, and replaced by others, every morning and evening.

It is now time that I revert to the proceedings which had taken place at the settlement during my absence. The increased confidence of the natives, and even violent proceedings, subsequently to our purchase of land and establishment of a market, have already been noticed: the numbers, indeed, which crowded within our boundary line, were immense; and their conduct in wandering about the settlement, with a view of inducing our people to make purchases, contrary to regulation, together with the irregularities arising from the temptation to sell their tools, to procure the means of privately feasting and tippling among the bushes, became so obnoxious, that Captain Owen determined to remove the market beyond the boundary line. He, therefore, directed the stakes to be removed, and took measures for preventing any number of natives from entering, in future, within the works, giving them to understand that no barter could be made, excepting at the place appointed for that purpose. The spot selected for the new market, was a point to the eastward beyond Hay River. Although much pains were taken to convince the chiefs of the advantages of this arrangement, it did not appear to give them satisfaction; as, for several days, few natives were to be seen on shore, and no canoes came off to the ship. It is probable that the chiefs were holding a conference respecting the affair, a mode of proceeding which they appear to adopt when any thing of moment occurs.

Two days afterwards Capt. Owen, accompanied by Capt. Harrison and Mr. Jeffery, went to examine the shore to the eastward of Hay River, and observing two canoes making towards a small cove, followed them, until they landed at a village near the beach, the inhabitants of which received him with every demonstration of friendly feeling, pawing the gentlemen of the party with their clayey hands, and pressing upon them so close, that they were also rubbing their bodies against their clothes. At the same time, that they thus expressed their welcome, they did not forget to solicit for iron, knives, and other presents. The chief occupation of the people of this village was fishing; and as, contrary to all other assemblages of the natives we had yet witnessed, the larger proportion present consisted of women, it is probable that the men were, at the time, engaged in that employment. Captain Owen purchased a few articles from them, and expressed his intention of establishing a market at the place; after which, he returned to his boat, both parties appearing satisfied with each other.

Our market was for some days afterwards carried on at the above village with reciprocal satisfaction, the supply of the several articles being abundant. It was soon, however, evident, that the tribes who were excluded by this arrangement, were by no means contented: and, as Captain Owen was anxious to do justice to the whole, by giving each a fair opportunity of barter, and as the immediate neighbourhood of the settlement was more convenient for the greatest assemblage of persons from the different tribes, he ordered, after first having a clear understanding with the chiefs, a new market-place to be fenced in, near the boundary line, which, from its situation and circumstances, ought to be regarded as neutral ground. This establishment of a neutral ground, was a measure of great importance and advantage, as we had now discovered that the natives are not only divided into distinct tribes, but that each tribe possesses a distinct portion of territory, and is extremely jealous of admitting others within its boundaries. The new market having been completed to-day, and a pole erected for the purpose of hoisting a flag, during the appointed hours of barter, it was opened about noon, with some ceremony, in consequence of hoisting, for the first time on this island, an Union-jack, under the hearty cheers of a large assembly, composed, perhaps, of as great a variety of people as ever before witnessed the first display of the British flag in a foreign land; comprising, besides our own countrymen and the inhabitants of the island, natives of various parts of Africa. The ceremony concluded by drinking palm-wine.

Monday, Nov. 26.—A circumstance unfortunately occurred to-day to interrupt the good understanding so lately established. One of our black labourers, who was occupied by himself in cutting wood within our lines, had drunk some palm-wine, which had been offered to him, without his having the means of paying for it; the natives, in consequence, forcibly took from him the bill-hook he was using. The theft having been communicated to Capt. Harrison, he assembled the chiefs who were at the market, and explained the affair, when two of them, Chameleon and Cut-throat, formed their respective followers into lines, each being armed with his equipment of spears; a parley now took place between the chiefs, who addressed their respective parties, with a view, no doubt, of finding out the thieves. A man, having the appearance of a priest, next harangued the whole body: each party in succession sang a war-song, the chiefs going on one, and the men on both knees. Each party now marched three times round a space which described a circle; after which, those under Chameleon suddenly started off at full speed, and were immediately followed by Cut-throat and his party, to the boundary of Hay River. The stragglers of the former, in their flight, disencumbered themselves of their yams, and calabashes of palm-wine, which the others, on coming up, amused themselves with breaking to pieces. Thus ended this curious specimen of war-like movements, which might appropriately be called the Battle of the Calabashes; and is sufficient to prove that a system of organization exists among the people, and confirms our former opinions on this subject: for, on our first landing at Baracouta, we perceived they had guards regularly stationed to watch and follow our movements. This system, I have some reason to believe, extends itself into the heart of the country, for, during my visit in the interior, I was sensible the people were running about at all hours of the night, ready for action. This may probably be the result of necessity, as the different tribes, if we are to judge from the numerous large scars in various parts of the body, are evidently engaged in frequent warfare with each other.

Tuesday, 27.—Mr. Jeffery held a market to-day, at the village near the beach; but an old chief, who had been named Bottle-nose, was apparently, out of humour, probably in consequence of the affair at the border-market the day before.

Wednesday, 28.—At the conclusion of the market, which was held at the Bottle-nose village to-day, a party of chiefs came hallooing after Mr. Jeffery, at the moment of his leaving the shore, but he did not offer to return. They then followed along the beach in the direction of his boat, until they nearly reached Hay River. He now perceived they held something in their hands, which they gave him to understand, by signs, was intended for him. This induced him to pull for the shore again, when he found they had brought back the unfortunate bill-hook that had been carried away on the preceding Monday: the men who had stolen it, however, were not forthcoming. Mr. Jeffery conducted them to Clarence, where an interview took place between Captains Owen and Harrison, and some of the chiefs, at which the former directed a couple of iron hoops to be given as a reward for the recovery of the bill-hook. After this, several chiefs came on board, bringing with them a sheep as a peace-offering, which the Captain immediately ordered to be killed for their own entertainment. In this operation, they assisted very effectually; for one of them took his knife, and after skinning the head and neck, the animal being yet alive, cut its throat and extracted the windpipe, which was given to our friend Cut-throat, who first slapped it for some time about his shoulders, and afterwards, having merely warmed it on the fire, devoured it voraciously. The skin being removed, others of the natives tore off with their teeth, and ate the portions of raw flesh which remained attached to it; while some cut off portions from the animal, and disposed of them in the same manner. The remainder of the body was partially dressed on the coals, and dispatched by the party generally. Notwithstanding this demonstration of their high relish for raw meat, it is remarkable that two of the chiefs, Cut-throat and Good-tempered Jack, who were honoured with a second dinner at Captain Owen's table, when presented with meat supposed to be done to their taste, shewed a repugnance to it, and wished it to be put on the fire again. Cut-throat had shewn so much disinterested zeal in our favour, on various occasions, and particularly in the affair of the bill-hook, that Captain Owen took the opportunity of rewarding him for it, by presenting him with some iron, and a pair of shoes. It is singular, that he is the only native we have, as yet, been conversant with, who never begged for any thing.

Thursday, 29.—Our little establishment (considering the few hands, and the many irons we have in the fire,) is making a rapid progress. The greatest activity pervades every department. The whole of our people, whether ashore or afloat, live uncommonly well, having plenty of yams and palm-wine served out to them daily, with fowls and fish occasionally, which are extra provisions, supplied gratuitously; the former being purchased from the natives with iron hoop, the latter taken by our fishermen. We have also caught a few hawksbill, and green turtle, and occasionally dig turtles' eggs from the sand on the beach.

Saturday, Dec. 1.—Our establishment has hitherto been remarkably healthy; the sickness which has occurred, being almost entirely the result of accidental wounds, or the bites of musquitos and sand-flies; the latter, being irritated by rubbing, have produced, in some instances, very serious sores, which have baffled the greatest attention of our surgeons: one feature in these ulcers is, that frequent changes of applications are required, no individual remedy appearing to agree, at farthest, for more than five days; generally, but three or four; nor has any kindly disposition to heal shewn itself, until a degree of salivation has been produced, by giving the patient a grain of calomel, night and morning. Both my companions in the country are unfortunately on the sick list,—Elwood, with remittent fever, with which he was seized immediately after his return; the other, Debenham, in consequence of getting his legs bitten by insects. I have myself, thank God, escaped without illness or injury of any kind.

Sunday, 2.—Two chiefs, Cut-throat and Bottle-nose, with some other natives of consequence, dined with Captain Owen to-day, who was entertaining a party of the officers and other gentlemen attached to the establishment. The natives always appear particularly gratified in being allowed to dine on board, and Captain Owen, as a matter of policy, in tending to promote a friendly intercourse, frequently indulges them in this way; it is offering, however, no trifling sacrifice at the shrines of the gods of friendship and cleanliness, to sit down with them, for their bodies not unfrequently emitted a most offensive odour, particularly when much heated by exertion, and the influence of a tropical climate. Imagine the action of these upon a mixture of perspiration, rancid palm-oil, clay and dust, the whole producing an effluvium little inferior to that which Sir John Falstaff describes to have been generated in his ducking-basket, 'The rankest compound of villanous smells that ever offended nostrils.' Besides, as our guests were all dressed in buff, it was necessary to clean, after them, the chairs and other places on which they might happen to sit. Cut-throat, and one of his tribe, slept on board, on a sail placed between two guns.

Monday, 3.—After breakfast, our visitors took their leave, accompanied by Mr. Jeffery, who, in consequence of a previous arrangement, was going to spend a couple of days with them, at a village about eight miles in the country, and from which he returned at the expiration of the appointed time, well pleased with the attention and hospitality that had been shewn him. A remuneration of bar-iron was the price of these civilities.

Our fishing party have taken in their seine to-day, two flying-fish of the gurnet species, and a hawksbill turtle. A party of natives from King Cove, headed by a chief named Toby Limp, came on board with a native woman, who was far advanced in that happy teeming state which is peculiar to females in all parts of the world. This was, in fact, one of the few instances of any female coming on board: for, although old Bottle-nose had once brought two alongside the ship, he kept them concealed at the bottom of his canoe: we have some reason, however, to believe that his original intention was to have honoured us with a full introduction, but that he waived it in consequence of finding the chief of another tribe in close conference with Captain Owen. With respect to Mr. Toby Limp's lady, the general opinion, drawn from various signs and appearances, was, that she was intended as a sort of present, or peace-offering, to the Captain; and what amused us exceedingly, was the peculiar mode which Toby adopted of recommending her more fully to his good opinion, by frequently passing his hand over her abdomen, while, regarding Captain Owen with a most animated countenance, he seemed to express something like the following: 'Look here! surely this is worthy of your attention.' But, however powerful the native charms of this lady might have been, and in spite of the above felicitous mode of 'showing her off,' the speculation proved totally ineffectual. Another circumstance concurred in diminishing the effect of any impression that might have been made, namely, that three or four clay-coloured chiefs appeared to be co-partners with Mr. Toby in the affections of the lady. The whole party passed the night together on board, between two guns. So much for the delicacy of sentiment among savages.

The following is a specimen of the delicacy of this people in another respect. On the occasion of Captain Owen visiting the brother of the King of Baracouta, a calabash of palm-wine was produced, which, in consequence of some imperfection in the vessel, leaked out its contents; in order to cure this defect, the hospitable chief took off his hat, and, scraping with his thumb-nail a portion of the clay and grease from his head, effectually checked further leakage, with this *veritable* Fernando Po cement.

Tuesday, 4.—An increase in the number of the sick has been reported to-day, several of the men on board, and of the mechanics and labourers on shore being affected with ulcers of the hospital gangrene kind. One seaman of the Eden, has had his leg amputated above the knee, in consequence of the nature of the ulceration. Having gone on shore this morning, I had the pleasure of finding the works in rapid progress; the floor plates were being laid in one of the frame houses; the roof of a large saw-pit was also being put on; while a great part of the labourers were occupied in bringing up some frames of houses which had lately been landed from the transport. We were treated to-day with a monkey for dinner, cooked in the manner of an Irish stew, with yams as a substitute for potatoes: I must admit that I found it by no means a disagreeable food, which is not to be wondered at from its being a very clean animal, living on vegetable substances. Our fishermen have taken one green, and one hawksbill turtle; also a skate, weighing ninety pounds; and two buckets full of other fish of various descriptions, principally mullet.

Lieutenant Vidal brought a native on board, charged with the following crimes: namely, stealing a dinner knife from on board the steam-vessel; and an attempt, in conjunction with others, to plunder our forge, on Adelaide Island. Lieutenant Vidal, fortunately passing in that direction, observed a canoe lying on the beach. This he secured. The men belonging to it, however, contrived to make their escape in another canoe, but left behind them two of their hats. The prisoner had the audacity to venture on board the steam-vessel, in hopes of recovering the lost canoe; he was immediately attempted to be seized, but he contrived, in consequence of his greasy skin, to give our men the slip, and effect his escape. Yet he was not deterred from making a second attempt, having, as he imagined, sufficiently disguised himself with a different hat and head-dress; but he was immediately recognised, and, having been enticed into the cabin, effectually secured. Captain Owen ordered him to be put into irons, with the intention of keeping him under confinement for a week, and then dismissing him with some slight punishment.

Wednesday, 5.—A brig was observed in the offing which had the appearance of a slaver. The steam-vessel was immediately ordered in chase, and returned in the evening, reporting her to be an English brig, from Liverpool, bound for the Cameroons.

Thursday, 6.—Our tender, the Horatio, sailed this week for Sierra Leone. Among other supernumeraries sent in her, were a serjeant and two privates of the Royal African Corps. The conduct of these men was so notoriously bad, that Captain Owen apprehended their example would corrupt the black soldiers with whom they were associated. I cannot avoid again calling in question the policy of our Government in sending out condemned soldiers to the Colonial African Corps; for nothing tends more to degrade the general character of our country, in the opinion of the native Africans, who are too apt to form their estimate of our morality, from these specimens of their masters.

Friday, 7.—The unloading of the transport which came with us from England was completed to-day. Among other stores, she brought out the frames of a block-house; six large and ten small dwelling-houses; six long eighteen pounders, and two long nines.

Saturday, 8.—Lieutenant Caldwell, of the Royal Marines, died this morning, and was buried at four in the afternoon. He had never been in health since our departure from England, or even been on shore, excepting for an hour or two at Sierra Leone. He was to have returned by the first opportunity to England, and, with that view, had, previously to his death, been removed from the Eden to the steam-vessel.

Monday, 10.—Our fishing party took to-day no less than ten turtle in their seine. The native prisoner having now been confined six days out of the seven awarded him. Captain Owen thought it better to inflict his intended punishment of thirty-nine lashes to-day, in order that his immediate rage might have time to subside, before being set at liberty on the morrow. It was accordingly carried into effect; and, although he made a most lusty bellowing on the occasion, the whip-cord appeared to make very little impression on his thick skin. I believe he deemed himself peculiarly fortunate in coming off so well, as, judging from his signs, he expected, at least, to have had his throat cut. During his confinement, he roared and blubbered frequently, particularly whenever he was sensible of any canoe approaching the ship. His countrymen, however, appeared to care little about him; on the contrary, they frequently mimicked his noises, as if in ridicule. His father, indeed, and one or two other relatives, took some interest in his fate, and offered ransom for him.

Tuesday, Dec. 11.—Captain Owen, at an early hour, went on board the steam-vessel to commence his intended survey of the island, and did me the honour of inviting me to accompany him. At seven o'clock we left Maidstone Bay, and proceeded towards a place to the eastward of Point William, where Captain Owen intended to land his native prisoner, and from whence he was expecting to receive on board Cut-throat, Bottle-nose, and another chief, known by the name of Good-tempered Jack. The two latter only kept their promise, but, on coming on board, they were so impressed with fear and astonishment, particularly when the paddles began to move, that their hearts failed them, and they retreated to the boat with all possible celerity. The prisoner was allowed to accompany them; but no sooner did the boat approach the shore, than, doubting the reality of his freedom, until entirely out of our reach, he jumped overboard, and, alternately swimming and diving, as if to elude pursuit, he, at length, reached the shore. About a week afterwards, he ventured to make his appearance on the beach, accompanied by Bottle-nose, but was careful not to approach our party, until the officer on duty threw out a signal of encouragement, when he came forward, exchanged his palm-wine for iron hoop, and afterwards joined in the laugh with those around him.

Pursuing our voyage, about noon, a party of natives were observed on the beach, and Capt. Owen determined on paying them a visit, ordering a boat to be lowered for the purpose. Unfortunately, however, it being necessary, while in the act of lowering, to make a few retrograde strokes of the paddle, the boat was drawn into the vortex on the right hand, and nearly cut in two. By this accident, one of the seamen who were in it, was thrown within the paddle, but, miraculously, taken out unhurt; another made his escape on board the vessel; while two more were set adrift in the sea; they were, however, soon picked up by a second boat, which was instantly lowered, and which also succeeded in recovering the wreck of the first. On approaching the shore, the surf was found to be so strong, that Captain Owen was obliged to communicate with the natives from the boat.

A few yams were purchased for some pieces of iron-hoop, which the natives were so eager to become possessed of, that, daring the exchange, they trembled exceedingly from the intensity of their desire. A piece was intentionally thrown into the sea, with the view of giving them a scramble: they all immediately darted with the utmost eagerness into the water, and exerted themselves most strenuously, until one had the luck to find it; when the remainder left him in quiet possession, without evincing the slightest disposition to deprive him of his treasure.

A small island lay off the shore of this place, which Capt. Owen did not consider of sufficient importance to induce him to give it a name. We now continued our survey along the south-eastern side of the island, advancing at the rate of six or seven miles an hour, until half-past five in the evening, when we arrived a-breast of the south-eastern point (Cape Barrow): we then took our bearings, let the steam down, and stood off the land, under easy sail, for the night.

Wednesday, Dec. 12.—An hour after midnight we tacked, and stood towards the land; at daylight, got the steam on, and furled the sails, and at eight in the morning we were off the same point at which our survey of the previous evening had concluded, the current having, during the night, carried us to the south-west, at the rate of about a mile and a half per hour. The part of the island we were now coasting along, was possessed of a very considerable degree of sublimity, the shore being bold and rocky, with various picturesque cataracts descending from the mountains; and the whole face of the country having a wild appearance. During the forenoon, we had two high peaks in view, one of which Captain Owen named after Dr. Burn, the surgeon of the Eden, who first observed it. About half-past ten, we passed a snug little cove, where the natives were occupied in building canoes, and where we observed a considerable quantity of wood piled up, intended for making paddles. Soon afterwards, we passed the entrance of a river, which, out of compliment to myself, Captain Owen named Holman River. A remarkably large stone lay on the beach near its mouth. At noon, we were off a bluff cape, which received the name of Cape Eden. At this time our previously fine weather disappeared, and we had, throughout the remainder of the day, a very hazy atmosphere, with occasional rain.

About one o'clock, a rakish-looking schooner made her appearance, which, from her manoeuvres, such as frequently altering her course, as if she wished to avoid us, we suspected to be a slave-vessel; we, therefore, made full sail in chase, and at three o'clock, had approached near enough to fire a gun at her, when she immediately hoisted English colours, brought to, and proved to be the African, Captain John Smith, twenty-five days from Sierra Leone, and seven from Cape Coast Castle, laden with provisions for the colony, and having on board Hospital-Assistant Cowen, of the Medical Staff, who had volunteered to join the establishment. Captain Owen, having received his letters, ordered her to proceed to Maidstone Bay, while we stood in for George's Bay, on the western side of the island, where we came to anchor soon after four o'clock.

Thursday, Dec. 13.—Soon after breakfast, Dr. Burn landed with three men, and proceeded to a native village, about three miles from the beach, where he was kindly received by an elderly chief, who appeared well acquainted with our countrymen. He could pronounce 'King George,' and a few other English words, and wore as an ornament, suspended from his neck, a brass plate, which had belonged to the cap of a soldier of the Royal African Corps; he had also another brass plate with G.R. upon it. This chief, with his son, accompanied Dr. Burn on board, and was entertained by Captain Owen with fish, yams, and palm-wine; at length, he began to express much anxiety to be gone, and was sent on shore. During the morning, Captain Owen and Lieutenant Badgeley occupied themselves with surveying the bay: after this, we went ashore, when many of the natives assembled round us, and behaved themselves very civilly, although they were, as usual, importunate for iron; offering in exchange yams, palm-wine, fowls, &c. &c. Only one canoe came off to us at this place, containing twelve men, who had a few yams with them, which they appeared very indifferent about parting with; at least, they demanded very exorbitant prices, as a piece of iron for a single yam, for which, at Maidstone Bay, we could have purchased eight or ten. We caught here a large dog-fish, a species of ground shark.

Friday, Dec. 14.—At day-break we were again under weigh, and stood out of George's Bay, making a little to the southward of it, for the purpose of resuming our survey at the point where we left off on the preceding day, in order to give chase to the schooner; we then returned into the bay, running close along, and surveying its shores, leaving it at its northern extremity, and passing round Goat Island; we then stood for Maidstone Bay, where we anchored at one in the afternoon, having surveyed the intermediate coast, as well us the whole extent of the bay, from Cape Bullen to Point William, from whence we had commenced the survey. Thus we completed the circumnavigation of the island.

I shall conclude my account of this short voyage, by giving a few of the geographical and meteorological observations, which have been made since our arrival, with every due attention to accuracy.

Names of Places.	N. lat.			E. lon.		
Cape Bullen	3°	47'	3"	8° 39'	4"
Point William, or Clarence Town	3	45	8	8 45	0
Cape Horatio	3	46	25	8 54	4
Cape Barrow	3	11	5	8 40	4
Point Charles (S.W. of St. George's Bay)	3	26	9	8 27	7
Goat Island (N.E. of St. George's Bay)	3	26	9	8 32	8
Cape Badgeley, or West Point	3	19	0	8 24	7
Cape Vidal, or East Point	3	39	3	8 56	3
Peak of Clarence Mountain	3	34	6	8 41	5
Peak of the Cameroon Mountain, on the Mainland of Africa	4	13	5	9 9	5

The Cameroon Mountain bears, from Clarence Peak, N. 32 deg. 30 min. E. at a distance of 48 miles; and from Clarence Town, N. 27 deg. E., the distance being 31-1/2 miles; while the nearest point from the mainland is only about 20 miles. From the proximity of this island to the equinoctial, there is only 14 minutes difference between the longest and shortest day; and the temperature is so equable, that the thermometer, throughout the year, never varies more than 10 degrees in the 24 hours. The spring-tides have a rise and fall between seven and eight feet; and it is high water all round the island, at the full and change of the moon, at half after four o'clock. During our absence, the first house erected in the settlement, had been completed; and Mr. Glover, who was to inhabit it, had invited his friends to the house-warming on the day of our return. This house consisted of only one floor, twenty feet square, and built on piles, with a store-room beneath, the sides of which are constituted by the piles. Ten other houses, of similar form and dimensions, are in progress of construction, besides six larger ones, of forty feet square, and the block-house, which measures fifty by thirty; the whole consisting of single floors, with store-rooms underneath.

Saturday, Dec. 15.—The system of labour among the workmen is, to commence at six in the morning, and leave off at eleven for dinner, recommencing at one, and concluding at half-past five; after which, during the remainder of the day, they are allowed to amuse themselves. The labourers and mechanics have been formed into a militia corps, under the command of Capt. Harrison, with the rank of Major, and are occasionally taught to march *en militaire*, and exercised with the pike, which is, at present, their only weapon; the Eden, having but twenty muskets to spare, which have been distributed among the artificers who came out with us from England.

This afternoon, our transport, the Diadem, sailed for Cape Coast Castle. In the evening, the bugles at Clarence sounded an alarm, in consequence of the flames of some burning brush-wood accidentally communicating with one of the huts. It was fortunately soon extinguished, without any serious injury having been sustained.

Monday, Dec. 17.—The Diadem, which sailed on Saturday, was detained during the whole of yesterday within sight of the island; but, about noon to-day, a fresh wind springing up from the eastward, she was soon out of sight. A few days since, our gardener, while digging in Paradise, turned up a Spanish copper-coin of Charles III., dated 1774, probably a relic of some ship which had touched here for water.

Tuesday, Dec. 18.—Anderson, a black soldier of the Royal African Corps, whom I have previously mentioned as an interpreter on our arrival here, was to-day found sleeping on his post, and committed to the guard-house, from whence he contrived to escape into the woods, with a view of seeking protection from the natives. Another black soldier was punished this morning for having quitted his post, and lost his musket, a few days since, in the following manner. A party of Kroomen being employed in cutting down wood, some of the natives contrived to steal an axe and bill-hook. The theft, however, was immediately detected, and a scuffle ensued, during which this soldier, who was a sentinel near the spot, threw down his musket, and ran away. The musket was taken possession of by a native, but subsequently recovered by a Krooman, not, however, without his first receiving a severe cut on his hand by the knife of the native. After throwing a few spears, one of which slightly wounded the head Krooman, the natives got clear off with the bill-hook and axe. A spear was also thrown at Mr. Davis, the master's assistant, who was accidentally passing at the time, and whom one of the natives had even the audacity to attempt to make prisoner; a fate which he only escaped, from his shirt giving way under the grasp.

When this affair was made known to Captain Harrison, he immediately proceeded to the market-place, and finding some chiefs there, communicated to them what had happened. Cut-throat, who was present, instantly arose, and, after making a speech to his countrymen, formed them into line, each being armed with the usual number of spears. After singing a war-song, and making three circular tours, or evolutions, the whole started off in quest of the thieves, and, in less than an hour, returned with the axe and bill-hook. Some few days after this event, one of the natives, who had taken an active part in it, had the effrontery to enter our lines for the purpose of selling his palm-wine, when he was immediately secured by the Kroomen, and conducted a prisoner to Captain Harrison, who sent him on board the Eden, where he was put into irons; however, this man had committed a previous offence, namely, having struck Mr. Jeffery two severe blows with a stick, about a month since, which compelled him to give up the pursuit of a fellow, who had been endeavouring to impose two calabashes of water upon him, instead of palm-wine.

During the last week, we have had little communication with the natives, and our supplies of palm-wine, &c., have consequently run short. This circumstance, we are informed, is attributable to their being occupied in the yam-plantations. I am inclined to infer, that, if the necessity really exists for thus employing the whole of the inhabitants in the culture of this root, the population of the island is not so great as we have been led to consider it.

Wednesday, 19.—At half-past one this morning, a loud splash was heard in the water, succeeded by the cry of, 'A man overboard.' A boat was immediately sent, and from the phosphorescence of the water, some one was discovered swimming towards the shore. On approaching him, he turned round in the direction of the Eden; and, when within twenty yards of the ship, he all at once disappeared, and was not seen afterwards. On inquiry, it was found that the native prisoner who had been confined in irons on the forecastle, for his participation in the affray I have so lately described, had contrived to effect his escape. To accomplish this, he had put his hand down the scuttle over the coppers, and taken from thence the iron that turns the handles of the dischargers. With the point of this he had contrived to break off one of the sides of the padlock which secured his fetters, and thus setting himself at liberty, he crossed the deck to the gangway, opposite to where the sentry was placed, when he mounted the railings, and immediately plunged into the sea. It is singular, with respect to this prisoner, that his countrymen shewed very little solicitude about him: and we therefore had reason to think that he was no favourite with them. When they did inquire after him, it was to know whether we had not cut his throat. The King of Baracouta's brother once asked Captain Owen what he intended to do with him; and, on being informed that he meant to keep him for a time in irons, and then, after a gentle flagellation, dismiss him, expressed his astonishment at this lenity, and made signs that we ought to cut his throat. It is true we sometimes had, as might be expected, very different versions of the signs of these natives; but, in the present instance, they could not well be misunderstood.

Captain Owen, attended by a small party of marines, went on shore at an early hour, to hold a Court of Inquiry on twelve African soldiers, for refusing to attend the punishment of their comrade (an Ashantee) on the preceding day. They were found guilty, and sentenced to receive three hundred lashes each. After a part of this punishment had been inflicted, they were sent on board the Eden.

Thursday, 20.—Anderson, the African soldier, who escaped from confinement on Tuesday, was met in the woods this morning by a serjeant of his company, to whom he immediately surrendered himself, and who placed him under charge of another soldier. Apprehensive, however, of the consequences of his double offence, he shortly after contrived to give his guard the slip, and again effected his escape. The above mentioned serjeant also detected a labourer in the act of lowering a piece of iron from a cliff, with the intention of selling it to the natives, whose canoes were lying off the beach. Having first secured the offender, he then fired his musket at one of the canoes, without injuring, or intending to injure, the men whom it contained, and the aim was so unerring, that the ball penetrated through the bottom of the canoe, in such a manner that it immediately began to fill with water; this terrified the natives so much, that they all leaped overboard, and swimming to another canoe, left their own, with her cargo of sheep, fowls, &c. to its fate. This might truly be termed a good hit.

In the afternoon I went on shore at Adelaide Point, where, it is said, the Spaniards had a battery. Whether this be true or not, the spot is well adapted for one; it is now entirely covered over with remarkably thick brushwood, which Captain Owen has ordered to be cleared off, with the intention of forming a road, through the woods, to Longfield. Hospital-Assistant Cowen found to-day a silver Spanish coin, in Paradise, near the same spot where the copper one before mentioned was discovered, and which bears the same date.

Friday, 21.—This morning, Matthew Elwood died, after an illness of 25 days. His complaint was a remittent fever, taken on our short journey into the interior. On the third day after our return, he took to his bed, from which he never rose again, excepting on the day previous to his death, when, under a state of mental aberration, he secretly took off his shirt, and threw himself from out of the port-hole near his bed into the sea; he was soon taken up, but his delirium continued until he expired. At five this afternoon he was buried in Paradise. My other companion, John Debenham, has also been ill ever since our return, with an ulcerated leg, occasioned by the bites of insects, and which, at present, shews little disposition to heal.

Saturday, 22.—A sheep was killed this morning, one of whose hind quarters weighed four pounds and two ounces, and which, although not fat, was the largest native sheep we have yet met with. About a fortnight since five were slaughtered, which altogether weighed but sixty pounds, and, consequently, averaged only twelve pounds each.

Sunday, 23.—During the last week we have experienced much thunder and lightning. Our fishermen attribute their want of success to this cause; for the fishery has been unusually unproductive. Early this morning it began to rain, and for an hour continued to do so more heavily than any of us had before witnessed, after which; a smaller rain continued until eleven o'clock, when it cleared off, and the remainder of the day was fine. In the evening, a number of native fishing boats assembled between Point William, and the Eden, and as their proceedings on the occasion particularly attracted our attention, I shall take this opportunity of describing the peculiar method of fishing which they make use of.

A number of canoes, containing from three to twelve men, put out to sea, to look for a shoal of fish; when discovered, they surround it on all sides, shouting and splashing the water with their paddles in every direction, endeavouring to drive it towards a centre. This done, they commence fishing, using for the bait a small fish with which they are previously provided, and they occasionally throw a few of these into the midst of the shoal. The fish appear to take this bait very eagerly; but, as the hooks which the natives use, are made of bone or nails, and without barbs, [32] not more than half the number struck in the first instance, are eventually secured. Two men paddle the canoe in the direction of the shoal, while the remainder are occupied in fishing. Captain Owen went in his boat, and pulled towards the party; we were much interested with their operations and success. At his invitation, after the fishing had concluded, one of the canoes brought us some very fine ones, a species of bream, weighing from two to three pounds each. This was the first time I ever knew fish caught, in deep water at sea, with a rod and line.

Monday, Dec. 24.—In the course of the day, a party of natives brought on board three black men, inhabitants of the Island of St. Thomas, who, six months before, had taken refuge in Fernando Po, under the following circumstances:— During the time they were engaged in fishing, a strong wind arose, which drove them out to sea. Unable to contend against the power of the gale, they deemed it prudent to keep the canoe before it, and even assist with their paddles, in hopes of sooner falling in with land, and thus escape starvation. In this manner they continued drifting for eight days without fresh water, or any kind of provisions, excepting the few fish they had caught before the gale arose, the greater part of which were thrown overboard, in consequence of their getting into a state of excessive putridity. At length they came in sight of Fernando Po. Some of the natives came off to them in their canoes, and took them ashore on the eastern part of the island. Here they had been compelled to remain, devoid of all hopes of returning, until they saw our steam-vessel making its late circumnavigation of the island. This opened to them a new and cheering prospect; and they determined to attempt reaching our settlement overland, by travelling at night, and secreting themselves during the day, in order that the natives might not interrupt their escape. Previously to the discovery of our steam-vessel, they had frequently heard the reports of our morning and evening gun: this had led them to the belief, that some Europeans were resident on the island, and now afforded them the proper line of direction for their march. After travelling for three nights, and at the time of their approaching our settlement, they were discovered by the natives, who, in the first instance, attempted to force them back to their former residence. The poor creatures, however, made so much noise and resistance, that, apprehending the fact would transpire and excite our displeasure, it was at length determined to conduct them to us. One of them was a Fantee, and had resided at the Dutch settlement of Elmina, where a black man of our party, who was no less a personage than a son of the King of Cape Coast, although now discharging the humble office of gun-room steward of the Eden, had frequently seen him.

At the time these men arrived on board, several natives were with us, and among the rest, our friend Cut-throat. No sooner did the Fantee fix his eyes upon him, than, to the astonishment of all present, they began to flash with

[32] We have met with some hooks made from the part of the solid wood of a prickly tree, or shrub, whence the thorn grows, and which process formed the pointed part of the hook.

indignation, while the countenance of Cut-throat assumed proportionably the expression of sheepishness. The cause of this proved to be, that, when they first landed on the island, our old friend had stolen a shirt from him; in other respects, however, I believe they had little reason to complain of the treatment they experienced: for they had not been compelled to work, excepting occasionally assisting in fishing, and they had been permitted to reside by themselves; it is true, on the other hand, that they had little hospitality to be grateful for, having been compelled to subsist on a scanty supply of yams and palm-wine.

During the last week, the natives had, without any apparent reason, absented themselves from the settlement; to-day, however, they returned in great numbers, and among the rest, our old friend Cut-throat, exhibiting a large gash on his forehead. He gave us to understand, that there had been some warfare between the various tribes, concerning a quantity of iron, probably that which Chameleon's party had stolen from Messrs. Vidal and Jeffery.

Tuesday, Dec. 25.—This being Christmas-day, Captain Owen selected it for taking formal possession of the settlement, in the name, and on behalf of his Sovereign, George the Fourth. At seven o'clock in the morning, accompanied by most of his officers and ship's company, he went on shore for this purpose. The different parties of our colony being assembled, the whole marched in procession, from the border parade, in the following order, with bugles, drums and fifes, playing alternately:—

Captains Owen and Harrison,
Surgeon Cowen and Lieutenant Holman,
Messrs. Jeffery and Carter,
The Surgeon and Purser of the Eden,
The European Volunteers, commanded by Lieutenant Glover,
Lieutenant Vidal, with half the Eden's ship's company,
and the Midshipmen of his division,
The Colours, carried by Mr. Wood,
The Band,
Lieutenant Badgeley, with half the Eden's ship's company,
and the Midshipmen of his division,
The Marines and Royal African Corps, under Lieutenant Mends,
The Clarence Militia, under their respective Officers:
First Division—Lieutenant Morrison,
Second Division—Lieutenant Abbott,
Third Division—Ensign Matthews,
Tom Liverpool's party, under Bell,
Ben Gundo's party, under Miller.

On arriving at the Point, the different divisions were formed around the flag-staff; and the colours having been first hoisted, the following Proclamation was read:—

'*Proclamation*,—By William Fitzwilliam Owen, Esq. Captain of His Majesty's ship Eden, and Superintendent of Fernando Po.

'His Majesty, George the Fourth, King of Great Britain and Ireland, has been graciously pleased to direct that a settlement by his Majesty's subjects should be established on the Island of Fernando Po, and his Royal Highness the Lord High Admiral having selected me for the performance of this service, the formation of the said settlement has been entrusted to me, under the title and denomination of Superintendent.

'In obedience to the orders of his Royal Highness the Lord High Admiral, I directed the first operations of clearing the land on this point (Point William) to be commenced on the first day of November last, and on the tenth and twelfth following, purchased from the native chiefs, and from the tenants of one small part of that ground which I desired to occupy, the full right of property and possession, for which iron was paid to the amount of three bars, and land-marks fixed by the native chiefs, to shew the extent of ground so bought.

'*Therefore*, in the name of God, by whose grace we have been thus successful, and for the sole use and benefit of his most gracious Majesty, George the Fourth, King of Great Britain and Ireland, I do, by this public act, take possession of all the land bought by me as aforesaid, under the future name of *Clarence*, being all the land bounded on the north by the sea, on the east and south by Hay-brook, and on the west by a line running from the sea due south, by the magnetic needle, or south-south-east, by the pole of the world, until it joins Hay-brook, the Peninsula of Point William included in the same, being in north latitude about three degrees and forty-five minutes, and east longitude from the Observatory of Greenwich, about eight degrees and forty-five minutes, and the aforesaid western boundary being taken from a tree marked by the natives, which is two hundred and eighteen yards from the gate of the ditch across the gorge of Point William, and bearing, therefore, south twenty and a half degrees west by the magnetic needle, or south two degrees and thirty minutes east by the pole of the world.

'And, in testimony of this public act, I command all persons present to attach their names to this Proclamation, as witnesses of the same.

'Done by me on Point William, in the settlement of Clarence, on the Island of Fernando Po, this one thousand eight hundred and twenty-seventh anniversary of the birth of our blessed Saviour and Redeemer, and in the eighth year of the reign of his present Majesty.

'WILLIAM FITZWILLIAM OWEN,

Captain of his Majesty's ship Eden, and Superintendent of Fernando Po.

'GOD SAVE THE KING.'

The following additional Proclamation was then read:—

'*Proclamation,*—By William Fitzwilliam Owen, Esq. Captain of his Majesty's ship Eden, and Superintendent of Fernando Po.

'It has become necessary to extend our lines for the purpose of keeping the natives more separate from our working parties, which are, at times, much incommoded by them, and for the purpose of possessing ground enough for our own establishment.

'*Therefore,* I do, by this act, formally take possession for his Majesty, of all unpossessed lands lying between a line running south, by the compass, or south-south-east by the pole of the world, from Cockburn-brook on the west, to Hay-brook on the south, and the coast-line between the said Cockburn and Hay-brooks, including therein the two islets named Adelaide; guaranteeing, at the same time, to the natives of Fernando Po, perfect security, and unmolested possession of all such grounds within the said limits as are now settled or appropriated by them, being apparently four small spots where they have parks for store yams, which grounds are to be purchased whenever the chiefs can be assembled for that purpose, and the said natives are disposed to receive an equivalent for their value.

'Given under my hand, at Clarence, this twenty-fifth day of December, one thousand eight hundred and twenty-seven.

'WILLIAM FITZWILLIAM OWEN,

Captain of his Majesty's ship Eden, and Superintendent of Fernando Po.

'GOD SAVE THE KING.'

The above Proclamations having been read, three general cheers were given, on a signal from the boatswain's pipe, after which the band struck up 'God save the King,' succeeded by a *feu de joie* from the volunteers, marines, and African corps, which was immediately responded to, by a royal salute, from His Majesty's ship Eden, the Steam-vessel, and the African (a merchant schooner), and afterwards from small cannon at the settlement.

The ceremony being thus concluded, the different parties marched off in the same order as before, and were dismissed to their respective quarters, the band playing 'Rule Britannia.' On returning to the Eden, Capt. Owen performed divine service, Captain Harrison doing the same to the civil establishment on shore; after which, Capt. Owen gave a dinner, at Mr. Glover's house, to the whole of the officers engaged in the establishment. It only remains to be added to the events of this day, that many of the natives, including our friend Cut-throat, were present during its different ceremonies.

Tuesday, January 1, 1828.—During the past week nothing of importance has occurred, excepting that our works are rapidly advancing; as respects our general pursuits, and intercourse with the natives, much sameness must necessarily exist.

Soon after eight o'clock this morning. Captains Owen and Harrison, attended by a party of marines, proceeded to a native town, eight miles to the eastward, for the purpose of meeting an old chief, who was said to be the principal one on that part of the island. After they had waited a considerable time at the place appointed, the chief made his appearance, accompanied by 150 spearmen, who entertained our party with an exhibition of warlike evolutions, when Captain Owen, in return, directed his marines to go through their military exercise; but, before they had proceeded far, the chief became evidently much alarmed, and requested them to desist: his apprehension appeared to be more particularly excited by the bayonets. Having spent a short time with the chief, partaking of his palm-wine, and inviting him to return the visit on the following Tuesday, Captain Owen took his leave.

In the course of the afternoon Chameleon came to our market, accompanied by nearly 150 of his followers, all well armed with spears, and walked up to Mr. Jeffery in a menacing and insulting manner, as if to demand satisfaction for some injury he had sustained. He even carried his daring so far as to make a seizure of Mr. Jeffery's person; that gentleman immediately despatched a messenger to Captain Owen to communicate what had happened, requesting at the same time that some soldiers might be sent to his assistance, in order to prevent further aggression on our lines. Captain Owen immediately hastened to the spot with a party of the Royal African Corps, and at length succeeded in conciliating the natives, although, for want of a good interpreter, he could by no means satisfactorily ascertain the cause of their violent proceedings. It probably originated in the discontent of the chief, who had, on the day preceding, in consequence of some misconduct, been excluded from the market.

At five o'clock I had the pleasure of accompanying Captain Owen on shore to a banquet, that had been prepared in honour of him by the civil and military officers of the establishment. On this occasion the Eden's band attended, and we were also favoured by the presence of many of the natives, who were thus enabled to gratify their love of music. The following ludicrous instance of their enthusiasm in this respect, occurred one day while the band were playing on the quarter-deck of the Eden. A chief, named Good-tempered Jack, while listening to the music, was so absorbed in his feelings, that he became totally insensible to the circumstance of a native woman, who stood behind him, giving way to her own raptures, by beating time, with no little vehemence, on his back.

Thursday, 3.—Lieutenant Vidal, Captain Smith, of the African, schooner, and others, made an excursion, about eight miles up the Baracouta river, this morning. They proceeded partly by walking along the banks, and partly by wading up the bed of the river. They met with little of interest, excepting that, at about three miles from the mouth, they observed some fine basaltic pillars: they also shot a few snipes, and saw the tracks of many deer.

Friday, 4.—Our old acquaintance, Bottle-nose, was to-day found guilty of an indirect mode of stealing, by demanding payment a second time, with the greatest possible coolness and effrontery, for a sheep, and a goat with its kid, for which he had previously received the stipulated price. Mr. Jeffery, of course, resisted the demand, and brought forward several persons who most satisfactorily proved the former payment. Mr. Bottle-nose, however, would not be satisfied with this, and had even the presumption to complain to Captain Owen, who, on inquiry, was convinced that he was guilty of an intentional attempt at imposition; he, however, ordered the animals in question to be returned, but gave directions that he should never in future be permitted to enter the market, or in any shape trade with our establishment. This man had also, on the very same day, been detected in two or three attempts to steal a knife, and various pieces of iron. It is evident, from the above and other traits, that the natives of this island, like all other savage nations, are naturally addicted to thieving: from the fear of detection, however, the instances of their venturing to indulge the propensity, do not appear to be numerous.

Monday, 7.—After breakfasting on board the steam-vessel, I accompanied Lieutenant Vidal and Mr. Cowen on shore, for the purpose of making observations. In the first place, we investigated the process for making a beautiful lake-red pigment, which is conducted by the women, the paint being used as an ornament for their skins. On entering the hut of an old chief, to whom our visit was more particularly directed, we found him sitting on the ground, with one of his wives in the same position holding a calabash, containing a mess of fowl and palm-oil, which he was eating with one hand, while the other held a roasted yam, which he also occasionally partook of. Having finished his repast, he took a draught from a large calabash of palm-wine, which he then presented to us, having, however, previously poured some into another vessel, which he gave to his wife. When the lady had finished her draught, she went to a tree near the hut, whose leaves and berries resembled those of our laurel, and plucking off about a dozen of the younger leaves, made them up into a bundle, which she first dipped into water, and afterwards into wood-ashes; they were then ground into a pulp on a stone, whose surface formed an inclined place, from which the material was allowed to run off when sufficiently prepared. On rubbing a portion of this pulp on our hands and faces, it became, after drying, a most beautiful and delicate rose colour, which required several times washing with soap and water before it could be removed, and which, if allowed to remain without washing, would retain its brilliancy for a comparatively long time. Mr. Cowen professed his intention of preparing a quantity of this dye, to send to his fair friends in England.

We also observed the process for preparing the palm-oil which I have before described. This oil, from the great number of palm-trees in the island, will, without doubt, ultimately become a considerable article of trade; indeed Captain Smith, of the African, schooner, has already opened a traffic for it, giving iron in exchange.

Two of the Kroomen to-day knocked down a fine buck deer, one of the haunches of which weighed six pounds.

Tuesday, 8.—Our market at Longfield, which of late has been held only twice in the week, when the natives are summoned by the sound of the bugle, has been well attended to-day. Hitherto Mr. Jeffery has had the superintendence of it, and it is impossible to pay too high a tribute to his exertions, and the manner in which he has discharged the very arduous task of conducting the barter with the natives. The system acted upon has now become so well defined, that Captain Owen deems it sufficient to commit the future charge to a corporal of marines, who has to-day entered on this duty.

Thursday, 10.—A native afflicted with insanity came within our lines this morning, and continued there until the afternoon. The conduits, or shoots from the watering-place to the beach, were this day reported to be completed.

Saturday, 12.—We have for some days been experiencing close warm weather, which I regret to say has proved unfavourable to our invalids, the ulcerations having in consequence been apparently aggravated.

Monday, 14.—Mr. Abbott, the store-keeper at Clarence, and John Earle, seaman of H.M.S. Eden, who had charge of the ordnance at the settlement, died this afternoon from intermittent fever.

Thursday, 17.—At daylight, the African, steam-vessel, got up her anchor and steam; when she stood out of the bay and parted company for England, intending to call at Sierra Leone, for a fresh supply of coals. She was under the command of Lieut. Vidal, who was charged with despatches relating to the proceedings of the settlement, &c. Mr. Bremner, master of the Eden, as well as several invalids, went home passengers in her: and I availed myself of the opportunity of sending home numberless specimens of articles used by the natives, amongst which were the following—the model of a canoe, spears, fishing lines, and stone slings, made from the fibre of the bark of a tree, bracelets, armlets, and other trifling ornaments worn about their person; a knife, made out of an iron hoop, and fitted into a wooden handle; a bell-shaped wooden rattle, some small boxes, made of split cane, monkey skins, &c. &c.

A building, composed of the frames of two small houses, each twenty feet square, having been erected, near Point William, for an hospital, it was this day reported to be ready for the reception of the sick, and 17 seamen of the Eden, with bad ulcers, were sent on shore to occupy it, leaving 15 on board with the same complaint, besides a few fever cases; there were also eight more ulcer cases that had been on shore for some time under a tent, near Point William. This situation was chosen by Capt. Owen for the hospital, as it was near the extreme point of a small peninsula, on which the prevailing wind blows transversely, therefore, if any spot on the settlement, or near the sea-shore of any part of the island was healthy, it is reasonable to suppose that this would be. The house consisted of only one floor, with a good broad verandah all round it, shingled in the same way as the roof of the house. [33]

Friday, 18.—This morning, one of the African Corps followed the example of our interpreter, Anderson, with this difference, however, that when he ran away, he took his musket and accoutrements with him. I do not see what advantage they proposed to themselves by going amongst the islanders, as they did not speak their language, and could not expect to procure the means of support, without working hard for it. The only point in their favour was, that they were of the same colour.

This afternoon the Eden's boats were sent after a vessel in the offing, which proved to be a sloop laden with palm-oil, from the Old Calabar River, bound to Liverpool. A few guanas have been seen here, and the Kroomen caught one a few days since, which they considered a great treat, and had cooked agreeably to their taste; but no venomous animal, except a few snakes, has yet been discovered. The guana is harmless, and, in some countries, is used for food. It is common to Asia, Africa, and America. Fortunately the alligator has not been seen in any of the rivers here, notwithstanding that they are native to all the rivers of the proximate continent. The cause, no doubt, is, that the rivers on the island, are mere mountain streams, which are very unfavourable to the retreat or repose of those reptiles.

Saturday, 19.—Soon after midnight, I accompanied Lieutenant Badgeley from his Majesty's ship Eden, on board the schooner African, Captain Smith, when we got under weigh to proceed round the coast of the Bight of Biafra, between the Camaroon River and Cape Formosa, for the purpose of cruising off, and entering any of the rivers, in quest of vessels trading for slaves, where we might have reason to believe that the inhuman traffic was pursued. The weather was very unpropitious during the night, for we had it squally, with heavy rain, thunder and lightning; but it cleared up in the course of the morning, and, at noon, it was calm and fine;—soon after which we saw a strange vessel, which we supposed to be a slaver: we, therefore, used every effort to overtake her, getting out our sweeps, and sending the Eden's pinnace a-head to tow; which

---

[33] Wood is seldom found to be desirable for building in a hot country, from the numerous ants and other insects that assail it, particularly where the changes are so frequent from very dry to very moist weather, if we had had time, it would have been much better to have erected our buildings with brick or stone. There is, indeed, plenty of fine clay for the former; but building stones are scarce in that neighbourhood, and we had not sufficient lime,--as we had to procure burnt lime from Sierra Leone, or shells from Accra, both of which we obtained for the building of an armourer's shop and a bakehouse. Indeed, we were obliged to use the utmost exertion to get any thing erected to shelter the Europeans and African soldiers, before the rainy season set in. As for the African mechanics and labourers, they built their own huts, in certain lines, that we called streets.

boat, with a good crew of English sailors, Lieutenant Badgeley had brought with him, to assist in performing the service. We had not advanced far towards the strange sail, before we observed two boats coming from her, which came alongside of us about three in the afternoon, when we found that they belonged to his Majesty's brig Clinker, which was well manned and armed, and that they entertained the same suspicions of our purpose as we had held of theirs. The Clinker was in the very best order, and was commanded by Lieutenant Matson, a most active and experienced officer.

I would here remark, that if we desire to be eminently successful in putting down the slave-trade, our Government ought to select vessels of a peculiar description, I mean vessels constructed principally for sailing; for, in the first instance, the very service on which they are employed is that of chasing vessels that have been built with a special regard to swiftness on the water. The consequence of the unfitness of our ships for this particular service, is, that of the number of slavers that we descry in these seas, the captures make but a small proportion.

If we had a few of the large class of Baltimore schooners, with a long 12 or 18 pounder a-midships for a chase-gun, and a few carronades for close action, with a good crew well trained to the sweeps; and a few brigs similar to the well known Black Joke, I would venture to say, that they would be more successful, and less expensive to Government, than the class of vessels that have hitherto been employed on this service. Instead of a large frigate, with a Commodore's Pennant, we might have a first class flush-deck sloop of war, built principally for fast sailing, with a distinguished young Post Captain to command her; for activity and experience on this coast are more wanted than large ships and officers of high rank, as there is not much diplomatic business to be carried on with the African nations. It may also be observed that it is a very safe coast to navigate, for if you will but sound in time, you may always be apprized of danger soon enough to avoid it. The worst weather is during the tornado season, and these squalls, of which there is always timely notice, generally come off the land, and do not last, on an average, more than a couple of hours.

At six we anchored off the entrance of the main channel into the old Calabar river, in company with H.M. brig Clinker; entrance of the Rio del Rey bearing E.N.E.

Sunday, 20.—We got under weigh at an early hour this morning, with the intention of proceeding up the old Calabar, so far as Duke's Town, off which place the palm-oil vessels, and slavers, generally anchor. H.M. brig Clinker also got under weigh at the same time, with the intention of accompanying us a short distance within the bar, where she was to have anchored; while her boats were to have gone with us, for the purpose of assisting in the capture of any slave-vessel that might be up the river, but it unfortunately fell calm about 9 o'clock, when Lieutenant Matson came on board and acquainted Lieutenant Badgeley that he was afraid the expedition up the river would detain him longer than he had expected, and he must therefore relinquish his intentions, and proceed direct for Fernando Po, in order to obtain a supply of provisions, of which they had much need. At noon there was a moderate breeze, and fine clear weather. East point of the old Calabar N.N.E. 7 miles: but the wind being down the river, we were employed working up all the afternoon, and having no pilot on board, we occasionally got rather too close to the mud banks on either side, and once we tacked in two fathoms water, which is just as much as would keep the vessel afloat. She was fortunately a very beautiful American pilot-boat schooner, that with the least breeze was as manageable as a boat. We scaled the guns, and otherwise prepared for action, for there was no doubt but that any slave-vessel would resist to the utmost, if there was the least chance of escape. We were afraid that they might obtain information of our movements, before we got up to Duke's Town, where they generally receive their slaves on board, for when they are nearly ready for sea, they always keep a canoe on the look out at the mouth of the river, to report when any men-of-war appear on the coast, so that they might have time to disembark their slaves, before men-of-war, or their boats, can reach them; for although vessels may be fitted up with a slave deck, and have every preparation on board for their reception, you cannot condemn them, unless you actually find slaves on board.

At 4 the east point of Old Calabar river W.N.W. 7 miles. Anchored at midnight.

Monday, 21.—Unsettled weather and wind variable. At daylight got under weigh. At noon light breezes and hazy.

From 4 to 6 this evening we passed between two lines of fishing-stakes, indeed we found that a number of large stakes were driven into the mud banks, in different situations, outside the entrance of the Old Calabar, some of them a considerable distance from the land; and there were long lines of them a short distance from each other.

I endeavoured in vain to find out the reason for placing these stakes in such situations, many of which were covered with water at the highest time of the tides. They are called fishing-stakes, and boats certainly do sometimes go and make fast to them for that purpose, as well as to wait the turning of the tide, when they are going to places at any distance along the coast, yet one would think that they would hardly take so much trouble as to bring, and place so great a number as there are, and many of them several miles from the land, merely for the above purposes. They make it very dangerous for boats, or small vessels, navigating those places in the dark, who are not acquainted with their existence. If I were allowed to hazard a conjecture on the subject, I should think they were placed there for the above reason, as men-of-war often send their boats up the rivers at night in quest of slave-vessels, for the purpose of coming on them by surprise, and thereby prevent them from landing the slaves which might be on board preparatory to sailing; also to get quietly alongside of them in any part of the river, where they might have anchored for the night, or the turning of the tide, with their slaves on board, on their way to sea. About 9 o'clock we unexpectedly found ourselves within the bar of the Old Camaroon river, where we anchored for the night.

The tide was running strong, taking the various directions of the coasts and rivers, and very perplexing to strangers. Unfortunately, there was no one on board who had ever been here before, and not having been able to procure a pilot, we were compelled to grope our way, both by night and by day, with only a rough sketch of a chart to guide us.

Tuesday, 22.—At daylight we got under weigh, and endeavoured to regain the channel of the Old Calabar river, but we found the tide stronger than the wind, and that it had carried us on a mud-flat off little Quay river, which, at about half ebb left the schooner aground, this obliged us to get some spars out, to prop her up on each side. At which time we were in the following situation: West point of Old Calabar river, W. by S. Fish Town point N. by W. 1/2 W. and the entrance of little Quay river N.N.E. At 5 in the afternoon we got the spars in and laid a small anchor out, with the assistance of a boat, by which, and other aid, we hoped to get the vessel entirely clear of the bank: but we only partly succeeded that tide, for on the return of low water, we were obliged to have recourse to the same means of propping her up, from there not being two feet water left on the bank.

CHAP. X.

Slave Canoe—Duke's Pilot—Old Calabar Town—Consternation on
Shore, and disappearance of the Slave Vessels—Fruitless Pursuit of the
Slavers—Eyo Eyo, King Eyo's Brother—Old Calabar Festivals—
Attempted Assassination, and Duke Ephraim's Dilemma—Obesity of the
King's Wives—Ordeal for Regal Honours—Duke's English House—
Coasting Voyage to the Bonny—Author discovers Symptoms of Fever—
The Rivers of St. Nicholas, Sombrero, St. Bartholomew, and Sta.
Barbara—"The Smokes"—Capture of a Spanish Slave Vessel in the River
St. John—Nun, or First Brass River, discovered to be the Niger—Natural
Inland Navigation—New Calabar River—Pilot's Jhu Jhu—Foche
Island—Author Sleeps on Shore—Bonny Bath—Interview with King
Peppel—Ceremony of opening the Trade—Rashness of a Slave Dealer—
Horrible Fanaticism—Schooner at Sea—Return to Fernando Po

Wednesday, January 23, 1828.—Fortunately the wind was light, for had it
blown hard, the result might have been fatal to the vessel. At seven in the
morning, we found the vessel afloat, and attempted, with a small anchor and
cable, assisted by the sails, to get her over the mud: but, at eleven o'clock, we
were again stuck fast. In the afternoon, we sent a letter by a Krooman, in a small
canoe, to Captain Cumings, of the brig Kent, lying off the town of Old Calabar,
commonly called Duke's Town, as the king of that country is generally known
by the name and title of Duke Ephraim. In about a couple of hours, the
Krooman returned, in consequence of having met with a very large canoe
coming down on her passage to the Camaroon river, to purchase slaves. He
induced the Captain to come on board, but the appearance of a schooner, with
so large a boat and so many hands, evidently created some suspicion in his mind.
He was too much a man of the world, however, not to affect a confidence,
which we were all persuaded he did not feel:—he drank some rum, and carried
himself with consummate self-possession; gave us all the Calabar news he could
recollect, and demanded our latest intelligence in return. When the conversation
was exhausted, and a good opportunity occurred for taking leave, he departed;
heartily rejoiced, no doubt, at escaping with so much tact. His canoe was about
fifty feet long, with a small thatched house built on a platform in the centre. The
paddles were worked by boys, under the direction of two men, who gave out a
song when pulling. There were two poor creatures, whom we supposed to be
slaves, confined in irons, at one end of the boat.

About nine we got clear of the mud-flats, after a great deal of trouble, with
hawsers and a small anchor; we then stood up the river, and at eleven anchored
for the night.

Thursday, 24.—Fresh breezes from the northward, and very hazy. The wind
coming from the Camaroon mountains, increased the haziness of the
atmosphere, and made it feel very cold. Soon after daylight, when the tide
answered, we got under weigh, and beat up the river. About eleven, we came to

an anchor off Parrott Island, the north end of which bore S.W. 1/2 W. and the north end of James's Island N. by E. At three in the afternoon, a pilot came on board, and, at five, Captain Smith, with Lieutenant Badgeley, went up to the brig Kent, off Duke's Town, to procure information.

Friday, 25.—At three this morning, the same party returned; and, soon after daylight, we got the schooner under weigh, to beat up the river, and the Duke's head pilot came on board, when to prove the confidence that might be reposed in him, he brought a certificate from Lieutenant Corry, of H.M.S. North Star, which stated that he had piloted that ship's boats up the river, as well as conducted them down, with a slave-vessel that they had seized. We blackened the schooner's yellow sides with a mixture of gunpowder and water. This, however, was not a very safe pigment, for if a spark of fire had happened to have come in contact with any part of her side, it would have communicated from one extremity to the other: but it served for a temporary disguise, which was all we required.

About noon, we came abreast of the town of Old Calabar, where we observed the greatest confusion. Armed men, of different colours and nations, were running about in all directions, preparing, as we imagined, to oppose our landing, for it was evident they were alarmed at our appearance, which sufficiently indicated our intentions. The slave-vessels, afraid of being seized, had disappeared from before the town, and gone farther up the river before we arrived, so that, however we might have been otherwise disposed, we did not drop anchor, but continued to advance as long as the tide served, which was till half-past one, when the wind failing, we were obliged to anchor. The Duke's pilot, when we were off the town, requested to leave us for a short time; he said, he "must go tell Duke news, and come back directly." We afterwards discovered that his pretence to go ashore, was merely a subterfuge to get away altogether, for he never returned, and we had good reason for believing, that all the people, from the Duke (or King, which is the same thing) to the meanest of his subjects, secretly abet the unlawful proceedings of the slavers, by whom they realize much larger profits than by the regular traders. At three, we sent the small canoe, with two Kroomen, up the river, to ascertain the situation of the slave-vessels, and soon got under weigh to follow them; but the wind dying off towards sunset, we were obliged to anchor again. About an hour afterwards, our canoe returned, with information that three slave schooners, and a brig, had gone still farther up the river, indeed, as far as the navigation of the river would allow, where they had fortified themselves in the strongest manner, to resist any attack on our part: having also the support of all the authorities of the native towns and villages that could, with any show of prudence, be extended to them. We also understood, that they had not a slave on board of either of them, which was likely enough, as it is not customary to put them on board until they are on the point of sailing. These circumstances determined Lieutenant Badgeley to return to the town, in which resolution he was also influenced by the consideration of the inferiority of our force. A schooner of 120 tons, with no more than twenty Europeans on board; the crew of the vessel being Africans (as the crews of most of the colonial vessels that navigate this coast are,) could have but a poor chance against five vessels, mustering not less than 150 white men of different nations, and reckoning 30 guns to our six. The caution evinced by this step, however justified by circumstances, did not, I must confess, appear to me to be very creditable to our character, and must have made us look very foolish. After having chased the slavers so far up the river, we ought to have brought the matter to an issue, particularly as we had the eyes of all the country upon us, and were regarded with great anxiety by the people of Old Calabar town, as well as by the crews of the British merchant-vessels in the river. The affair gave the slavers an opportunity of exulting over our failure, and their own good fortune; which, I think, was to be regretted. On going down the river, a large canoe came alongside with one of the great men of the country on board, named Eyo Eyo, a brother to King Eyo; when he asked for a present, and something to drink, the customary demand of the natives. We presented him with a few leaves of tobacco, which appeared to amuse him exceedingly: he held them up with a contemptuous sneer, and asked if that was a present? This man was as shrewd a fellow as any we met with, in Old Calabar, and had long been accustomed to trade, and receive presents, from captains of slavers, and palm-oil vessels.

At nine, we arrived off Robin's Town, where a canoe met us, with a note from Captain Cumings, of the Kent, informing us, that a Frenchman had entered his palm-oil house, and deliberately shot his second mate through the body.

There are two grand festivals here, which take place every eighth day in succession. Old Calabar day, which was yesterday; and Duke's day, which happens to-day. The succession of these festivals is curious enough; that which takes place on Thursday in this week, will be on Friday in the next week; and the one on Friday this week, will be on Saturday in the following week, and so on.

Saturday, 26.—We got under weigh, and dropped down with the ebb tide, abreast of Duke's Town, a distance of three miles, where we anchored. We had not been long here before the Duke, attended by a number of his black gentlemen, and followed by Captain Cumings, of the Kent, came on board to have a grand palaver with Lieutenant Badgeley, concerning the attempted assassination of Captain Cumings' mate, on the preceding day. The Frenchman's name was Ferrard, and this monster was no less than the Captain of a slave-vessel. The cause of this palaver, was an imperative demand, on the part of Captain Cumings, that the Duke should deliver the Frenchman into our hands, in order that he should be given up to justice in the event of the mate's death: but the Duke made great difficulties concerning the practicability of securing this man, and offered many excuses to escape the acknowledgment of any responsibility in the matter. It was clear enough that he wished to protect the assassin, as indeed it was his policy to shield the slavers, whose trade was more lucrative to him, than that of any other class of persons. Finding himself somewhat embarrassed in the conversation, he made an apology for leaving the vessel, saying he would go on shore and see what could be done, inviting us at the same time to finish the palaver at his house. Accordingly we all went on shore, after breakfast, attended by two marines. A second palaver took place, which was merely a repetition of the first, and when it terminated, he presented us with some excellent Champagne, and then exhibited a quantity of fine clothes, with a variety of other articles, all of which he said he had received as presents. The only dress His Majesty wore, when he came on board, was a cotton cloth round his middle, and a fine white beaver hat, bound with broad gold lace. Captain Cumings, at our request, asked permission of the Duke to allow us to see his wives, who live in a square formed of mud huts, with a communication from the back part of his house. The Duke very courteously complied with our wishes, and sent persons to attend us. There were about sixty Queens, besides little Princes and Princesses, with a number of slave-girls to wait upon them. His favourite Queen, the handsomest of the royal party, was so large that she could scarcely walk, or even move, indeed they were all prodigiously large, their beauty consisting more in the mass of physique, than in the delicacy or symmetry of features or figure. This uniform tendancy to *en bon point*, on an unusual scale, was accounted for, by the singular fact, that the female upon whom His Majesty fixes his regards, is regularly fattened up to a certain standard, previously to the nuptial ceremony, it appearing to be essential to the Queenly dignity that the lady should be enormously fat. We saw a very fine young woman undergoing this ordeal. She was sitting at a table, with a large bowl of farinaceous food; which she was swallowing as fast as she could pass the spoon to, and from, the bowl, and her mouth; and she was evidently taking no inconsiderable trouble to qualify herself for that happy state, which Pope tell us is the object of every woman's ambition, that of being Queen for life, the royal road to which, in this country, lies through a course of gormandizing. The same custom extends to the wives of the great men, who undergo a similar operation before marriage. On the morning of their wedding-day they are seated at a table, to receive presents from their relations and friends; a yard of cloth from one, some silk from another, some beads from a third, according to the taste incapacity of the donors. My companions were not much struck with the beauty of the Queens, for they declared that some of the pretty young slave-girls had much more lovely looks. Each of the Duke's wives bring, or send, a jug of water for his large brass-pan bath every morning, and his favourite wife remains to assist in his ablutions.

On leaving the Queens' Square, we were invited to go over the Duke's English house, as it was called, which, in fact it was, having been sent out in frame, from Liverpool, with carpenters to erect it, by Mr. Bold, formerly a merchant of that town. This wooden edifice stood by the side of his mud hut, in which, by the bye, such was the force of habit, he preferred residing. In the English house there was a grand display of European articles, consisting of furniture, mirrors, pictures, a quantity of cut-glass on the sideboard, and to crown all, there was a large brass arm-chair, weighing 160 pounds, a present from Sir John Tobin, with an inscription engraved on it, to that effect.

About two o'clock we took leave of the Duke, and went on board the Kent, where the poor mate was lying dangerously ill, and we all apprehended the worst result, not having any medical man to dress the wound, or tell the exact nature of it. After dining with Captain Cumings, we returned to the Duke's house, to learn if he had ascertained the name of the vessel the Frenchman commanded. The reply was unsatisfactory, as he still declared his ignorance on the subject. It is not unusual for the blacks (like the Chinese) to identify the ship in the Captain, for instance, if they want to speak of the Jane, Captain Brown, they say, 'that Brown's ship.' It was, therefore, possible that the Duke might really have spoken the truth in protesting that the name of the vessel was unknown to him.

Finding there was nothing more to be done with the Duke that evening, we left him, with an assurance that we should persist in our demand of having either the Captain, or his vessel, delivered up to us; that we should go and report the circumstance to the Governor of Fernando Po, who would send a frigate to blockade the port, stop all the trade of the river, and perhaps come and burn the town. These threats were not apparently without their effect, although his Majesty was as much afraid of opposing the slavers, as he was of quarrelling with us. The following morning at daylight we left Duke's Town, and proceeded down the river, not however, with the intention of going to Fernando Po, but merely to visit all the rivers between the Calabar and Cape Formosa, in quest of slavers, first going to the celebrated Bonny, off which river we arrived on *Thursday, 31.* Here we saw a brig at anchor, which proved to be the Neptune, of and from Liverpool. She had been lying here ten days, waiting for clear weather to enable her to pass the bar, and get into the river.

On the day we left Old Calabar town, I had all the symptoms of approaching fever, such as headache, foul tongue, hot and dry skin, loss of appetite, prostration of strength, &c. I, therefore, took calomel, and adopted prompt measures of regimen, abstaining from all food, taking nothing but diluents, keeping myself quiet, and occupying the mind with amusing thoughts. By following this practice, at the expiration of three days, I found myself quite convalescent, after which I soon recovered my former health and spirits.

At noon, we parted from the Neptune, and stood to the westward, for the river St. Nicholas, having had information that two Spanish vessels, trading for slaves, were in that river. At six, we passed the entrance of the Sombrero river, and, at midnight, that of St. Bartholomew's river.

Friday, February 1.—In the afternoon, the Eden's pinnace went to examine a small river, which was found to be the Sta. Barbara, but there were no vessels there, and about sunset, we anchored off the river St. Nicholas.

Saturday, 2.—At daylight, the Eden's pinnace, the schooner's boat, and a canoe, manned with Kroomen, all well armed, left the schooner to go in search of the two vessels said to be in the river; but they returned on board, having examined a large river, three creeks, and one town, without success. All they saw on the banks of the river, was a large dog, and a rattle, like those at Fernando Po.

Sunday, 3.—At daylight, weighed and stood to the westward. About nine o'clock we anchored off a long line of breakers, but no land in sight, in consequence of the haziness of the weather. That peculiar state of the atmosphere, which we call hazy, is, perhaps, more characteristically designated "the smokes," on these coasts. Lieutenant Badgeley and Capt. Smith, went in the schooner's boat to sound, and trace the passage into the river St. John, at the entrance of which we supposed ourselves to be situated. In the afternoon, the party returned, having not only found the entrance of the river St. John, but also one of the vessels of which we were in search. At half-past four, the pinnace, schooner's boat, and Kroo canoe, were despatched, well manned and armed, to bring the schooner out of the river. At eleven, Captain Smith returned on board, and informed us, that, at sunset, they boarded the Spanish schooner Victoria Felicita, armed with one long nine-pounder and twenty men, and that they took possession of her with scarcely a show of resistance. The Spaniards endeavoured to get the gun ready, but the boats came so suddenly upon them, by rounding a point close to their moorings, that they were completely taken by surprise, and boarded before they could carry their measures of defence into effect. There were but two slaves and a part of the crew on board, the rest of the slaves and the remainder of the crew, being at the Barakoom, or Slave-yard, to which place they are always consigned so soon as they are purchased, and left until the vessel is ready for sea, to escape from the responsibility which would fall upon the commander of the vessel, in case any slaves were discovered on board. There were many slave-dealers on the schooner's deck when the boats came in sight, but they all jumped overboard, and swam to the shore.

Monday, 4.—At daylight, Captain Smith left us to assist in bringing the prize out of the river, but the day being calm, she was not removed. We burnt blue lights, at intervals, during the night, as signals to the prize, or any boat that might be sent from her.

Tuesday, 5.—At nine, we saw the Spaniard under weigh; and, at ten, she anchored close beside us. She was well supplied with water, of which we stood in need, and of which we availed ourselves. A midshipman, with some men, was then appointed to take charge of her to Fernando Po. We parted company, and proceeded on our further examination of the rivers on this coast, when we stood to the westward, anchoring off Nun River, [34] at nine in the evening.

Wednesday, 6.—After breakfast, we sent on shore to procure information of slavers, in consequence of having seen the smoke of a fire, which is a well-

---

[34] "The river Nun, or First Brass River, is the main branch of the Quorra, from whence you pass (in about two hours) through a creek, in an easterly direction, into the Second Brass River, which is also a large branch of the Quorra."—*Lander*, vol. iii. p. 224. "Brass, properly speaking, consists of two towns of nearly equal size, containing about a thousand inhabitants, and built on the borders of a kind of basin, which is formed by a number of rivulets, entering it from the Niger, through forests of mangrove bushes. One of them is under the domination of a noted scoundrel called King *Jacket*, who has already been spoken of; and the other is governed by a rival chief, named King Forday. These towns are situated directly opposite to each other, and within the distance of eighty yards, and are built on a marshy ground, which occasions the huts to be always wet."—*Lander*, vol. iii. p. 234.

known signal on the coast, to invite vessels to trade with them. The fire is made by night, and the smoke forms the signal by day. Our boat returned, bringing a poor Spaniard from a small town, just within the entrance of the river, called Pilot's Town. [35] He was a native of Manilla, and had been left behind by his vessel, but from what cause he did not state. He told us, the blacks informed him, that there had been a man of war on the coast, but that she had left some days since.

Thursday, 7.—Light airs. At daylight we got under weigh, and came to an anchor, off the mouth of the Bonny river again, soon after sunset.

We had now examined the entrances of all the rivers between the Bonny, and Cape Formosa; all of which communicate with each other in the interior; some being navigable by vessels, but all by canoes; for instance, a vessel may go in at St. Nicholas, and by passing through a creek, come out at the St. John's. This piece of intelligence had the effect of occasionally placing us in some perplexity as to our movements; for, according to one person, a vessel freighted with slaves was on the point of coming out of one river; while, at the same time, agreeably to another informant, the same vessel was stated to be coming out of another river.

There is, however, but little doubt that the interior of the country is intersected by very extensive water communications lying between the bight of Benin and Biafra, and I heard Captain Owen say, that, in his opinion, the Niger would be found to discharge itself in one of these bights, a fact, which I have the satisfaction to learn, is now proved by the recent discovery of the Landers.

Friday, 8.—At daylight, we made sail. At ten, we received a pilot on board, and in three hours, entered the channel of the New Calabar river, which must be passed, before an entrance into the Bonny can be effected. This position of the Calabar is, however, on the coast usually denominated the Bonny, in reference to the superior trade of that river.

The pilot here requested the Captain's permission to make a "jhu jhu," which is a superstitious rite performed by the natives in these rivers. The object of the ceremony is to propitiate their deity for a safe passage and a good trade; the operation consists of spilling a wine glass full of rum, twice on the bowsprit (upon which the operator stands), and once on each side of it, into the water. They practise a similar rite when they anchor, cutting some bread and meat into small pieces, scattering it in like manner on the bowsprit, into the river, and also on the deck, while those who stand around, mingle in the act, by tasting their offerings. The objects worshipped by the people of the New Calabar, are the tiger and the shark; while the Bonny people worship the shark and the guana.

---

[35] "A place, called Pilot's Town by Europeans, from the number of pilots that reside in it, is situated nearly at the entrance of the First Brass River (which, we understand, is the Nun River of Europeans), and at the distance of sixty or seventy miles from hence. This town acknowledges the authority of both kings, having been originally peopled by settlers from each of their towns."—*Lander*, vol. iii. p. 234.

At half-past four, we anchored, for the night, off Foche Island, inside the first bar of the river, and the pilot went on shore. The town on this island had been burnt to the ground only a few days before we arrived, owing to the carelessness of some new slaves, and the people of the town had determined upon selling the woman to whom the slaves belonged, as a punishment for her own neglect.

The dogs on Foche Island were observed to bear a close resemblance to those of Fernando Po, (a common sort of small cur.) I mention this, because it has been thought that the Fernandians have had very little connection with the people of the Continent, as a proof of which, we have never found any one (out of all the varieties of the African nations) who could speak with, or understand, the language of the natives of Fernando Po.

Saturday, 9.—Soon after daylight the pilot returned on board. We found the natives of Foche Island very cautious in coming off, even the pilot would not reply to our signals, until we had sent a messenger to tell him what we were, nor would he even then consent to sleep on board. I have little doubt, from the timidity he exhibited, that the slave-vessels have occasionally enticed pilots and their people on board, and carried them off for slaves.

Our breakfast this morning consisted of smoked and dried herrings, corned mackerel, fresh prawns, beef steaks, cold roast beef, cold ham, roast and boiled yams, eggs, and toast: a supply that will not be thought despicable for the passengers of a merchant schooner, in the Bight of Biafra, where the sun was so powerful, that our anchor was hot enough to serve the purposes of a heated oven.

At four in the afternoon I accompanied Lieut. Badgeley, with six Kroomen in a small boat, to visit the town of Bonny, and the English shipping in the river. Soon after dark we went on board the Neptune, which was lying off the town of Bonny, and was the same vessel we had boarded outside the river. After refreshing ourselves with tea, we accompanied the Surgeon on shore, to look for Captain Cudd, whom we found visiting one of King Peppel's great men. We wished to call upon the King, but were informed that we could not be allowed to do so, as his Majesty was too drunk to receive company, and exceedingly dangerous in his cups; a state of bliss to which he commonly arrived by that hour, every evening. We, therefore, contented ourselves by passing the night at the house of the prime minister, with the intention of waiting upon his Majesty the following morning. I slept in the same apartment with the Doctor. Our beds, by courtesy so called, were made on a mud floor; they consisted merely of a mat spread for each, with a coya-cushion (the outside shell of the cocoa nut) for a pillow; fortunately the climate is too hot to require any covering; we therefore lay down without removing our nether garments; sleep was, however, quite out of the question, for so soon as the lights were out, the rats and mice came in, and assisted by myriads of cockroaches and ants, contrived to keep us constantly employed driving them away from our bodies, until we were in so feverish and exhausted a state that we anxiously longed for the return of day.

On the following morning, *Sunday, 10*, I was invited to take a Bonny warm bath, which I accepted with pleasure, for after such a night the very name of a bath was refreshing; the Doctor therefore kindly conducted me into the open space where I was informed that every thing was prepared. I was seated in an arm chair, with a large brass-pan before me full of tepid water, about two feet deep, into which I was requested to put my legs: two or three attendants provided with bowls of warm water, soap and cloths, now began to operate on my body; the sensation produced by this process, was similar to the effect of champooing. After they thought they had sufficiently polished me with their cloths, they began to pour cold water over me, which was the most refreshing part of the business; but the reader may imagine what my feelings were, when to my utter surprise I discovered that the whole ceremony had been performed by women, many of whom, although black, were both young and handsome. I had detected a good deal of giggling from the beginning, and objected to the presence of so many persons; but I was indifferently told, 'Oh! it was the custom of the country.'

We accompanied Captain Cudd on board his vessel to breakfast, after which we all came on shore, to wait upon the King, to whom we were conducted by our friend Bill Peppel, at whose house we passed the night, and whom I understood to be the King's most confidential minister. His Majesty received us in a very easy friendly manner, and in what he perhaps considered a fine dress, consisting of a neat striped fine calico shirt, a pair of white trowsers, and a silk cap with a long tassel. We talked on a variety of subjects, selecting those which we supposed were interesting to him, such as the regular trade in palm-oil, and the illicit one in slaves, but our conversation principally turned on England, in courtesy to the King who had been at Liverpool, in the capacity of cabin boy, with one of the Captains of the palm-oil vessels. He ordered some Membo (palm-wine) to be presented to us; we found it flavoured with a strong bitter, produced by the use of a native nut. To our European palate, this taste was by no means agreeable. It is with palm-wine so prepared, however, that his Majesty contrives to get tipsy with such punctuality. When this liquor first exudes from the tree, and before the process of fermentation has drawn its intoxicating qualities into action, it is a sweet and not unpleasant beverage.

Our interview lasted about an hour, when we took leave of the King, to return on board. In passing through one of the streets, we saw a guana climbing up a tree, the Doctor advanced and seized it by the tail, a proceeding by no means dangerous as regarded the animal, whose nature is extremely gentle. The natives, however, witnessed this act with horror, this creature being to them an object of worship. As these animals are protected by the superstition of the people, and are allowed to enter their houses at pleasure, they become extremely bold, and frequently help themselves to a chicken, or any thing else for which they have a fancy, upon which occasion the owner feels himself highly favoured, and imagines that some good fortune will attend him in consequence. I was informed that they have been known to devour young infants. A guana was once killed on board an English vessel, upon which the trade with that vessel was immediately stopped, and a grand palaver held, when the Captain was sentenced to pay a fine of 500 bars, this was afterwards commuted to 200; and when it was paid the ship was permitted to recommence trading.

The ceremony of opening the trade with each vessel is as follows: a day being appointed by the King, a dinner is prepared, and His Majesty is entertained by the Captain and his officers, on board the trader. The black gentlemen who form the royal suite are obliged, upon this occasion, to trust to chance, and the good-nature of the ship's crew, for their share of the feast. In order that no point of courtesy may be wanting, it is requisite to send a boat from the ship to meet His Majesty, as he comes out of the creek in his own canoe. The King, upon joining his entertainers, immediately enters their boat; which condescension is acknowledged by a salute of seven guns, fired from the ship. On arriving alongside, His Majesty throws an egg at the vessel's hull; he then ascends to the deck, which is usually covered, from the gangway to the cabin, with a piece of cloth; an arm chair, covered and ornamented with the same material, being placed ready for his accommodation.

The only beverage used by King Peppel is his favourite Membo, which is brought on board by his attendants. His Majesty commonly returns about sunset to the shore, when a second salute of seven guns is fired from the ship, and the trade is declared free to all his subjects.

Shortly before our arrival a circumstance occurred which serves to illustrate King Peppel's good-nature and forbearance. About the middle of December, 1826, Capt. Lawrenson, a slave agent, arrived at the Bonny, to purchase a cargo of slaves, which he accomplished in about two months, and sent them away to the West Indies, remaining behind himself, with a quantity of goods to make further purchases, having written his owners to send vessels, and take the slaves away. In the meantime he contrived to ingratiate himself so much with King Peppel, that His Majesty allowed him to live in his house, and consulted his opinion, upon all matters of importance, relative to the white people. Many months elapsed before any vessel arrived, but when they did, the slaves were not ready, and the King continued to delude him with promises for two months longer, at the end of which period, finding his hopes still unrealized, the impatient Frenchman became enraged at what he considered the King's deceit, and resolved on taking summary vengeance. Accordingly, one evening, he went on shore with a cigar in his mouth, and a few squibs in his pocket, when he deposited the latter in the thatch of several houses, and set fire to them. The huts being composed of bamboo, palm-leaves, and reeds, soon burst into a flame, which spread so rapidly in all quarters, that nearly the whole town was destroyed. The people were greatly exasperated and wished to kill the Frenchman, who had not attempted to effect his escape, but King Peppel forbade them to injure a hair of his head, permitting him to return to his vessel, which immediately sailed for France; the Captain still vowing vengeance against the King, and threatening to return with a much larger vessel, well armed, to commit greater ravages, and to carry off all he could lay his hands on, until he considered that he had received compensation for the fraud which he averred had been practised upon him.

There is a superstitious ceremony performed at the Bonny river, about once in three years, which consists of offering the most beautiful virgin they can find, as a sacrifice to their Jhu Jhu, whereby they hope to propitiate the evil spirit, and avert the dangers to which vessels are liable in crossing the bar. The victim is taken in a boat to the mouth of the river, where, after a preparatory ceremonial, she is made to walk to the extremity of a plank, from which she is precipitated into the water, where in a few seconds she is devoured by sharks. The mind of the poor wretch is prepared for this fate: which, indeed, appears to be a source of pleasure, rather than of terror, from the idea that she is going at once to Paradise, to become the wife of Jhu Jhu; and towards the conclusion of the ceremony, it is not uncommon for the victim to display extravagant transports of joy. One of the English captains remonstrated with a native for going to witness such an exhibition. "What?" replied the indignant black,—"What you tink?—Why! she now married to Jhu Jhu—got large house—more big than any in Liverpool—plenty copper-bar—plenty rum—plenty clothes—what you tink she want?—noting!" These articles being the principal objects of the trade from England, are consequently most desired; and as the majority of the trading vessels come from Liverpool, where some few of the Bonny people have been, they consider that town the ultimatum of magnificence and splendour.

We went on board the Neptune about noon, where we took an early dinner, and returned to the schooner about sunset, when we learnt that a grand deputation of black gentlemen, from New Calabar Town, had arrived, to invite Capt. Smith to bring his schooner up their river to trade; they requested him to lose no time, and offered to leave a large canoe for our use, when we returned from the Bonny; however, Captain Smith would not agree to their request; and when they discovered, that, instead of being a trader, we were looking out for slavers, they were glad to get away. Our pilot partook of their alarm, and, on the following morning, he sent back the casks empty, with a message, that he could not come on board again.

There is much enmity between the Bonny and the New Calabar people, arising principally out of their rivalship in the trade with foreign vessels. A short time ago, they had a fight on board an English ship, under the following circumstances.

The New Calabar people had got on board the ship Huskinson, and were taking her up to their town. On the passage, they were attacked by a number of large canoes, well manned and armed, from the Bonny: a desperate struggle ensued; the Bonny people lost many lives, but they succeeded in boarding the vessel, dislodging their opponents, and triumphantly carried the ship into their river; thus securing all her trade to themselves. This fight did not, on the present occasion, produce war between the rival people, as such incidents usually do; it merely had the effect of suspending their intercourse for a short period. Their war canoes are very large, and will carry from 50 to 100 men, well armed with muskets, pistols, sabres, and sometimes a small gun in the bow.

We got under weigh in the afternoon, without a pilot, and worked the schooner over the bar, which is very narrow, and stood out to sea that evening, notwithstanding there was a fresh breeze against us, through a very intricate navigation. It was at the entrance of this river that one of the boats of H.M.S. Maidstone was upset. She had come to an anchor in the evening, with the tide running in, which made the water very smooth; but, in the middle of the night, at the turn of the tide, they found the boat rolling about very uneasily. This very much surprised them, because the wind had not arisen; the sea soon began to break over them, when the boat upset, and the surgeon's assistant, with several other persons, was drowned. This proceeded from the ebb tide encountering the ordinary set on the land. We left the Bonny with the intention of visiting our friends in the Old Calabar, in the hope of meeting the Frenchman, who had shot the mate of the Kent.

Tuesday, 12.—At five this morning, we came to an anchor. The weather had been squally during the night, and at daylight the wind increased; the squalls becoming more frequent and heavy, with continued thunder and lightning; and so heavy a swell, that if we had not taken in the boat from the stern, she would have been washed away. At daylight, we discovered that Tom Shot's Point bore N.E. by N. six or seven miles.

Wednesday, 13.—At daylight, saw a vessel at anchor, outside of us, which proved to be H.M.S. North-Star, and immediately after, Lieut. Mather came on board to examine us. On that officer's return, Lieutenant Badgeley and myself went on board the North-Star, to wait on Captain Arabin, who gave us a most friendly reception. He pressed us to remain and dine, but Lieutenant Badgeley's anxiety to return to Fernando Po, obliged us to decline an invitation which otherwise would have proved extremely agreeable, and as Captain Arabin had sent his boats up the river (under the command of his first lieutenant) in search of slavers, it superseded the necessity of our going; we therefore got under weigh, and sailed to rejoin Captain Owen.

CHAP. XI.

Reverence for Beards—Native Shields—Petty Thefts—Tornado Season—
Author departs for Calabar—Waterspout—Palm-oil Vessels—Visit to
Duke Ephraim—Escape of a Schooner with Slaves—Calabar Sunday—
Funeral of a Duke's Brother—Egbo Laws—Egbo Assembly—
Extraordinary Mode of recovering Debts—Superstition and Credulity—
Cruelty of the Calabar People to Slaves—Royal Slave Dealer—Royal
Monopoly—Manner of Trading with the Natives—Want of
Missionaries—Capt. Owen's Arrival—Visit Creek Town with King Eyo—
The Royal Establishment—Savage Festivities—Calabar Cookery—Old
Calabar River

Thursday, 14.—ARRIVED in Maidstone Bay, at ten o'clock, when we learnt
that Commodore Collier, in the Sybille, with the Esk and Primrose, had been in
the bay, and left it only on the preceding day. We also heard of the decease of
Captain Clapperton, Richard Lander, who was the bearer of the melancholy
tidings, being on board the Esk, for a passage to England. Received some letters
and papers from England, that had been left for me by my old friend Captain
Griffenhooffe, of the Primrose, and whom I was unfortunately doomed never
to meet again in this sublunary scene; for having suffered from fever, he was
invalided, and died at Ascension, on his way home. We found the Diadem
transport here, which had arrived a few days before, with government stores
from Cape Coast Castle. A remarkable occurrence took place between the agent
(Lieutenant Woodman) and the natives, on their first interview. That gentleman
had, like Captain Owen, and some of his officers, allowed his beard to grow
from the time he had left England, having been induced to do so for the sake of
the advantages, which, from experience. Captain Owen considered were to be
derived from it. In the first place, all the Arabs wear long beards, and they are
held in much respect wherever they sojourn among the various African nations:
not altogether for their beards, but from their intelligence; however, the beard is
naturally identified with their character. They also command respect, because
they are generally worn by the old men of their own country, and, on our first
arrival, the chiefs of Fernando Po advanced with delight to rub beards, with all
those among us who wore them. When Lieutenant Woodman left the island for
Cape Coast, his beard was of considerable length, but meeting with Commodore
Collier at Accra, that officer would not receive him in his Fernando Po costume;
and being unequal to contend with the higher powers, yielded to the alternative
of removing his beard, in preference to subjecting himself to the consequences
of his superior officer's displeasure. But, mark the effect!—when he came back
to Fernando Po, the native chiefs turned from him with contempt, believing that
he could not have lost so dignified an appendage, without having committed
some crime. This reminds me of a passage in the 15th chapter of Gibbon's
Decline and Fall of the Roman Empire, viz. "The practice of shaving the beard
excited the pious indignation of the Fathers of the Church, which practice

(according to Tertullian) is a lie against our own faces, and an impious attempt to improve the works of the Creator."

I was sorry to learn, that there had been some altercation between Commodore Collier, and Captain Owen, on the subject of wearing beards.

Saturday, 16.—Went on shore at day light, and remained till evening, when I returned on board in the midst of a tornado, which, however, did not last long, and fortunately had no great strength. We observed a glare in the mountain, which the natives informed us proceeded from a fire of considerable extent, made by them for the purpose of driving the wild oxen, or buffalos, to a certain spot, where they are hamstrung, and afterwards slain. We never saw any animals in the island, larger than sheep or goats. I have more than once, in a native hut, found a shield made of hide, about four feet high and two broad, with a stick passed longitudinally through each end; but whether they procured these shields from vessels touching at the island, or from the wild animals described as being in the mountains, we had no means of ascertaining.

Sunday, 17.—Captain Owen had some of the officers of the Eden, as well as civilians from the establishment, to dine with him to-day: our dinner consisted of green turtle, a variety of fish, small mutton, fowls, &c. all the produce of the island.

Monday, 18.—The weather was now getting very close, hazy, and oppressive, as the season approached for the hot winds from the Continent, named, on this coast, the Hermattan, similar to the Sirocco of the Mediterranean; yet, the thermometer was only 88°. F. in the shade.

Tuesday, 19.—Mr. Galler ran after, and secured, a native who was making off with an iron hoop.

> But, lo! what dangers doth environ,
> The man that meddleth with cold iron,

for, on the following day, Captain Owen ordered the thief to have his head shaved, for the purpose of shaming him out of the repetition of his crime, thus making him an object of ridicule, among his own, as well as our people; and, as the natives display no small degree of dandyism in dressing their hair, he hoped that this 'rape of the locks,' would have a beneficial effect: he, however, considered an additional punishment necessary, in consequence of the frequency of the offence, iron-stealing having become a very common practice; he, therefore, ordered the offender to receive thirty-nine lashes; but at the twenty-fifth he fainted, from fear, no doubt, certainly not from the severity of the chastisement; however, he was immediately taken down and carried into the guard-house, where he continued bellowing, in a most frightful manner, for a long time.

Monday, 25.—We have had very close weather for several days, with much thunder and lightning during the whole of last night. At eight o'clock this morning, a heavy tornado came on, the rain and wind continuing for more than three hours; the greatest force of the hurricane was, however, expended in the first hour, from which time it gradually diminished; this produced a very agreeable change in the state of the atmosphere, the thermometer having fallen, during the tornado, from 91°. to 78°. F. being the lowest degree we have yet experienced.

Wednesday, 27.—The Diadem, transport, Lieut. Woodman, agent, sailed this morning for Sierra Leone, and England, by which conveyance I sent letters, and a few curiosities.

Friday, 29.—Mr. Wood was sent, with a party of men, to assist the gunner in erecting a battery on Adelaide Island. Having made bankrupts of the natives in the yam market, the African, schooner, sailed to-day for the purpose of procuring them, in other parts of the island.

Saturday, March 1.—Some days since, a native having been detected stealing a knife out of Capt. Smith's store, he was sent on board the Eden to have his head shaved, and be kept in irons for a week; the time having expired this morning, he was ordered to receive thirty-nine lashes previously to his dismissal. He bore his punishment well, and was going away, when, about 300 yards from the place, he fell down in a fainting fit, doubtless from the apprehension that he was not yet quite out of our power. Mr. Cowan, the surgeon, ran to his assistance, but the natives surrounded the patient, and would not allow him to receive medical aid from us; this was of the less consequence, as their method of proceeding proved completely effectual. They first bound a strong narrow leaf around the sufferer's body, stuffing as many more leaves within the bandage as it would contain: they then chewed some vegetable substance until it was reduced to a pulp, and when this preparation was blown up into the nose and ears of the patient, it almost immediately produced the desired effect.

There had been much thunder in the distance, and we had seen a good deal of lightning playing about the Camaroon mountain for several days past; but more particularly towards the morning.

Saturday, 8.—This being the tornado season, we have experienced one almost daily, lasting however only a few hours, the rest of the twenty-four being in part, very cloudy; and in part, very fine. The Lady Combermere, of Liverpool, which anchored here last night, sailed this afternoon to prosecute her voyage along the coast.

The African, schooner, Captain Smith, intending to sail this evening on a trading voyage up the Calabar river, principally to procure bullocks for our little colony, I was glad to avail myself of the opportunity of going as a passenger, for the purpose of making further observations on the habits and peculiarities of the people.

We left Maidstone bay about ten o'clock in the evening, taking with us, by way of experiment, three native youths from the island, an event which certainly augured well for the future advancement and civilization of these islanders.

Sunday, 9.—We this morning saw a very large waterspout, which broke within 200 yards of the vessel, and it is remarkable, that before it broke, we observed it raining in five or six different parts of the horizon, while it was quite fair, with the sun shining, in the intermediate spaces. Soon after four in the afternoon, we entered the Old Calabar river, and at sunset we anchored in three and a half fathoms water; east end of Parrot Island, N.N.W. four or five miles.

Monday, 10.—Weather still variable. Got under weigh at daylight, but it soon fell calm, and we made use of our sweeps. At noon, abreast of James's Island; and at three, we anchored off Old Calabar, or Duke's Town.

We found the brig Kent, Captain Cumings, still here; also, the ship Agnes, Captain Charles, from Liverpool, for palm-oil; and a Spanish schooner, from the Havannah, waiting for slaves. Captain Smith and I accompanied Captain Cumings on shore to pay a visit to Duke Ephraim, with whom Capt. Cumings was a great favourite, which proved a fortunate circumstance for us. The schooner having last visited the place as a man of war, she was received with suspicion, and it was extremely difficult to convince the Duke and his people, that there was not a *ruse de guerre* intended by her reappearance as a mere trader.

Tuesday, 11.—A fine but very hot day. Paid a visit to the Duke after breakfast, and in the afternoon went three miles down the river to visit the Lady Combermere on her way up the river. In the evening we paid another visit to the Duke, at which period, every day, he holds a sort of levee for supercargoes, and Captains of vessels, to talk over "news." Upon these occasions he discovers an acute knowledge of his own interest. Remained on shore, and passed the night in the Duke's English house, where his visitors always sleep, but none of his family, except a few domestics in charge of it. This evening a tornado came on with heavy rain.

Wednesday, 12.—A schooner, that had secreted herself further up the river; dropped down and anchored off the town last night, after it became dark, intending to take in her cargo of slaves during the night. She completed her object before daylight, when she got under weigh, and sailed down the river, without shewing any colours.

This day was the Calabar Sunday, but it was not kept as the usual holiday, in consequence of the recent death of the Duke's favourite brother. The funeral ceremony is horrible, but I feel bound to describe it for the sake of shewing the extraordinary superstition and bigotry that still exists among a people, who have not only been visited, but regularly traded with, by European nations, for nearly two centuries. I shall introduce this individual case by premising that human sacrifices are lavishly made, not only in honour of the blood royal, but in a more or less degree upon the death of *great* (or I should more properly say *rich*) men; for riches constitute greatness here, even in a higher ratio than they do in more civilized countries; the riches of these parts consisting in the possession of slaves.

At the funeral obsequies of the Duke's brother, six human victims were destined to the sacrifice; namely, three men and three women, who, however, were, with a strange mixture of mercy and cruelty, rendered insensible to the terrors of their fate by previous intoxication. Five of these poor creatures were hung, and placed in the grave of the Prince, while the sixth, a young and favourite wife, was reserved for a destiny still more horrible; being thrown alive into the grave, which was immediately closed over the whole.

These people practise many other superstitious customs, equally dreadful, and I am persuaded it needs but a recital of them, to prove how much they stand in want of the benevolent instructions of Christian missionaries.

The laws of the country are worthy of attention, being, perhaps, the most curious, as well as the most prompt, and effectual, of any that we are acquainted with, amongst the African nations. The whole of the Old Calabar country is governed by what are termed the "Egbo laws." These are laws, enacted by a secret meeting, called the Egbo assembly, which is held in a house set apart for that purpose, called the Palaver house; of this assembly the Duke, by virtue of his sovereignty, officiates as the chief, with the title of Eyamba. There are different degrees of rank in the subordinate Egbo members, and each step must be purchased successively. They sometimes admit Englishmen into this assembly: Captain Burrell of the ship Haywood, of Liverpool, held the rank of Yampai, which is one of considerable importance, and he found it exceedingly to his advantage, as it enabled him to recover all debts due to him by the natives.

The following are the names, and prices, of each step:

1.	Abungo	125	Bars.
2.	Aboko	75	Bars.
3.	Makaira	400	White copper rods.
4.	Bakimboko	100	Bars.
5.	Yampai	850	White copper rods,

also some rum, goats, membo, &c. &c.

The Yampai is the only class of Egbo men that are allowed to sit in council. The sums paid for the different titles of Egbo are divided among the Yampai only, who are not confined to a single share, for a Yampai may have his title multiplied as often as he chooses to purchase additional shares, which entitles the person so purchasing to a corresponding number of portions in the profits arising out of the establishment.

Their mode of administering justice is as follows: When a person cannot obtain his due from a debtor, or when any injury has been received, personally or otherwise, the aggrieved party applies to the Duke for the Egbo drums; acquainting him at the same time with the nature of his complaint: if the Duke accedes to the demand, the Egbo assembly immediately meet, and the drums are beat about the town; at the first sound of which every woman is obliged to retreat within her own dwelling, upon pain of losing her head for disobedience: nor until the drum goes round the second time, to shew that council is ended, and the Egbo returned, are they released from their seclusion. If the complaint be just, the Egbo is sent to the offending party to warn him of his delinquency, and to demand reparation, after which announcement no one dares move out of the house inhabited by the culprit, until the affair is settled, and if it be not soon arranged, the house is pulled down about their ears, in which case the loss of a few heads frequently follows. This extremity, however, rarely occurs, for if the offender be not able to settle the matter himself, it is generally made up by his relations and friends.

The Egbo man—that is the executive person wears a complete disguise, consisting of a black network close to the skin from head to foot, a hat with a long feather, horns projecting from his forehead, a large whip in his right hand, with a bell fastened to the lower part of his back, and several smaller ones round his ankles. Thus equiped he starts from the Egbo-house, runs through the streets with his bells ringing, to the house of the offender, followed by half a dozen subordinate personages fantastically dressed, each carrying either a sword or stick.

I one day asked King Eyo who this Egbo was, who ran about with the bells, "What? you tink Egbo be man, no, he be debil, come up from bush, nobody know him," was his reply.

It is their custom upon the death of a great man, to have one of his slaves, male or female, taken down to the side of the river to make what they call a devil, which means, I presume, an offering to the Evil Spirit; this is done in the following manner. A stake is driven into the ground close to the water's edge, to this the poor wretch is fastened, the head being pulled as high as possible to stretch the neck for the sword, by which he is to be decapitated, and after the deed is accomplished they carry the head through the town rejoicing.

These frightful orgies used to take place in the daytime, but in consequence of the repeated remonstrances from the Captains of vessels, who were shocked by the frequency of these horrid scenes, performed in sight of all the ships in the river, they now take place in the night; for my own part I think that the noise occasioned by their savage merriment, and their running about during the stillness of night, produces a more appalling picture to the imagination, than even the reality of the scene in broad day; the only difference is that there are fewer spectators, as the greater number of those on board the vessels are wrapt in profound repose.

The practice of burying the youngest and favourite wives with the corpse is by no means uncommon, [36] and they resort to a variety of cruel practices for maiming and destroying their slaves; thus they cut off parts or the whole of their ears, a part of the nose, a finger or a hand. One of the servants who waited upon us at the King's house, had lost an ear in this way, for some trifling offence.

After a recital of these facts, it is scarcely necessary to observe that the Calabar people are extremely cruel, indeed I am informed that they frequently cause their slaves to be put to death for a mere whim; a practice which they endeavour to excuse, by saying, that if the slaves were not thus kept in awe of their masters, they would rise in rebellion: they also plead the necessity of it, for preventing them becoming too numerous. These reasons form also their apology for countenancing the slave-trade, a traffic which is most strenuously supported by the Duke, who also trades largely in palm-oil.

His method of procuring slaves is worthy of remark. He induces the Captains to deposit a quantity of goods in his hands, which he sorts into such portions as would form an ordinary load for a man to carry on his head. He then

---

[36] It is the custom here to bury their dead in their own houses.

sends his agents into the country with the goods to purchase slaves, promising the Captains their cargoes, amounting to any given number, within a stated time; in the meanwhile he employs other persons to collect in his own town and neighbourhood, and if he is very hard pressed, (for the Captains of slavers are always very impatient), he obliges his great men to furnish him with a certain number each. This is done by sending him every individual from the neighbouring villages, who have committed any crime or misdemeanor; and should he still continue unable to make up the specified demand, they sell their own servants to him. The Duke has profited largely by this system, for he has several warehouses full of goods, some of which he has had in store for years, such as wines, spirits, liqueurs, sail-cloth, cordage, manufactured goods, copper rods, iron bars, &c. &c.

The palm-oil he collects in small quantities from his subjects, in the neighbourhood of the Calabar, and other small rivers that fall into it. The Duke, however, does not engross the whole trade, for the commerce being once regularly opened, may be carried on by any person who has property to barter. Their mode of proceeding is as follows:—Those who desire to traffic, come on board and select whatever they want, making their agreement with the captain as to what they are to bring in return. If the captain knows them to be honest men, they are allowed to take the goods away at once; but if they have not sufficient credit with him, they must get the Duke, or some trustworthy person, to be responsible for them. I was fortunate enough to be present during the time they were carrying on business.

The principal part of the cargoes of the Liverpool vessels who trade for palm-oil, is salt, of which the natives are very fond; but they consider it more a luxury, than a necessary condiment; the article next in estimation is rum; after which, they eagerly desire all descriptions of manufactured articles; such as cotton cloths, especially those printed with fancy patterns: all sorts of beads, glass or china-ware, umbrellas, hats, &c. for which they frequently send orders on board the vessels, written in the following style.

NOTES.

(NO. 1.)

"Captain Cummins Sir please Let the Bearer have fifteen and the 13 Crew Cask to fill at Toby Creek.

"Duke Epbraim."

(NO. 2.)

"Captain Image Sir Please Give King Eyo Trust for 800 Crews of Oil be down for it if his no pay I will pay.

"Duke Ephraim."

(NO. 3.)

"Dear my good friend Captain Halmaga Sir I have send you this letter to let you know that I send you 1 Goat and I send my Dear John to send me that Rum you promised me yeseday and I thank you to let me know what Hour you want me to come down to take my Trust.

"I am your Best friend

"King Eyo Honesty at Old Creek Town."

(NO. 4.)

"Dear friend Captain Cummins Sir I have to thank you to send me 8 Empett Cask for to go for Market.

"I remain your friend Eyo Eyo Honesty." [37]

(NO. 5.)

"My friend Captain Commins if you please send me that Rum I been beg you and thank you for lettle Beef too if you got any.

"Toby Tom Narrow."

(NO. 6.)

"Captain R. Commings Sir I mush obliged to you for please spear me some nails for make door do my friend I remain Sir

"Tom Duke."

(NO. 7.)

"Captain Cummins Sir I let you know but I want to go to Market for me self in I send you Book to give me 50 Iranba for 110 Crew Salt then now I want 70 Crew Salt in them Bring me Book for 40 Crew Salt again then now I thank you to Down hose head for my 2 small hatt I am your Humble Servant

"Antega Ambo."

---

[37] Brother to King Eyo.

If the Christian Missionaries were to establish schools in the towns on the banks of these rivers, they would be very likely to prove eminently beneficial to the people, who are very desirous of, receiving every kind of instruction, more particularly a knowledge of writing, which, at present, the head men teach each other in an imperfect manner, of which the above notes form an example. There is not one of them who ever read English, or any other language in print; and I have heard the Duke express great regret at not being able to read the newspapers, of the contents of which, although he had seen many, he still remained ignorant.

Thursday, 13.—The Eden's prize (a Spanish schooner taken last voyage by the African) arrived this evening from Fernando Po, with Capt. Owen on board, to whom Captain Smith and myself immediately went to pay our respects.

Friday, 14.—Captain Owen visited the Spanish slave schooner, the ship Agnes, the brig Kent, and mustered the crews of the two palm-oil vessels, when he met with several volunteers for the Eden. In the afternoon, he went on shore to see the Duke, who received him very civilly, but suspiciously, for, notwithstanding their great professions of friendship for the English in general, and their real regard for some particular individuals, who are regular traders to the country, the consideration of the profits they derive from the slave-trade, prompts them to feel no little annoyance at our interference in their lucrative commerce. They already perceive that our new settlement at Fernando Po, is calculated to interfere with their proceedings, and they have clearly expressed their sentiments upon the subject; not, however, without clothing their observations so cunningly as to avoid giving offence.

"What for," said one, "white man come to live in black man's country? What for can't white man stop in own country? Much better for white man, than black man's country."

Mr. Cowan, the hospital assistant at Fernando Po, and myself, accompanied King Eyo, this evening, in his large canoe, up the river, to Creek Town, a distance of twelve miles, where his Majesty resides.

The town is built on the edge of a creek, a short distance from the river. On our arrival, we found that King Eyo had a larger wooden framed English house, than the King of the Old Calabar, but not in such good repair: it was also sent from England by Mr. Bold, of Liverpool, to the King's father. In the largest room there was an elevated seat, in humble imitation of a throne, where the King sat to hear and give judgment in cases of dispute, and other causes that required his interference. He had a number of articles of English furniture, for instance, drawers, sofas, chairs, &c. The principal articles in glass, were a chandelier, suspended in the centre of the room, several mirrors, glass shades, for lamps or candles; rummers, wine-glasses, &c.; but, like the Duke, his Majesty does not sleep in his English house, preferring a native hut, where he was surrounded by his wives and domestics; the latter, of course, being his slaves. King Eyo is more moderate in his conjugal establishment than the Duke, having only twenty wives, while Duke Ephraim's number amounts to sixty.

The captain of an English vessel calling on the Duke one day, he exclaimed, "Oh, my friend, you come very good time, I just send away some of my wives, that I have had to entertain me!"—The captain replying, that he regretted he had not come sooner, as he should have liked to see them. The Duke answered, "Oh! no, my friend; you could not; it is not Calabar fashion!" How many were there? questioned the captain—"Oh!" replied the Duke, "only twenty-five!"

Saturday, 15.—There was so much noise in the town all night, that we imagined it must proceed from drunkenness, or else some desperate rencounter; indeed, it was impossible to think otherwise, for they were screaming, hallooing, and blowing cows-horns, or conchs, which produced so horrid a din, that there was no possibility of sleeping, and we expected no less than that a party would rush into the house where we were. The uproar, however, died away towards morning, and we learned afterwards, that it was nothing more than the ordinary savage enjoyment of the natives.

Captain Owen arrived this morning to pay King Eyo a visit; he remained a couple of hours, and then returned to Old Calabar Town.

In the afternoon, we left Creek Town, with the King, in Tom Eyo's canoe, to return to Old Calabar; we had been very hospitably entertained by his Majesty, who gave us what is called Calabar chop, a dish consisting of any sort of meat stewed in palm-oil, and highly seasoned with pepper.

The idea of palm-oil may be unpleasant to an English reader, but when it is fresh, it is not unpalatable, and I must confess, that I greatly relished a dish of fish and yams which was brought on board the Kent, as a present to the captain: of course it was cooked in their best style. I remember, at one time, having as much prejudice as any of my countrymen against oil; but when I went to France, I partook of it insensibly, until I began to like it; and, when in Italy, I fell into the custom of using it with vegetables, as a substitute for melted butter: fresh oil, in warm climates, being generally preferred to butter, even where both are to be had, which is not always the case in southern latitudes.

There are very few good fish in the Old Calabar river; the best I met with was a species of sole, but very thin, which, I suppose, is owing to the muddiness of the river itself, and to the extensive mud-banks which flank the channel. The water in the river is also so bad as to be unfit for use, in consequence of the quantity of decayed animal and vegetable matter that must constantly be mixed with it, in a climate where the progress of putrefaction is so rapid; however, fortunately for the shipping, there is a good spring on the bank of the river, about a mile below the town, where it is usual to send for supplies.

King Eyo went on board the African, schooner, and remained with Captain Smith to select goods, equal in value to twenty bullocks.

CHAP. XII.

Captain Owen's Departure—Runaway Slave—Egbo again—Duke's Sunday—Superstitious Abstinence—Anecdote of a Native Gentleman—Breaking Trade—Author's Visit to Creek Town—Bullocks embarked—Departure from Calabar—Chased by mistake—Dangerous Situation—Mortality at Fernando Po—Detection of a Deserter—Frequency of Tornados—Horatio hove down—Capture of a Slave Vessel—Loss of Mr. Morrison—Another Slave Vessel taken—Landing a part of the Slaves—Author's Daily Routine—Garden of Eden—Monstrous Fish—Continued Mortality—Market at Longfield

Monday, 17.—After breakfast, Captain Owen sailed in the Victoria for Fernando Po. The Lady Combermere also departed for the same destination; the latter vessel, being on a trading voyage along the coast, contained a number of articles in her freight, much required by the people at the settlement.

Soon after these vessels were out of sight, two parties of slaves came down from the Baracoons, to wash themselves in the river; they were chained in pairs, the right leg of one to the left leg of another. Before the Victoria arrived, they were brought down daily; but were not seen during the time she remained, notwithstanding there were several depôts for slaves in the town.

Some black gentlemen came on board to-day to barter for bullocks.

The brig James, from Liverpool, arrived this afternoon. About eight in the evening, a Calabar man was brought on board from the Kent's oil-house; he wanted to be secreted until we sailed, as he wished to make his escape; for, he said, his master wanted to cut his head off, or to make him chop nut, i.e. to oblige him to eat a poisonous nut, which produces speedy death, because he had free-mason (meaning witchcraft), and that his master had been sick ever since he had last flogged him.

Picked up floating about the harbour, the long-boat of a French slaver, that had been taken while at anchor here, by a French man-of-war brig.—Ther. at 1 P.M. 93°. F. in the shade.

Wednesday, 19.—We saw from the vessel to-day, that Egbo was running about the town. A small canoe, with a couple of the Eden's Kroomen, came up the river this evening with a letter from the Eden's tender, for information respecting the Spanish slave-vessel that was expected to sail.

Thursday, 20.—Fine day, with a fresh sea breeze, which felt quite reviving after several hot days. Egbo again in action to-day, having been sent from Old Calabar to Robin's Town, a distance of three miles, to recover a debt for the Duke.

Friday, 21.—Old Calabar being yesterday, this was Duke's Sunday; but neither of these holidays were kept with the usual festivity, in consequence of the prescribed time of the mourning for the Prince, not having yet expired. When these holidays are observed, it is usual for the Duke to invite all the captains and super-cargoes of vessels in the river, when he gives them an excellent dinner, with plenty of palm-wine. The dinner consists, generally, of goats, wild pigs, monkeys, fish, plain yams, foofoo, &c. The latter dish is a preparation of boiled yams, which are pounded in a mortar until they obtain a tenacity that will admit of being drawn out like birdlime. While the Duke is at dinner, or breakfast, he usually has some foofoo before him. This he rolls in his hands into small balls, of about two inches in diameter, before he partakes of it: it is, however, but justice to remark, that his Majesty always washes his hands both before and after each meal.

There is a superstition, prevalent among these people, concerning food that is forbidden, which is pointed out to them from time to time by their doctor, or rather by the fetish men, who are the interpreters of his supposed will; the doctor himself being a mere wooden image; one of which is always carried about in the suite of the Duke. At the time of our visit, the Duke was forbidden to eat beef or fowls, consequently he never allowed them to be put on his table. He was occasionally permitted to eat fish, because, I presume, he was supposed to have a fancy for it. At these times, the Duke's attendants are forbidden to taste fish. Although the Duke does not eat beef or fowls, he occasionally orders the animals to be sacrificed as an offering to the devil: for the Calabar people say, that "God is a good man, and will not hurt them; but the devil is a bad man, and it is therefore necessary to appease him."

The natives of this country all shave on the day previous to Calabar Sunday; and it is curious enough that they all do so according to the Mahommedan mode, excepting when they make devils, that is, go into mourning, at which period, they not only omit shaving, but put on their worst clothes.

The captain of an English vessel, calling one day on a black gentleman, with whom he was on very friendly terms, opened the door suddenly, without ceremony, breaking a slight fastening, and found his friend under the hands of one of his wives, who was performing for him the office of a barber; a discovery which so offended the prejudices of the native, that he could never summon courage after that circumstance, to look the captain full in the face.

The Duke, King Eyo, and several black gentlemen, breakfasted, and began their trade, on board the James to-day. The form of breaking trade here is not so ceremonious as at the Bonny, being merely done by the Duke's visit a few days after the arrival of a vessel, when refreshments are provided for him and his suite, after which he selects whatever goods he wants, and the trade is then open to all his subjects.

Sunday, 23.—There were four guns fired in the town this afternoon, the object of which was to announce the death of a rich old lady; as they were not minute-guns one would suppose her relations were rejoicing at the event which had taken place.

Monday, 24.—This evening I accompanied Captains McGhar, Charles, Coxenham, and Smith, (all commanding English vessels in the river) to visit King Eyo at Creek Town, but our visit was rather of a different character to that which would be paid to crowned heads in Europe; in this instance our host was the gainer, as well as the honoured party, for his guests came amply provided with the luxuries of life, and he was only required to furnish a few necessaries, which are also presented to him by his subjects, or his particular slaves. The excursion, however, procured us a little variety, and terminated satisfactorily to all parties, but after the novelty of a first visit has passed away, there is little interest to be found in a black town, the huts are all on the same plan; and the streets rugged and narrow.

Tuesday, 25.—About noon we left Creek Town, to return on board our respective vessels. Early in the evening we experienced a slight touch of a tornado, which in a few hours after was followed by a very violent one, and a good deal of heavy rain.

Friday, 28.—We completed our cargo of bullocks this afternoon, which we began to receive on board the preceding day. Our whole deck was now crowded with these animals, divided into compartments, with bamboo and other spars, leaving only a small space in the fore and after parts to work the vessel. There was also a platform made in the hold for a further number. Took leave of our friends at Old Calabar, and dropped down the river just below seven fathom point, where we anchored for the night. Had a slight tornado this evening.

Saturday, 29.—Got under weigh at daylight, but were obliged to anchor again before noon, both wind and tide being against us. We here found the Haywood, Captain Burrel, at anchor; she was from Liverpool, bound to Old Calabar, for palm-oil. The larger Liverpool vessels have generally a small one, for a tender, to collect palm-oil, ebony, and ivory, [38] at different places on the coast, as the ships generally remain in one river until their cargoes are complete. There was a dreadful accident happened to one of these tenders. She was boarded by a number of piratical blacks in canoes, belonging to an island near the mouth of the Camaroon river, when they murdered all the trader's crew, and after plundering the vessel of every thing they thought worth carrying away, they got clear off with their booty.

At 5 in the afternoon we got under weigh, and at 8 crossed the bar, where there was a heavy surf and only 15 feet water, so that we and our live stock were in some danger. Soon afterwards we were chased, and had two shots fired at us, being taken for a slaver escaping under cover of the night, and when the vessel was ranging up alongside, with the intention of pouring in a heavy fire and boarding us in the smoke, our assailants, to their great mortification, heard the bellowing of our oxen, and we discovered the vessel to be the Eden's tender, commanded by our friend Lieutenant Badgeley, who came on board, when we enjoyed a good laugh at his disappointment, in taking our horned cattle for slaves. We soon parted company, leaving him our best wishes.

Sunday, 30.—Soon after midnight the weather, from being very calm and clear, became overcast, and at 2 o'clock a tornado came on, which continued with frequent, and most violent gusts of wind, rain, thunder and lightning, till

---

[38] Ebony is plenty in this country, but the high duty that is imposed upon its importation, renders it an unprofitable article in the English market. At Liverpool it sells for no more than £4 per ton, the duty out of which is £2 per ton.

between five and six in the morning; our situation was not at all enviable, as we had both the deck, and hold, crowded with cattle. The violence and variableness of the wind soon raised a very rough and cross sea, which frequently broke over us, making every thing fly from side to side, and producing the greatest disorder. All this time I was in a small moveable bed-place on deck, expecting every instant that the sea would overwhelm us, and wash me and my bed-place overboard, for I was in no danger of being washed out of my bed, as it required no little management to emerge from it at pleasure. This berth of mine was commonly called a doghouse (a box about six feet long, four high, and two broad,) containing a mattress fitted about 18 inches from the deck, above which there was a sliding door and curtain, scarcely large enough to admit an ordinary sized man. I found it, however, much more pleasant in fine weather than sleeping below, where the cockroaches were so numerous that a large dishful might be obtained in a few minutes, by putting a little treacle in it, to serve both for bait and trap. I used to think, that if the old story were a fact instead of a fiction, namely, that the Chinese make Soy of these animals, a very lucrative trade might be carried on between them and the natives of these coasts.

Our schooner was a low, sharp, fast sailing vessel, but in an irregular sea she was tossed about like a cork. At daylight the weather cleared up, and the day turned out fine with a moderate breeze, which died away towards noon, when being in sight of the vessels at anchor in Maidstone Bay, Captain Smith and I left the schooner, to pull thither in a boat, and got on board the Eden about two in the afternoon: we also went on board the Louisa, from Sierra Leone.

The accounts we received of our infant settlement were not so favourable as we could have desired, not with regard to the progress of operations, for that was greater than could be reasonably expected, but from the sickness that had prevailed, and the consequent loss of several valuable lives. Mr. Glover, the master of the house-carpenters, died only the preceding evening, and it is much to be feared that the panic which took place on the first symptom of illness, (from a deficiency of that moral courage which every Christian ought to possess) proved more fatal than the disease itself. This morning we had a most convincing illustration of this fact. One of the stoutest and healthiest of our Plymouth artificers, who exhibited no previous symptoms of illness, on hearing of the death of Mr. Glover burst into a fit of crying, and exclaimed, "Oh my wife! my children! I shall never see you again!" From that moment he drooped, and in a few days died from despondency.

Good Friday, April, 4.—About 11 o'clock last night, the sentinel over the provision store at Newmarket, observed a man lying on the ground, tearing away the watling off one side of the store. On being challenged, he rose up, either to make his escape, or to resist the sentinel, who was advancing with fixed bayonet. In the scuffle that followed, the culprit was wounded in his left breast, notwithstanding which he succeeded in releasing himself from the grasp of his adversary. The sentinel, however, returned to the charge, and following him up closely, felled him to the earth with a blow from the butt-end of his musket. Still, however, the thief struggled violently, and prostrate as he was, endeavoured to bring down his opponent by seizing his legs: the soldier was now compelled, in self-defence, to transfix his prisoner to the ground, by running his bayonet through his left arm, until the serjeant came up, who took him to the guard-house, whither he walked, notwithstanding his severe wounds, and great loss of blood. His appearance was that of a native, his body being coated with red clay, and the fore part of his head shaved, while he wore the usual ornaments, a girdle, and armlets, of beads: but he was soon discovered to be a soldier of the African Corps, named Gott, who had run away four months before, taking with him his arms, accoutrements, and clothes.

The African, schooner, sailed this afternoon, for the purpose of procuring yams and live stock from other parts of the island, our people having bought up the whole stock of the natives in the neighbourhood of the settlement. We found here a few oysters on the Mangrove trees near the sea-shore, within reach of the tide.

Saturday, 5.—The Eden's tender, Victoria, returned from the Old Calabar this afternoon. A heavy tornado this evening, but as it is almost a daily occurrence, it is scarcely worth noticing.

Sunday, 6.—The Eden's tender, Horatio, with Captain Harrison on board, returned this afternoon from a week's trading voyage for stock round the island. A seaman belonging to the Eden was drowned through carelessness, in upsetting a small boat on leaving the Horatio. The Victoria sailed this evening, under the command of Lieutenant Robinson, to blockade several slave-vessels that were daily expected to sail from the Old Calabar river.

Monday, 7.—The armourer of the Eden died this afternoon. I had been myself affected with feverish symptoms during the last fortnight, but, although so many persons were dying around me, I still maintained my cheerful spirits, to which circumstance I attribute the restoration of my health, which was now daily improving. I mention this solely for the sake of impressing upon others the importance which cannot be often urged, of not giving way to despondency in this insalubrious climate.

Thursday, 10.—The Fame, brigantine, arrived here on her way from the Camaroon river, bound to Liverpool with palm-oil, which afforded us an opportunity of sending letters to England: she sailed on *Saturday*, on which day the Horatio filled, and sunk in Clarence Cove while in the act of heaving down. This event occasioned much trouble, and it required the assistance of two vessels to get her up again. The weather had been very unsettled throughout the past week, with a tornado during some part of each day or night.

Monday, 14.—The African sailed for the island of Bimbia to procure as much stock and vegetables as they could obtain. I regretted that a temporary indisposition prevented me from going, occasioned by a large boil in a highly irritable state, which is very common on this coast.

Tuesday, 15.—Mr. Mercer, midshipman of the Eden, who had sailed from hence in the Victoria, returned to-day in charge of the Elizabeth schooner under French colours, with upwards of 100 slaves on board. He had taken possession of her from the Eden's pinnace, while Lieutenant Robinson in the Victoria, went in chase of a suspicious vessel in another direction.

The Elizabeth was said to be from Guadaloupe, but from the testimony of her crew, and other circumstances, it appeared, that she had only got her French captain and papers from thence, and that she had sailed from St. Thomas's, under Spanish colours, where she engaged a part of her crew; the rest, with her Spanish captain, having previously joined her at Porto Rico. The Spaniard, who acted as captain in the outward bound voyage, remained at Old Calabar, to go back in another vessel, while he sent the Frenchman, with false papers, for the voyage home, knowing that the Eden's tender and boat were on the look-out for him at the mouth of the river.

Wednesday, 16.—Captain Owen employed himself in the examination of the papers and crew of the schooner brought in by Mr. Mercer. A short time before midnight, there was an alarm that a man had fallen overboard: every exertion was made to pick him up, without success. On inquiry, the unfortunate person proved to be Mr. Morrison, who had left England as schoolmaster of the Eden, and who, after the death of Mr. Abbott, was appointed acting store-keeper to the settlement. For want of lodging on shore, he used to come on board every night to sleep. Upon this occasion, he had laid down in the hammock netting on the gangway, a favourite place with the young gentlemen, as most of the ship's company, as well as the Kroomen, and black labourers, slept on the deck. It is supposed, that on awaking, he intended going below, but being drowsy, he mistook the outside for the inside rail, and fell into the water. He struggled a very short time before he sunk, and it was therefore thought, that he must have struck himself against a gun, or the side of the vessel, in his fall.

Thursday, 17.—We this day hove the Horatio down alongside the Eden to a pinnace filled with iron ballast: the pinnace sunk during the night in a squall, in consequence of her iron ballast not having been taken out at sunset. Eighty-one adult female slaves, and some female children, were landed this afternoon from the Elizabeth.

Sunday, 20.—About two o'clock in the afternoon, Lieutenant Badgeley arrived in a Brazilian schooner, Ou Voador (The Flying-fish), which he had taken with 230 slaves on board.

Monday, 21.—The Victoria, Lieutenant Robinson, returned from Old Calabar to-day, without having met with any further success. Landed this afternoon, at the settlement, from the Voador, sixty male slaves, with forty-two women and children, who were to be employed, with an allowance of sixpence per day, and their provisions.

Wednesday, 23.—Fired a royal salute from Adelaide Island, in honour of St. George's day. The African returned with stock from the island of Bimbia. Landed sixty-four sick children, of both sexes, from the Voador, their complaints being sore eyes, scurvy, craw-craws (itch), &c. The black mechanics and labourers, and their wives, shewed the greatest anxiety to take one, two, or more of these children under their protection, although they had been previously told that they would not receive any additional allowance for their support. One woman remarked, that as she had left her child at Sierra Leone, she wanted another in its place, to carry at her back; and before they obtained the Governor's permission for the indulgence of their wishes, they took the beads off their own necks to decorate their newly-adopted favourites. This philanthropic disposition was happily not confined to people of colour, (most of whom had fallen under the protection of the British flag, from similar situations, i.e. the holds of slave-vessels), as most of the naval, military, and civil officers, who resided on shore, also received boys under their protection.

Thursday, 24.—The Wanderer, transport, Lieutenant Young, agent, from Deptford, arrived this afternoon, with stores for this and Ascension island; and in the evening, the sloop Lucy, from Sierra Leone, with provisions for the settlement.

Friday, 25.—This afternoon, the two prizes, Ou Voador and Elizabeth, sailed for adjudication at Sierra Leone. The African left this evening for Old Calabar.

Saturday, 26.—This evening the Victoria sailed to blockade the Old Calabar river.

Monday, 28.—The French captain of the Elizabeth, having offered his services to superintend one of the working parties of black labourers on shore, commenced the performance of that duty this morning. The last of the two horses brought from Sierra Leone, died to-day from a disease in the mysenteric glands. The Munroe, an American whaling brig, arrived this evening. Two men, who were taken ill with fever, were ordered on board the Eden, and there were still five of the Plymouth artificers ill with the fever on shore; one of whom was in a state of delirium. We had likewise several seamen suffering from fever on board.

Wednesday, 30.—Ware, a fine boy, about fourteen years of age, whom Captain Owen had appointed to attend me, was unfortunately taken ill with fever to-day, which gave me great uneasiness.

Thursday, May, 1.—Went on shore soon after daylight, with the working parties, attended by a new servant, and returned to breakfast. Went on shore again before dinner, this being my accustomed routine. I occasionally remained on shore the whole day, and sometimes at night; but I preferred sleeping on the deck of the Eden, where, on the top of the Captain's skylight, I weathered out many a tornado. In this situation, I was tolerably protected by the sloped awning from the violence of the wind and the heavy rain, by which it is always accompanied: but even a wetting, now and then, would have been preferable to sleeping in a close cabin, between decks, where, in spite of every precaution, the heat was intolerable.

Saturday, 3.—We have had either a tornado, or heavy rain, with thunder and lightning, at some part of every twenty-four hours since I last noticed the weather. Another of the artificers departed this life. We had cucumbers from the Garden of Eden for dinner.

The following is a list of the seeds that have been sown there by the order of Captain Owen, who gave it its poetical appellation.

Many of them were planted in December, 1827.

Early York Cabbage.
Emperor ditto.
American Cabbage.
Custard Apple.
Sour Sop.
Sierra Leone Plum.
Tomato.
Orchilla Weed, from St. Vincent's.
Do. St. Antonio.
Do. The Cape.
Do. Madeira.
Fruit Stones, from England.
Canna, or Indian Shot.
Large and small Pepper.
Balsams.
Pride of Barbadoes.
Madeira Broom.
Rose Apple.
Dahlia.
Sunflower.
Four o'Clock.
St. Jago Lilac.
Marigold.
Malta Turnip.
Spanish Onion.
Kidney Bean.
Lettuce.
Mustard and Cress.
American Cress.
Leek.
Cucumber.
Pumpkin.
Lime.
Lemon.
Orange.
Cocoa-nut.

Sunday, 4.—The American brig, Munroe, whaler, sailed to-day, on her return to her fishing ground.

Monday, 5.—The African, schooner, arrived from Old Calabar, with a cargo of bullocks, seventy-six in number; also a small cutter from Sierra Leone, with rice, &c. for the settlement.

Tuesday, 6.—Captain Hurst, of the Wanderer, towed a very large fish on shore, and hauled it up on the beach for examination, the mate of that ship, after some difficulty, having killed it with a harpoon. The sailors called it a Devil Fish, because, perhaps, they had never seen one so ugly, or so large of its kind before. They endeavoured to describe it to me, as I was too late to examine it myself; many of our black labourers having carried away pieces of it immediately after it was brought to land. The head was formed like the concave of a crescent, with an eye near the end of each point, and a small orifice just behind each eye, like an ear. In breadth, it measured fourteen feet and a half, that is, from the extremities of the fins, or flaps, which resembled those of a skate; in length, seven feet in the body, and six feet in the tail.

A very pretty young native girl, about fifteen years of age, took refuge in our settlement this afternoon, and placed herself under the care of a fine strapping young Krooman, servant to Capt. Smith, of the African.

Wednesday, 7.—Forster, the marine, who was superintending a party on shore, was sent on board in a high fever to-day; and Thomas Welling, another of our Plymouth artificers, died this morning. We also found that our bullocks began to die very fast, without our being able to discover the immediate cause.

My poor servant lad has continued in a high fever ever since he was first taken; and this evening, about nine o'clock, his respiration became very low and quick (the rattles), and for a full hour no hope was entertained; but, at the end of that time, the alarming symptoms subsided; his respiration became more easy and natural, and after a composing sleep of several hours, he awoke with every prospect of recovery.

Saturday, 10.—The Lucy, cutter, sailed this afternoon to procure stock from the opposite coast.

Monday, 12.—Forster, the marine, died last night, after five days illness; and, although the sailmaker was called to sew him up in his hammock before he was quite cold, the work of decomposition had already commenced, and the corpse was so offensive, that he had much difficulty in completing his object. This was a case of remarkable despondency. He entertained an opinion, from the moment he was attacked, that his illness would terminate fatally, and it was impossible to inspire him with the least hope; a state of mind which certainly tended greatly to the accomplishment of his prophecy.

The Victoria returned from Old Calabar to-day.

Tuesday, 13.—In the middle of the night, a heavy tornado came on; after which it continued to blow very hard from the eastward till noon, when the wind died away to a light breeze, and we had a very fine afternoon. In the evening, the Horatio sailed for Old Calabar.

Wednesday, 14.—A tornado in the middle of the night.

Friday, 16.—A market opened to-day at Longfield, where our people were allowed to purchase what they pleased from the natives, paying a small duty for this privilege to the Colonial Government. Hitherto an officer had been appointed to make the purchases, and distribute the articles, gratis, to the establishment. The following were the rates of the impost:—

s.   d.

For every Gallon of Palm-Wine	0	8
Ditto Ditto of Oil	0	2
100 Yams	2	0
Fowl	0	1-1/2
Sheep, or Goat	2	0
Kid, or Lamb	0	9

For my own part, I cannot perceive the policy of imposing duties upon such trifling articles, the whole of which would amount to a very inconsiderable sum, when collected, and it had the bad effect of rendering the people dissatisfied: God knows, there were sufficient privations for those living in this infant colony, without imposing duties upon the few additional comforts of life, that were so scantily supplied by the inhabitants.

CHAP. XIII.

Saturday, May 17, 1828.—Mr. Craig, who had come from Sierra Leone to set
up a store, went into the country with a native chief this afternoon, for the
purpose of procuring palm-oil. He returned, however, the next evening, very
much fatigued and disappointed; for he not only found the journey very
harassing, in consequence of the badness of the paths, but discovered that his
mercantile project was fruitless, owing to the poverty of the natives. Indeed, the
people of Fernando Po are less abundantly supplied with provisions than the
nations of Africa in general; their principal dependance being on yams, which
are, of course, liable to occasional failure. They have very little live stock of any
kind, and the chiefs alone appear to indulge in the luxury of animal food. It is
only on particular occasions, however, that they treat themselves to a goat, or
sheep, as they are principally confined to fowls. That they are not plentifully
supplied with fish, is owing solely to their own negligence, as there are
abundance to be had by those who take the trouble of toiling for them; but for
many days together, not a canoe was to be seen. It is difficult to ascertain the
cause of this strange indifference; it may be that they are afraid to venture out to
sea, and this is not unlikely, as they appeared, on our first arrival, to entertain
much apprehension at the sight of a strange vessel on their coast; but, as they
became accustomed to our presence, and began to entertain a feeling of

confidence and protection in our friendship, this diffidence gradually wore off. It cannot be doubted, that their island has often been visited by vessels engaged in the slave-trade, as well as by men-of-war. A circumstance occurred a few years ago, which proves that they are not without hostile visitors; and which, in some measure, justifies the suspicions with which they regard all strangers. In the year 1820, or 1821, a Spanish vessel came over from the Camaroon river to this island, accompanied by King Aqua, with a number of war canoes, for the purpose of decoying the natives, or, in the event of failing in their artifice, to adopt hostile measures, with the ultimate view of seizing upon all they could capture, and selling them for slaves. They accordingly landed well armed, but met with a stout resistance, which proved, however, unavailing, the invaders succeeding in making about 150 prisoners, whom they carried off to the West Indies, and killing as many more in the skirmish. It is supposed that King Aqua received very little reward for his services on the occasion, or for the loss his subjects sustained in the fight. This anecdote was related to me by Captain Cumings, of the Kent, who was trading on the opposite coast for palm-oil, at the time it occurred.

Thursday, 22.—The Horatio, schooner (Eden's tender), arrived this afternoon with only her foremast standing, having lost her mainmast in a tornado. Mr. Craig has just opened his general store, which, with Captain Smith's, forms the second mercantile establishment in this infant settlement.

Friday, 23.—Mr. Adamson, the assistant-surgeon of the Eden, who had the charge of the hospital, as well as of the mechanics and labourers of the settlement, and who had resided on shore for the purpose of giving them his constant attendance, was sent on board the Eden to-day, in consequence of an attack of fever, which lasted five days.

Thursday, 29.—The weather has continued unsettled; sometimes clear and hot; sometimes cloudy and close; with alternate rain and cold. We fired a royal salute to-day on Adelaide Island, in commemoration of the Restoration.

Friday, 30.—One of the liberated Africans from the Voador, was brought in this morning by one of our black masons, having been absent, with three of his companions, ever since he was landed. We learned, that he, and his party, had lived in the bush by day, emerging at night to steal yams, and proceed on their journey, until, after an absence of four weeks, being at some distance up the mountain, they were fiercely attacked by the natives with spears, and stones thrown from slings. In this rencontre, one of them was killed, and another taken prisoner; while he, and his remaining companion, effected their escape, by taking different directions: they never, it appeared, met afterwards. From this circumstance, it is evident that the islanders are unwilling to give shelter to runaways; an occurrence by no means unsatisfactory, as the newly liberated Africans desert very frequently, and sometimes in small troops, so many as nine having been known to go away together.

Saturday, 31.—Captain Harrison, the superintendant of works, who had, up to this time, been living on board the Eden, gave a dinner to Captain Owen and a select party, at his new residence on shore to-day, to which I had the pleasure of being invited; but, alas! like most of those who accompanied the first part of the expedition to this settlement, his services have since terminated with his life.

The master of the ship Agnes, of Liverpool, trading for palm-oil, in the Old Calabar river, arrived in his long-boat this afternoon, for the purpose of obtaining men from Captain Owen, to navigate the Agnes to England, part of his crew having previously entered for and joined H.M.S. Eden.

Sunday, June, 1.—There has been scarcely a day during the last fortnight, that some vessel has not arrived at, or left the settlement, and one or more been seen in the offing; in fact, the little colony appears to become extensively known already, and it is expected that the large palm-oil vessels will find it more to their advantage to anchor in Maidstone Bay, and carry on their trade with their tenders only, than to take their vessels up the river, where the long period occupied in procuring their cargoes, affords time for the men to imbibe the pestilential disorders of the climate, frequently occasioning the sacrifice of many lives.

Tuesday, 3.—The day at last arrived on which I was to quit Fernando Po. Captain Owen, finding his crew much reduced in numbers from sickness, which appeared unlikely to diminish, and fearing also, that his operations would be retarded for the want of stores, determined to make a visit to Sierra Leone; by this step, hoping to re-establish the health of his men, and to procure the necessaries of which the Colony stood in need. Accordingly, making the requisite arrangements on the establishment, and committing it entirely to the charge of Captain Harrison, he got under weigh in the afternoon, when we made sail out of Maidstone Bay, and stood for the opposite coast, with the Agnes' long-boat in tow.

On looking back at this incipient colony, and reflecting upon the probabilities of its future destiny, a few thoughts arise, which this appears to be the proper place for inserting.

The formation of a new settlement amongst an uncivilized people must always be an event of interest, whether we regard it in a political or moral point of view, as extending the power of the parent nation, or spreading the advantages of improvement in regions hitherto sunk in the darkness of barbaric ignorance. The objects proposed by the British Government in establishing a colony at Fernando Po appear to have been three-fold, and not less connected with political than moral results.

First, to create facilities for promoting our commercial relations with the districts of tropical Africa, in which many valuable necessaries and costly luxuries are produced.

Second, to assist in carrying into effect the wise and benevolent regulations adopted by our Government for the suppression of the slave-trade, which has been so long the scourge and disgrace of our fellow men in this portion of the globe.

Third, to increase the means of advancing the civilization of central Africa.

The determination to endeavour to carry these leading objects into full effect, is sufficiently evidenced in the perseverance with which our Government has established the British name on the African Coast, in our different settlements at Sierra Leone, Cape Coast Castle, and other places. We have made as yet but slight progress towards the completion of designs so comprehensive in their purpose, we must look for the causes in impediments which time alone can conquer, and not in any lack of zeal on the part of those who were appointed to execute the plans of the Government. If firm resolution, meritorious conduct, and indefatigable diligence could have mastered the difficulties which meet the English residents on this insalubrious shore, the ends which it was desirable to attain must have been speedily accomplished: but unfortunately the laws of nature and the force of habit oppose us at the very threshold of our proceedings, and seem almost to render our labour a work of despair.

All our attempts to penetrate into Africa, to establish a friendly intercourse with the people, and to abolish the traffic in human life are repelled, and frequently rendered abortive, by the fatal influence of the climate, and the obstinate resistance of the natives to our projects of liberty, which they oppose because they derive a lucrative source of income from the slave-trade, while habit has made them insensible to its ignominies and miseries. This opposition to our progress would be of no moment, if the barbarous notions of the people were not favoured by the repulsive nature of the climate, which is even more pernicious than we originally believed when we ventured to form a British settlement within its range. It is so unpropitious to European life that the pestilential breath of death may be said to lurk in every calm, and to be wafted in every gale.

It has been supposed, and not without reason, that much of the insalubrity of the climate may be referred to local causes, and that if the soil could be completely cleared and drained, the operations of the air in the redeemed space would expel, or reduce, the baneful influences that at present produce such extensive mortality. But this would be a labour demanding almost an incalculable and indefinite period of time, and which the difficulty of procuring sufficient manual power must always render nearly impossible, to any great extent.

Hitherto, the situation and prospects of the settlement of Fernando Po have been discouraging, in consequence of the disease having been more universal in its ravages than we had anticipated. But it must not, therefore, be supposed that the place is more unhealthy than other parts on the coast, or even that the deaths which occurred, during the period to which I more particularly allude, were occasioned by the insalubrity of the situation. When the crew of the Eden suffered so much from fever, it broke out on board of that vessel while she was at Sierra Leone, and several of the officers and men died before she returned to Fernando Po: the mortality that ensued was in a great measure caused by the contagion which the infected sailors spread at the settlement. Several vessels also arrived before I left the Colony with invalids on board, but the deaths that took place in their number, certainly ought not to be introduced into the argument against the insalubrity of the island.

That Fernando Po must always be liable to considerable atmospheric changes, and become, at particular seasons, very unhealthy, there cannot be a doubt: but that is invariably the case in all low situations within the tropics, on the west coast of Africa, where the decomposition of animal and vegetable matter is so rapid in its progress. But the insular situation of Fernando Po, with its many local advantages and peculiarities, may ultimately have the effect of diminishing the production of miasmata, or at least of correcting their deleterious qualities, and preventing such immense and dangerous accumulations, as have on the adjacent continent produced so great a loss of European life.

Wednesday, 4.—At daylight we cast off the Agnes' long-boat, leaving her to prosecute her voyage up the Calabar to her own ship, while we stood to the eastward.

Thursday, 5.—Unsettled weather. In the afternoon we anchored off the mouth of the Camaroon river, where Lieutenant Badgeley and Mr. Wood went, in separate boats, to examine the river, for slave-vessels.

Saturday, 7.—Soon after daylight this morning our boats returned, reporting that there was a Brazilian brig, at anchor, some distance up the Camaroon river, waiting for a cargo of slaves; and a Brazilian schooner at the Island of Bimbia, near the entrance of the river, on the same service. At noon we got under weigh, and stood to the southward.

Wednesday, 11.—Lat. 2°. 4'. N. Wind from S.S.W. to W.S.W. Tacked and sounded occasionally, working up to Prince's Island, and also in chase of a brigantine.

Thursday, 12.—At 10 in the forenoon we tacked to the southward in hopes of falling in with the brigantine, which we supposed had stood toward the land in the night, and at noon our expectations were realized: we also saw her in a more favourable point for pursuit, she being a little under our lee. Finding that she could not escape us, she put a good face on the matter, and continued to stand towards us. Between one and two o'clock we sent a boat's-crew on board to examine her. She proved to be the Emprendadora, a Spanish brigantine from the Havannah, well armed, mounting one long eighteen-pounder on a swivel, and four 12 lb. carronades, and having thirty-two persons on board. Her outfit and general appearance were extremely suspicious, for she had not only a slave-deck, with irons, &c., but also two slaves, secreted in the forehold, from whom we learnt that they had been stolen from Po-Po, near Wydah. She had also a quantity of merchandise on board, without having any Custom-house certificate of clearance from the Havannah, or indeed any other account of it, which circumstances led us to believe that it had been plundered from some American vessel. It was evident that she had been along the Gold Coast, and round the Bights of Benin and Biafra. The Captain stated that he was going to Prince's Island to procure anchors, having only one remaining, and that one, with but a single fluke to it. We afterwards learnt from the crew that he had endeavoured to enter the river Lagos, but had been fired on and forced to retire, by several Brazilian vessels lying there at the time. We conjectured that she had left the

West Indies, on a pretence of going to the coast of Africa, upon a slaving voyage, without any cargo, except perhaps a small quantity of specie, in dollars and gold, but carrying an efficient crew, composed of persons from various nations, and a good stock of provisions. Vessels, thus equipped, frequently traverse these seas, and being generally very fast sailers, they contrive to keep away from ships better armed than themselves, and to board only those that they can approach, or run away from, at convenience; when convinced that they are not likely to encounter any resistance, they plunder such vessels at their pleasure: but should they arrive on the coast of Africa, without having succeeded in obtaining plunder on their voyage to enable them to purchase slaves, they entrap and steal such negroes as they can get into their power, and then return to the West Indies to dispose of their slave cargo. This is the general character of these pirates, that are occasionally met in different parts of the North Atlantic Ocean, and also about the equinoctial line. I have heard numerous instances of vessels, from Europe, bound to these latitudes, meeting on their voyages with one or more of such vessels. Prison ships going to New South Wales have been followed by them; and scrutinized with spy glasses from their decks: but they have never yet ventured to attack a prison-ship, the sight of soldiers being quite enough to deter them from any hostile attempt. Indeed, I believe the best plan in meeting these marauders is, to assume as bold an air, and make as much show of resistance as possible. Knowing the character of these craft, Captain Owen thought it right to detain the brigantine, and therefore sent Lieut. Robinson, Mr. Wood, midshipman, and twenty-two men, to take her into Sierra Leone, for adjudication. In the evening we parted company, but expected to find her at our rendezvous in Prince's Island.

Saturday, 14.—At daylight saw Prince's Island, towards which we continued to make our course. At eight came to anchor in Port Antonio, where we found Lieutenant Robinson with the captured brigantine, and also the Vengeance, a Brazilian brigantine on a slaving voyage, which had put in for Cassada root, or Mandioc, upon which these people principally feed their slaves. After breakfast I accompanied Captain Owen on shore to wait on the Governor, who received us very politely, and introduced us to his lady and family. On leaving the Government House, we proceeded to that of Mr. Ferraro, who was said to be the richest and only respectable merchant here, but he had gone into the country; we therefore walked about the town until our curiosity was satisfied. There were no inns in the place, only some public houses, where nothing could be got but spirits, and inferior wines. The sailors, however, considered it a very civilized place, because it afforded them the means of getting most agreeably drunk, a feat which they could not accomplish at Fernando Po. Captain. Owen having allowed some of his men to go on shore for amusement, one of the marines contrived to get into a drunken frolic, and was so troublesome, that it puzzled the whole guard of black soldiers to secure him. I regret to remark that in many foreign places, the people intentionally lead our sailors into disputes, merely to obtain a fee for releasing them.

Sunday, 15.—After divine service, I accompanied Captain Owen in a walk to a negro village, about two or three miles distant, and to which there was no distinct road, but merely a rough irregular path. There was little of interest to be seen there, and scarcely any refreshment to be procured; the blacks brought us a few young cocoanuts, of which we drank the milk. The only fruits to be had on the island, were pine-apples, plantains, bananas, lemons, limes, and a few more common kinds, all of which the blacks brought to the ship in their own boats; as also vegetables, namely, pumpkins, onions, cucumbers, tomatos, &c. The oranges do not come into season until September. The principal plantations were mandioc and coffee, and there was also a small quantity of cocoa; the coffee is rather celebrated for its flavour and quality. The prices vary a good deal, but we found the average from eight to twelve pounds for a dollar. The natives both roast, and sell, their coffee with a pellicle over the berry, and I should imagine it is to this circumstance that its singularly delicious flavour may be attributed. We found the place very gay, it being the festival of St. Antonio, the patron saint, which, considering it is a Portuguese town, and situated in such a demi-civilized part of the world, may be called rather a neat one. It contained about twelve hundred houses, and seven churches, most of these, however, were in a miserable state. There were not more than fifty Europeans on the island, the whole population of which does not exceed four thousand. The principal part of these were negroes, who, of course, were slaves [39], and the remainder were of different shades from black to white. This island has still the character of slave-dealing, in a small way, with some of the African nations. One of the gentlemen of the Eden, rode across the island to West-bay, about six miles distant, but the road was a mere footpath, and scarcely entitled to be considered a bridle-road. West-bay is where our men-of-war, on the African station, generally anchor to procure water. It is a place of no consequence, in a mercantile point of view, as it consists merely of a small negro village. We heard that the great merchant, Mr. Ferraro, had been at his house in town to-day, but he left it again without having shewn the courtesy to return Captain Owen's visit; perhaps, he feared that such an effort of politeness might lead to a demand upon his hospitality, a virtue for which the Portuguese are not very remarkable, especially in their intercourse with Englishmen; in this respect, the Governor was no less a niggard of his attentions than the rest of his countrymen, giving no invitation either to Capt. Owen or any of his officers, whose ceremonious visit cost him, no doubt, infinite annoyance, as, upon that occasion, his Excellency was obliged to appear clean shaved, and in his full uniform, a laborious sacrifice to cleanliness and grandeur, at the expense of his accustomed habits of luxurious indolence and personal ease.

We found the latitude of Port Antonio, by a good observation with stars, to be 1°. 38'. N. while, in most books on navigation, it is laid down in 1°. 27'. N.

[39] There are a good many runaway slaves living at the south end of the island, quite independent of all the Portuguese authorities.

Monday, 16.—Visited the Brazilian brigantine (Vengeance), with Signor Begaro, who was sailing-master of the Voador, slave-schooner, taken by Lieutenant Badgeley, in the Eden's boat, in company with the African, schooner. This gentleman had prevailed on his countrymen to accommodate him on board, for a passage to the Brazils, however, they had first to procure their cargo of slaves; and told us, that they were going southward of the line for them, but we thought, if that were the case, they would not have come to the northward of the line, merely to get provisions. [40] From this circumstance, we suspected it to be their intention to go to the Camaroon, or some other river in that direction, where slaves are not above one-third of the price that they are to the south of the line, and where children (which they always prefer to adults) are also more easily procured. Could I have believed their assurance that they were southward bound, I should have endeavoured to have made arrangements with the captain to take me with him, being anxious to get to St. Paul de Loando, for the purpose of visiting different parts of Angola, and in which view I had prepared myself with a letter of introduction to the Viceroy of that country, from a distinguished person in England: but although I had been about seven months at Fernando Po, and other parts of the Bight of Biafra, I had never met with an opportunity for proceeding to Angola; I was therefore obliged to leave that place out of my plan, and to make the Brazils the next point in my route; with this intention I thought it most desirable to return to Sierra Leone with Captain Owen, where I might meet with a captured slave-vessel, that had been bought up by the agents, to be sent to some part of the Brazils, from whence there would be no difficulty in my ultimately reaching Rio de Janeiro.

Captain Owen had a Portuguese Abbe, Signor Begaro, and some of his officers, to dine with him to-day.

Tuesday, 17.—As it was Captain Owen's intention to visit Ascension before he went to Sierra Leone, we parted company with the Emprendadora, desiring Lieutenant Robinson to make the best of his way to the latter place; she accordingly sailed this morning at daylight, passing round to leeward of the island, while we followed soon after, with the intention of working to windward.

Wednesday, 18.—We had a fine fresh breeze, veering between S. and S.W., and kept our course to the westward. Lat. 1°. 0'. N. On getting into the open sea, we found the weather much colder than it was at Fernando Po, notwithstanding we were 3°. nearer the equinoctial line, than at the former place, while the thermometer for the last twenty-four hours, has only ranged from 74°. to 78°. F. Indeed, it is very commonly remarked, that the poor slaves brought from the Bights of Benin and Biafra, for the Brazils, suffer dreadfully from the cold, when they get into the open sea, and approach the line.

---

[40] It should be explained, that these vessels are permitted to trade for slaves to the southward of the line; but are liable to capture, if found to the northward of the line with slaves on board. However, they frequently expose themselves to the risk, in a desperate spirit of speculation.

Thursday, 19.—There was a fine southerly breeze to-day, and we crossed the equinoctial line this forenoon, without observing the usual custom of shaving, having gone through that ceremony on passing the tropic, before we arrived at Sierra Leone, not expecting, at that time, the Eden would have occasion to cross the equinoctial line. Latitude, at noon, 0° 6'. S. steering W. by S. with the wind south. There have been numberless flying-fish, with a few bonetas and dolphins sporting round the ship at times, to-day; men-of-war are not very successful in taking these fish, but in a low, dull sailing merchant-vessel, it is otherwise, particularly if she is not coppered, and has been sometime in a warm climate. I consider the dolphin and flying-fish to be exceedingly palatable food, but the boneta is strongly flavoured, and very close grained, approaching to the solidity of animal flesh.

Sunday, 21.—Latitude, at noon, 28°. 19'. S. Still a fresh trade-wind, but as we advanced from the Bight of Biafra into the Southern Atlantic Ocean, increasing our distance, at the same time, from the continent of Africa, we found the wind gradually drawing from the westward of south, to the eastward of south, until it arrived at that point (S.E.), which is the prevailing trade-wind of the Southern Atlantic, from the equinoctial line to about the 28th degree of south latitude, varying a few degrees from these extremes, according to the season of the year. Being now in the regular trade-wind, I shall not think it necessary to trouble my readers with any farther remarks on the common routine of the duties of a ship, until we come within sight of Ascension,

> Whose rocky shores to the glad sailor's eye
> Reflect the gleams of morning.

Having run for this little island in the middle of the ocean, during the night, we saw it immediately on the break of day, of *Wednesday, 25th*, within a mile of the computed distance, viz. three or four leagues. At eight, we anchored in N.W. Bay, in eleven fathoms water, about half a mile from the landing-place, when the Governor, Lieut.-Colonel Nichols, came on board; and after breakfast. Captain Owen and myself accompanied him on shore, in the gig. We landed with facility, there being very little surf, and some marines ready to run the boat upon the beach the moment she touched the ground. The officers of the establishment were prepared to receive us, and we were introduced to them individually. We first visited the mess-room, which, with some apartments attached to it for the officers' quarters, is one of three buildings that are distinct from the general establishment, called Regent Square. The second building is a store-house, containing provisions for the African squadron, as well as the persons employed on the island; and the third, a house that was built for the Governor, but which Colonel Nichols allows Lieutenant Stanwell to reside in, he being a married man, with a family of five children. One part of Regent Square is composed of the barracks for the marines, and the other for the liberated Africans that are employed on the island. All these buildings are of stone, which is the cheapest material that can be procured. The coral that is found on the beach, makes excellent lime, and enhances the utility of the quarries. It is fortunate that the island contains these resources, as it is entirely destitute of brick and timber. There was a tank of considerable size in progress, not far from the establishment; close to the landing-place there was a large pond of salt water for keeping the turtle which are taken during the season, for supplies to the shipping, &c.; there were about eighty turtles in it, at the time of our arrival.

Colonel Nichols, Captain Owen, and myself, dined with. Mr. and Mrs. Stanwell, where, among other things, we had a large loin of wether goat, which, in my opinion, was equal to the finest mutton; indeed, had it been called mutton, I should not have known the difference, it was so fat and highly flavoured. There are about six hundred goats on the island, who are allowed to wander in herds, browsing on the sides of the hills, and feeding on whatever herbage they can procure in the valleys. In this way, no doubt, they pick up many aromatic herbs, [41] which give a peculiarly fine flavour to the meat; but the flesh of goats, is not the only description of fresh provisions on the island. Those who reside here, are much better provided, in this particular, than people in England imagine, for there is a moderate supply of cattle and sheep, for general consumption, while most individuals have their own private stock of domestic poultry. Turkeys arid fowls thrive well here; but geese and ducks, very indifferently, from the want of fresh streams and pools, so necessary to their nature, in consequence of which they lay their eggs, but do not produce young. They have also a few goats, and abundance of guinea fowls, [42] in a wild state, which, in flavour, greatly surpass those that have been domesticated; and some of the domestic poultry of the gallinaceous tribe, that have returned to their aboriginal state. These three species of Ascension game, with the hunting of wild cats, occasionally afford no little amusement to the officers of the establishment. A number of cats were originally introduced; in their tame state, to destroy the rats, which, at one period, overran the island; but, after routing the rats, the cats, like the Saxons of old, finding themselves masters of the soil, became greater usurpers than the foes whom they had been called in to vanquish. These treacherous animals, and most unworthy allies, discovering that they could sustain themselves in freedom, without the aid of the biped population, fled into the least inhabited parts of the island, where they lived most royally upon young guinea fowl, and other wild poultry; regaling themselves occasionally upon eggs, or such other dainties as fell in the way of their most destructive claws. So numerous had this band of quadruped freebooters become, at the time of our visit, that the inhabitants had been compelled to call in the assistance of a number of dogs, [43] for the purpose of putting them to flight; and the gentlemen

---

[41] Wild parsley is very abundant in the valleys, besides chickweed, thistles, wild mint, and other herbs.

[42] The guinea fowl feed principally on crickets and chickweed.

[43] Bull terriers.

sportsmen of the island declare, that a battle between these belligerent powers and natural enemies presents a scene of unusual excitement and interest to the lovers of animal gladiatorship.

The sale of spirits is prohibited on the island, but each man may purchase one pint of brown stout per diem. Butter, cheese, and other little comforts, were to be procured from a stock that had been sent out by dealers in England; having, it is said, ten per cent. profit on their exportation, and two per cent. to the corporal who took charge of its disposal. It had no freightage to pay, as the owners were allowed the privilege of sending it out in a transport, which annually brings stores to the island; and, I was informed, that the British Government allowed the Governor to exchange turtle with any vessel for such necessaries, or temperate luxuries, that may be required by the establishment.

The turtle season here, is considered to be the interval between Christmas and Midsummer-day, during which time parties are stationed almost every night on each of the beaches, [44] where the turtle are known to land, for the purpose of depositing their eggs; upon these occasions, they turn as many as are likely to be required for the use of the establishment, until the following season, and also for the shipping that may call for them; these are kept in the pond, to be taken out at pleasure: two pounds of turtle is allowed as a substitute for one pound of ordinary meat. [45] The Wide-awakes, or Kitty-wakes, [46] as sailors call them, are also very numerous, both on the rocks and plains, in the laying and breeding season: and, consequently, an immense number of eggs are deposited, which are much used by the persons on the island.

We returned on board for the night, to avoid putting the officers to an inconvenience for our accommodation.

Thursday, 26.—We went on shore to breakfast, landing in a smaller boat to-day than yesterday, namely, a four-oared gig instead of a larger one with six, and yet we landed with more ease. About eleven o'clock, I accompanied Colonel Nichols and Captain Owen on horseback to visit the Colonel's residence on Green Mountain, distant about six miles from Regent Square. The roads have been made with a great deal of labour under the direction of the Colonel, and considering circumstances, there is no little credit due to that officer for his indefatigable exertions, and perseverance in accomplishing what would, to ordinary minds, have appeared impracticable. When about four miles from Regent Square we arrived at Dampier's Spring, a stream of water that might pass through an ordinary sized goose quill, and if allowed to spread over the surface

---

[44] It is observed, a short time previous to the turtle season, that the sand rises on shore, near the beach, considerably higher than at other times.

[45] The turtle, generally, weigh about 400 lbs.; and, sometimes, as much as 700 lbs.

[46] A small species of gull.

of the ground in some climates, would evaporate as quickly as it flowed, but here, conducted into a cask, it affords no inconsiderable portion of the supply at Regent's Square. It is sent down in barrels on the backs of asses, or mules, and served out by measure, according to the quantity procured. There were a few habitations near this spring, cut out of the solid rock, for the residence of soldiers who were stationed here, with their wives and families. From Dampier's Spring we continued to ascend about two miles further, when we arrived at the Colonel's dwelling (which consisted merely of a ground floor), from whence all sterility ceases, the space between it and the top of the mountain being covered with a fine rich mould, partly cultivated with sweet potatoes, and partly covered with wild herbage, amongst which the Cape gooseberry is very abundant; this is an agreeable subacid fruit, pleasant to eat when ripe, and useful in a green state for tarts, &c.

Before dinner I took an opportunity of walking to the top of the hill, which is the highest on the island, being 800 feet above the Colonel's house, and 2,849 feet above the level of the sea.

After dinner Lieutenant Badgeley, Dr. Burn, and Lieutenant Carrington of the Marines, left us to return by way of Regent Square, to the Eden. These three gentlemen have all, since that time, paid the debt of nature on board that ship. I accompanied Mr. Butter round the side of the Mountain to the Black Rock, beneath which stretched a wide and deep valley. In this walk we passed various spots set apart for the cultivation of vegetables, to which the soil is exceedingly favourable, while the deposition of night dews, with light showers, and a genial climate, all combine to render vegetation here peculiarly luxuriant, so that the inhabitants are not only enabled to reserve an ample supply for themselves, but to spare a small quantity for most of the ships that call at the island. Colonel Nichols informed us that he had 1000 lbs. weight of vegetables, principally the sweet potatoe, ready to dispose of at this period. We had at dinner green peas, and French beans, besides the more common vegetables, likewise turnip-radishes with our cheese. In fact all European vegetables may be, and most of them are, produced here. The greatest range of the thermometer on the mountain in the winter months, which are August, September, October, and November, is from 58° to 70°, and in the summer from 70° to 82°, consequently the greatest range of the whole year is only 24° being from 58° to 82° F. The sweet potatoe, (of which there are a great many and very large [47]) was first brought here from Africa; the best method of cultivating them is found to be from shoots.

The following are the names and number of domestic animals now on the island, which is about 30 miles in circumference.

70 head of oxen.
60 sheep. (principally from Africa.)

[47] Some have grown so large as to weigh 5 or 6 pounds.

600 goats.
8 horses.
4 mules.
27 asses.

There are likewise the dogs lately imported, and a few rabbits from the Cape of Good Hope, which have been turned loose in the valleys to breed; it is feared, however, that the cats will destroy the young rabbits, if they do not the old ones. Two red-legged partridges have also been brought from the Cape, and there are a few pigeons, likewise the English linnet in a wild state.

Friday, 27.—Fine morning with a few refreshing showers. Thermometer at 6 A.M. 70°. F. Soon after breakfast we left the Colonel's house to return to Regent's Square, but we walked nearly a mile before we mounted our horses. The officers of the Establishment invited all Captain Owen's party, and their Colonel, to dine with them to-day at their mess, which consists of Lieutenants Evans and Barns, R.M. Mr. Mitchell, Surgeon, and Mr. Trescot, Agent-victualler to the African squadron.

The population of the island at that time was 192 souls, [48] all Europeans, except 40 liberated Africans, and they were then deficient of 10: the Government having allowed the number of 50 to assist in carrying on the required improvements and other employments, which consists of road-making, erecting buildings, gardening, conveying water, &c. &c. The officers of the Establishment, superintend the working parties, however, these only work four days in the week, Wednesday and Saturday being allowed them for fishing, [49] cleaning their clothes, and other private purposes, while the Sunday is of course kept holy. Their working hours are from daylight until eight o'clock, when they are allowed three-quarters of an hour for breakfast; after which they return to labour till eleven, they then rest until three o'clock; from which time they work until sunset. This arrangement, which throws open to repose the hottest portion of the day, is highly to be approved of in a warm climate.

At 7 o'clock we took leave of the Colonel and his officers, to return on board the Eden. When we got under weigh, and made sail out of Ascension-roads, for Sierra Leone, steering N.N.E.

In the year 1801, when I belonged to H.M.S. Cambrian, (the Honourable Captain Legge,) on our return voyage from St. Helena, we passed so near this island, that we sent a 24-pound shot among the hills, and saw it scatter the dust around the spot where it fell, but we did not send a boat on shore, for we knew it was then uninhabited, and our Commander was not disposed to lose his time in turning turtle, while he might be more gallantly employed chasing the enemy.

---

[48] About 50 of this number live at Dampier's Spring.

[49] They have boats belonging to the Establishment, which are on these days provided with hooks and lines, and sent off those parts of the island where there is known to be good fishing ground.

We merely fired as a signal to any one that might have been left on the island by accident, for on the preceding year H.M.S. Endymion took on board the crew of a brig that had been wrecked on the island: and the celebrated navigator, Dampier, was also cast away here in the Roebuck, of 12 guns, on his return voyage from New Holland. Little could I have imagined at the time of my first visit, that I should ever have landed here, under my present peculiar circumstances, or that after so many years I should find so much to interest me in a place that presented nothing to my recollection but utter desolation. The alteration in the island was indeed curious, and I am happy to learn, that the improvements still proceed with at least equal energy, and proportionate success. Since my last visit, I am told that, the inhabitants have greatly increased their facilities of obtaining, and preserving supplies of fresh water, an achievement which must necessarily add much to their daily comfort.

Saturday, 28.—Nothing material occurred on this or the following day, for we glided along pleasantly with a fresh trade-wind, varying only a couple of points from S.E. to E.S.E. until the morning of

Monday, 30.—When the wind got much lighter and we were afraid of losing the trade altogether, for although at this season of the year it prevails much further from the Southern towards the Northern Hemisphere, yet we can seldom hope to carry it beyond the equinoctial line, where we expect to get into what is very characteristically called "the variables": at one season of the year, these winds are very light and changeable, with frequent calms and occasional thunderstorms and waterspouts: at another season of the year, the weather is dark, gloomy, squally with occasional calms and much rain, until we advance to 12° or 14° N. latitude, where we usually fall in with the N.E. trade wind, however, ships are sometimes fortunate enough on leaving the Southern Hemisphere for the Northern, particularly in the months of May, June, and July, to carry the S.E. trade to the northward of the line, even until they fall in with the N.E. trade.

Between three and four this afternoon, we crossed the equinoctial line, at which time I took an affidavit before Captain Owen for my half-pay. I was induced to do this from the novelty of the circumstance, as well as a preparatory measure in case I should have an opportunity of forwarding a letter to England. Lat. at noon, for the last three days, 5°. 39'.—2°. 25'. and 0°. 13'. S.

Tuesday, July, 1.—There was a great change in the weather to-day. The wind was more unsettled, the clouds were heavy, and there was a general haze around the horizon. These were clear indications of our approaching the coast of Africa in the rainy season; there had also been a heavy dew last night, which aggravated these gloomy appearances. At sunset, we saw a vessel a few miles a-head of us, which we came up with in about an hour, she proved to be a Dutch galliot, from the island of Mayo, bound to Rio de Janeiro, with half a cargo of salt.

Immediately on receiving this intelligence, I requested the boarding officer to engage a passage for me to the Brazils, which being accomplished, I took leave of my kind and respected friend Captain Owen, after having been his guest for nearly twelve months; during which time I had experienced an unvarying series of unequalled attentions, a consideration for my interest and pursuits highly flattering, and had derived, from his conversation and society, an acquisition of truly valuable information; for which I desire to acknowledge myself deeply and gratefully his debtor.

CHAP. XIV.

Dutch Galliot—An Agreeable Companion—Strange Associates— Melancholy Account of St. Jago—Beauty in Tears—Manner of obtaining Salt, and Water at Mayo—Pleasures of a Galliot in a heavy Sea—Dutch Miscalculation—Distances—An Oblation to Neptune and Amphitrite (new style)—Melange, Devotion and _Gourmanderie_—Curious Flying-fish—Weather—Whales—Cape Pigeons—Anchor off Rio Janeiro— Distant Scenery—Custom-house Duties—Hotel du Nord—Rua Dircito— Confusion thrice confounded—Fruit Girls, not fair, but coquettish— Music unmusical, or Porterage, with an Obligato Accompaniment— Landing-places—An Evening Walk—A bad Cold—Job's Comforter— Shoals of Visitors—Captain Lyon's Visit, and Invitation to the Author— Naval Friends—Packet for England—English Tailors—Departure for Gongo Soco—The Party—Thoughts on Self-Denial—Uncomfortable Quarters—Changes of Atmosphere—Freedom by Halves; or _left_-handed Charity—Serra Santa Anna—Valley of Botaes—The Ferreirinho, or little Blacksmith—Dangerous Ascent of the Alto de Serra—Pest, an Universal Disease—An English Settler—Rio Paraheiba—Valencia—Curiosity of the People—Unceremonious Inquisitors—Comforts of a Beard—Castor-Oil for burning—Rio Prëta—Passports—Entrance to the Mine Country— Examination of Baggage—Attention without Politeness—The Green-eyed Monster, "An old Man would be wooing"

At eight o'clock, I found myself and baggage on board the Dutchman, under all sail, for Rio de Janeiro. I had the good fortune to meet with a countryman, in a fellow voyager, who proved to be excellent society, and who, consequently, became my principal companion, for although the captain and his mates were good sailors, and honest men, they were unskilled in the polite usages of society, and as the best linguist amongst them had but a small share of broken English, much conversation with them was out of the question.

Mr. Fearon (my fellow passenger), having left England, some time since, for Sierra Leone, the vessel in which he sailed, had called at St. Jago, where they found the Consul General for the Cape de Verds, lying dangerously ill with the fever. Mr. Fearon was solicited to remain and perform the duties of that office; and a few days after, had the melancholy task of attending the Consul to his grave, and very shortly after, of laying the widow by her husband's side. These melancholy duties being performed, he took upon himself the office of Vice Consul, until a reply to his report of the Consul's death could be received from the British Government; but, in the meanwhile, he was himself taken so ill with the endemic fever, and found it so impossible to regain health at St. Jago, that it was deemed necessary to send him to the island of Mayo for change of air; where he attained convalescence, but still continued much debilitated when we met on board the galliot. The Consul's sister at St. Jago, a most accomplished and attractive young lady, and whose acquaintance I had had the pleasure of making there at her brother's house, had also been, I learned, taken ill at the same time; I had, however, the gratification of meeting her afterwards at the Brazils, as a married lady, both happy and healthful, after she had surmounted a variety of difficult adventures, and many severe trials of fortitude, and presence of mind.

One of my first inquiries, was respecting the manner of preparing the salt at Mayo, for exportation. I learned, that during the summer a portion of low-land, near the sea, was inundated, between which and the sea, the communication being subsequently cut off, the water rapidly exhaled, leaving the salt in chrystals on the surface of the earth; these, in due time, were collected in heaps; but as, of course, the longer they remain, the more concentrated the chrystals become, it is necessary to observe considerable caution in loading vessels, to select that portion which has been the longest exposed to evaporation.

They procure water for the town and shipping at Mayo, by digging a number of pits (too shallow to deserve the name of wells), near the beach, between the salt-pan plain, and the sea: they thus collect a stock of brackish water, in small quantities from each pit: however, in the interior of the island, they are well supplied with good spring water.

Wednesday, 2.—We had a fresh trade-wind to-day, which made me feel the difference between H.M.S. Eden, and this pile-driving galliot: my sleeping-place too, happened to be at the furthest end of the vessel, which might be compared to one of the horns of a crescent, and while I was dancing in the air, others in the centre of the concavity, were scarcely out of the horizontal line. Fortunately, a very short repose is sufficient for me, as my bed was not the softest in the world, for as I had not brought one with me, I was obliged to lie upon an old sail, with a bag of clothes for a pillow: however, I have no desire to consider comforts, when I am travelling, lest feather-bed indulgences, and luxurious appointments, should divert my attention from more useful objects. The latitude at noon to-day, was 1°. 36'. N, and longitude, 16°. 28'. W. by the Eden's calculation (the correctness of which I might venture to swear by, for no ship ever kept a better), being 1°. 27'. E. of the galliot's reckoning.

Thursday, 3.—Still a fresh S.E. trade-wind, which enabled us to go a point free, (S.W. by S.) Noon, lat. 0°. 14'. S. lon. 17°. 29'. W. Having crossed the equinoctial line this forenoon, I have passed it for the third time, in as many distinct voyages, within a fortnight, namely,

1st. From Prince's Island, to Ascension.

2nd. From Ascension towards Sierra Leone.

3rd. From on board the Eden, on her way to Sierra Leone, more than 2°. north of the line, to Rio de Janeiro.

There being no one on board the galliot, who had ever crossed the equinoctial line before, except the chief mate, Mr. Fearon, and myself, the usual ceremony of shaving, &c. was dispensed with, but to prevent the circumstance passing entirely uncommemorated, Mr. Fearon presented us with some champagne, as an oblation to Neptune and his spouse, Amphitrite. About sunset, seven flying-fish fell on board, which we had for supper, and found them very delicious.

Friday, 4.—Still a moderate S.E. trade, lat. 1°. 56'. S. lon. 18°. 16'. W. Our mode of living is as follows:—Between six and seven in the morning, a cup of coffee is brought to us; at half-past seven, the whole crew assemble in the cabin to prayers; immediately after which, we all go to breakfast, ours in the cabin, consisting of boiled barley, of which the captain and his mates partake freely, mixing with each portion, a large table spoonful of butter; this is followed by tea, cold meat, and biscuit, and concluded with well buttered biscuits and cheese. At eleven, coffee again; and so soon after noon as the ship's place is ascertained by the reckoning, a glass of wine is presented to each person, [50] followed by dinner. At half-past three, tea; and at six, tea again, but combined with supper. At half-past seven, the crew again assemble to prayers; after which, all not employed on watch, retire to rest, with the exception of Mr. Fearon and myself, who were neither such *gourmands*, nor such sleepers as our Dutch friends.— They, however, were very moderate in their use of ardent spirits, or fermented liquors; they were also very moderate smokers, and seldom introduced smoking in the cabin.

This evening, three more flying-fish fell on board, one of which, having four wings instead of two, I preserved in spirits. Mr. Fearon informed me, that he had previously remarked this variation in the species, which, however, does not appear to be common, it having, as I think, escaped general notice.

Saturday, 5.—Saw a large ship to-day standing in the same direction with ourselves, but she did not approach us. At noon, Lat. 3° 52'. S. Lon. 19°. 18'. W.

Sunday, 6.—Fresh breezes and cloudy, with heavy squalls, and rain at times; four more flying-fish for breakfast. The sea getting up to-day made the vessel very uneasy. Lat. 5°. 47. S. Lon. 20°. 12. W.

Monday, 7.—Strong breezes and cloudy, with a heavy sea. Course continues the same, and but little variation in the wind, excepting force. Lat. 7°. 42'. S.

Tuesday, 8.—The wind moderated to-day, and the weather cleared up. Only two flying-fish for breakfast, which proved a sufficient relish for the passengers, but they would not have gone far towards satisfying our Dutch messmates. Lat. at noon, 9°. 34'. S. Lon. 22°. 17'. W.

Wednesday, 9.—Breeze freshened again to-day. Lat. 11°. 9'. S. Lon. 23°. 36'. W.

Thursday, 10.—Wind increased to a very strong breeze, with a good deal of sea, which made the vessel roll about and plunge in a most delightful manner. Lat. 13°. 13'. S. Lon. 25°. 7'. W.

Friday, 11.—Very squally weather, with a heavy swell. Lat. at noon, 15°. 9'. S. Lon. 25°. 7'. W.

Saturday, 12.—Fresh breezes and cloudy. Lat. 17°. 9'. S. Lon. 27°. 46. W.

---

[50] This was a very pleasant, light, sweet wine, made at Tours, and which the captain procured at Nantes.

Sunday, 13.—Wind and weather moderated to-day. Lat. 18°. 55'. S. Lon. 29°. 48'. W. Saw a few whales playing about.

Monday, 14.—Fresh breezes and very fine weather. At noon, Lat. 20°. 44'. S. Lon. 31°. 42'. W. Cape Frio, S. 76°. W. 564 miles.

Tuesday, 15.—Moderate and fine: wind N.E. Lat. 22°. 2'. S. Lon. 33°. 22'. W. Cape Frio, S. 82°. W. 472 miles. Afternoon, light breezes and variable, from N. to E.

Wednesday, 16.—Fresh breezes and cloudy, with squalls at times. Wind N.E. to E. A single flying-fish for breakfast. Lat. 22°. 23'. S. Lon. 35°. 9'. W. Cape Frio, S. 84°. W. 364 miles.

Thursday, 17.—Fresh breezes, and cloudy until noon. Afternoon, moderate and fine. Lat. 22°. 34'. S. Lon. 34°. 7'. W. Found a sore throat coming on, accompanied with fever, the effect of a severe cold caught by remaining on deck late at night. I had also frequently got wet during the blowing weather, by the sea breaking over the vessel: and, unfortunately, had not recommenced wearing flannel, having abandoned the use of it at Fernando Po, in consequence of the exhaustion it produced by the excessive sultriness of the weather.

Friday, 18.—Two Cape pigeons were hovering over the vessel to-day; they were the first we had seen; and it is very possible, that they had recently deserted some vessel which they had followed from the Cape of Good Hope. They are a small sea-fowl, about the size of a pigeon, from which resemblance they derive their name. They are to be seen in great numbers off the Cape, as well as in the higher southern latitudes.

At noon, Lat. 22°. 34'. S. Lon. 38°. 27'. W. Cape Frio, S. 82°. W. 200 miles. Soon after noon, the discoloration of the sea indicated the proximity of land, although, by our reckoning, it should have been far distant; however, we saw it at sunset, bearing N.W. by N. about 15 miles, which we supposed to be the Cape St. Thomas, when we sounded in 33 fathoms sand, with black and white specks. Stood to the southward for the night.

Saturday, 19.—Soon after daylight, we saw the land. At noon, Cape Frio, W.N.W. about 12 miles. Lat. 23°. 7'. S. Lon. 39°. 25'. W. At two in the afternoon, we passed a warlike looking schooner under Brazilian colours. At sunset. Cape Frio, E.N.E. about eight miles. Continued our course for the harbour of Rio de Janeiro till midnight, when we hove to for daylight.

Sunday, 20.—At daylight, we made all sail with a light breeze, for the harbour of Rio de Janeiro. At two in the afternoon, sounded in forty fathoms; Sugar Loaf Hill bearing N.W. At eight in the evening, we came to an anchor abreast of the forts, at the entrance of the harbour. [51]

---

[51] It is worthy of remark, that, notwithstanding the immense number of sharks in the harbour, the inhabitants are not deterred from bathing; these animals being so abundantly supplied with food from the offal of a large and populous city, as to be divested of their natural ferocity:—accidents caused by them, are absolutely unknown here, although they are frequently seen swimming near, and even among the persons bathing in the harbour.

Monday, 21.—At daylight, we found the most splendid scenery open to our view: a clear atmosphere, and a sky so serene, that the distant mountains blended softly into the heavens, while the picturesque grouping of objects in the vicinity, completed a beautiful *coup d'oeil,* which it is difficult to imagine, and scarcely possible to be surpassed. The wind and tide being against us until two o'clock, the sea-breeze then setting in, we got under weigh, to go into the harbour, but, at four o'clock, the Portuguese authorities obliged us to come to an anchor in the outer harbour, abreast of Fort Santa Cruz, in 22 fathoms water.

H.M.S. Blossom, Captain Beechy, dropped anchor here this afternoon, on his return voyage from his explorating expedition in Baring Straits, when she immediately saluted the flag of Sir Robert Otway, which was flying on board H.M.S. Ganges. H.M.B. Chanticleer, Captain Forster, was also lying in the harbour; an agreeable *rencontre,* I should imagine, for Captains Beechy and Forster, who were companions on the North Pole expedition; no small difference in climate and scenery from their present place of meeting. Captain Peters of our galliot (the Young Nicholas) and Mr. Fearon went on shore in the evening, but I was too ill with my cold, even to venture exposing myself to the night air, or to remove until I had secured a comfortable lodging; however, on the following afternoon I landed, but without my baggage, as it was detained until special permission for its removal could be received from the Custom-house; where every packet was examined and paid for, before I was permitted to take it to my lodgings.

Mr. Fearon and myself took up our quarters at the Hotel du Nord near the Palace, at one end of the Rua Direito (or strait street), which runs parallel with the sea. This is the broadest and best street in Rio de Janeiro, and as the Custom-house is situated in the centre, with the Palace and Dock-yard flanking the extremities, this street is an immense thoroughfare, especially as all articles of merchandise, not excepting the slaves, or any other object of traffic imported, or exported, must pass through it, on, or from, its way to the Custom-house.

But, as though the confusion necessarily attendant upon this continual bustle were insufficient, each group of porters as they pass along with their heavy loads, chant their peculiar national songs, for the double purpose of timing their steps and concentrating their attention on their employment. To these sounds are added the variety of cries, uttered in an endless alternation of tones, by the pretty negress fruit venders, who, smartly dressed, and leering and smiling in their most captivating manner endeavour so to attract the attention of the sons of Adam. These, with the gabbling of foreigners, hurrying on their several missions of pleasure or of business, the chattering of slaves waiting to be hired, and the occasional expostulations of those who are unceremoniously jostled from the pavement by the rude encounter of bales of goods, keep up altogether a din of discordance perfectly distracting.

There are three principal landing-places at the city of Rio, one in front of the Palace, one at the Custom-House, and one at the Naval-yard; where there are flights of stone steps for the convenience of the public. I took a walk in the evening with my friend Mr. Fearon to the Rua Pescadores (Fisherman's street, one of the many that branch from the Rua Direito), to find out Dr. Dickson, a naval surgeon settled in this city, for whom I had a letter of introduction, from my friend Captain Owen. He was not at home, but we were received by his partner, who appeared much concerned at my state of health, and advised me to return home and not think of leaving the house again until Dr. Dickson saw me, which he promised should be early on the following morning. I believed my catarrh had encreased to pneumonia, and the medical gentleman appeared to consider the symptoms much more seriously than I did myself.

Wednesday, 23.—My cough was much worse to-day, indeed it had become so troublesome that I was almost exhausted, especially as I dared not partake of any stimulating food, to support my strength. Neither could I obtain repose either by night or by day, indeed I found the horizontal position less endurable than any other. I, however, received in my bed room a number of gentlemen who called upon me. Among these was Captain Lyon of the royal navy, who had charge of a very large mining establishment in the interior, under the title of the Imperial British Brazilian Mining Company, at Gongo Soco. On hearing my intention to travel in the Brazils, this gentleman not only invited me to visit him, but also to accompany him to his establishment, to which he was about to return in a few days. This invitation was perfectly irresistible, and I promised to avail myself of it, if it were possible for me to sit on horseback at the time of his departure. This hope induced me to be doubly careful in promoting the measures judged advisable for my recovery. Captain Duntz, and his friend Mr. Edward Walker, one of the Directors of the Mining Company, also called with Captain Lyon; as well as Messrs. Luddington, Power, &c. in the course of the day.

Thursday, 24.—Captain Lyon most obligingly invited me to join a party, consisting of Mr. Gordon, our Minister, Captains Beechy and Forster, &c. &c. on a most interesting excursion to the Corcovada Mountain on the following morning, for the purpose of measuring its height; but I was most reluctantly obliged to decline it; first, because it would have been too trying for my cough; and secondly, because I wished to reserve all my strength for my journey into the interior.

Saturday, 26.—Captain Duntz paid me another visit, bringing his friend Sir T. Thompson of the Cadmus with him. Captain Lyon and his friend Mr. Edward Walker also favoured me in like manner.

Monday, 28.—The packet sailed for England to-day, calling at Bahia and Pernambuco on her way. Captain Lyon's friend Mr. Edward Walker went passenger in her. I heard that our journey into the interior was fortunately deferred for a day or two. My friend Lieutenant E. Belcher of H.M.S. Blossom, called on me to-day, as did several other gentlemen.

Tuesday, 29.—Captain Lyon called to inform me that he had determined on proceeding to the interior the following day; I therefore busied myself in preparing for the journey. Among the few articles of which I stood in need, were a jacket and pantaloons, which I was obliged to purchase, ready made, at a store of English slop-goods, the English tailors here being too consequential to accommodate any one on an emergency.

Wednesday, 30.—I took leave of my friend and fellow passenger Mr. Fearon, to join Captain Lyon at Mr. Raynsford's in Rua Pescadores, from whose house we were to set out. Every thing being ready about noon, we mounted our mules, and formed a very respectable cavalcade, our party for the interior consisting of Captain Lyon, Mr. Sharpe, Mr. A. Walker, and myself, with a train of loaded mules, we were also favoured by the escort of Messrs. Raynsford, and Lewis, on our first day's march. The latter gentleman is a Prussian Jew, and has amassed a considerable property in this country by dealing in precious stones, in addition to which traffic, he has a general store at Gongo Soco. He has also a brother a dealer in jewels who lives at Villa Rica. How is it that other men cannot succeed so well as those of the Jewish persuasion? Is it that their intelligence, penetration, and discrimination, are superior to other men? Or is it solely owing to their less scrupulous integrity? My own conviction has always been, that want of success in any particular pursuit or profession, has arisen in most cases, out of an absence of that firmness which enables a man to reject the pleasures of the world, and the world's frivolities, for the sake of the one purpose to which he should rightly devote all his energies. When men practise a rigid course of self-denial in this respect; immolating all vain desires upon the altar of science, or of interest, they seldom fail to attain the utmost point of their ambition.

I found myself very weak, and much reduced by the low regimen which I had necessarily observed during the violence of my inflammatory cough. A blister had also been kept open on my breast during the whole time of my sojourn at Rio de Janeiro, this had only received its first dressing just before I mounted my mule, and I had not got clear of the city before the inflamed state of my chest, so dried up the dressing, that the irritation produced was like a red hot iron applied to the surface: this torture I was compelled to endure for more than three hours, before I could obtain any relief. About four o'clock we arrived at Venda Nova, or Traja, also known by the name of Willis's, it having been kept by an Englishman of that name. It was much patronized by the English, who frequently made excursions of pleasure to this place, distant from Rio de Janeiro four Brazilian leagues or sixteen English miles. We were well supplied here with provisions, but our lodgings were of a very inferior description, all the party, excepting myself, being literally, and actually, necessitated to exclaim

"My lodging is on the cold ground."

The only imitation of a bed-place was considerately resigned to me. It consisted of a crib in a small room, no larger than a closet; however, as the horizontal position still continued most distressing to me, a bed of down could not have procured me repose, for I do not think I ceased coughing for three consecutive minutes the whole night. And it was no small aggravation to my misery, to know that I was the means of disturbing all my friends in the next apartment. Under these circumstances, I heard the summons for preparation, at a very early hour, with infinite satisfaction, and, ill as I was, though the morning was extremely raw and cold, I rejoiced to find that we were all in the saddle before daylight (half-past five)—Mr. Raynsford, on his return to Rio de Janeiro, and our own party for the Mine Country. Soon after noon, we arrived at Manganga, a distance of four leagues (16 miles), having passed over a very level country, where the heat of the day was equal in intensity, to the cold of the morning; the thermometer being, at one time, upwards of 90°. F. This change was to me delightful, as heat agrees with me at all times, and more particularly while suffering from an indisposition, the prevalent symptom of which is a sensation of chilliness. I found my strength very inadequate to bear much fatigue. Our accommodation, however, was better to-night than the preceding one, and Captain Lyon being well known on the road, acquainted with the language, and a man of very agreeable manners, we found every one ready to do their utmost to serve him, especially the fair sex. In speaking of the fair sex—or rather, in this case, the female, but not fair—a pretty young negress came to solicit charity, for the purpose of enabling her to make up a sum of money to purchase half her freedom, the other half having been left as a legacy, by her deceased master. This is doing things by halves with a witness: who would have thought of such piece-meal generosity, except a thrifty Brazilian Portuguese.

Friday, August 1.—Soon after daylight, we set off again with our whole party: and at eleven, we rested a short time to refresh ourselves at a venda, [52] which stands at the foot of a rugged and precipitous range, called the Serra Santa Anna (or St. Ann's Mountain), which we afterwards passed over, and arrived, about three o'clock, at a respectable farm-house, in the village of Botaës, where we remained for the night, having travelled four leagues to-day. Captain Lyon called my attention this afternoon, to the note of a bird in a wood, when passing over the mountain, named the Ferreirinho (little Blacksmith), from the resemblance of the note to the ringing sound of a smart blow from a small hammer on an anvil, terminating in a sharp whistle.

Saturday, 2.—Notwithstanding the inconvenience I had suffered during the journey of the two preceding days, I felt an increase of strength, and an abatement of my cough. Fortunately for me, we passed the night in a warm valley, and did not start this morning till nine o'clock, from which time our journey over the mountain proved very pleasant, for it must be remembered, that this is the winter season in this country; and that the coldness of the nights continues unabated until the rising sun begins to exert its influence. We left Mr. A. Walker, with the loaded mules, to follow; Capt. Lyon being anxious to proceed at a quicker rate. Almost immediately after leaving the farm, we began to ascend the Alto de Serra, where, in some places, a false step of the mule would have precipitated both the animal and its rider into one of the fearful chasms that occasionally yawned beneath our path. We were frequently placed in

---

[52] This is a shop, or store, by the road-side, where aqua-dent (spirits made in the country, and generally strongly flavoured with aniseed) and sometimes wine can be procured, with provisions, and a few other common necessaries.

very awkward situations, for we met with several caravans of loaded mules, winch were generally conducted by the voices of the muleteers, who dash on at a fearless rate; and, in some of these passes, at the imminent risk of overturning the travellers whom chance places in their way: I was frequently obliged to jerk my foot suddenly out of the stirrup, and allow my leg to pass behind on the back of the animal on which I rode, to avoid these unceremonious assaults; while, on the opposite side, I was pressed against the rugged surface of an overhanging ridge.

When we arrived at the top of the mountain, we made a halt at a blacksmith's shop, for the purpose of getting Captain Lyon's mule bled, the muleteer having declared that he had the pest; but the word *pest* appertains here to all sorts of animal ailments; for example, there was a fowl sick at this place, and on asking what was the matter with it, we were told that it had the pest; the fowl's disease proved to be the pip. Indeed, this convenient word pest, was indiscriminately applied to all diseases which the people did not understand. It reminded me of La Fleur, in the Sentimental Journey, who, when he could not get his horse to pass the dead ass, cried "Pest!" as the *dernier resort* of his vocabulary of exclamations. In the afternoon, we made a short halt at a venda within twelve miles of Botaës, to refresh ourselves, which was kept by an Englishman named John M'Dill, who had formerly lived at Gongo Soco with Captain Tregoning. He had recently settled here on a small estate, which he was clearing for a coffee plantation. About sunset, we crossed the Rio Parahëiba, over a long wooden bridge, about a mile beyond which we put up for the night, where we had but very indifferent accommodations. We had ridden five leagues, or twenty miles, to-day.

Sunday, 3.—We set off at five this morning, and arrived at the town of Valencia at nine, where we stopped for breakfast. Nearly all the inhabitants of the town collected to comment upon us, and it so happened, that I was the principal object of curiosity in the whole group: this unlooked for distinction, arose from two circumstances, first, my wearing a long beard; and secondly, my blindness. These peculiarities produced numberless exclamations, as, "How could I travel? Why did I travel? Why did I wear a long beard? Was I a Padrè?— or, a Missionary?" and so forth, until they became so pressing that we were glad to get housed, with closed doors, to keep these troublesome inquisitors at a respectful distance.

I can well understand, that a simple people, whose experience is limited to their own habits, and who have never had an opportunity of inter-mixing with other nations, must have been startled by the novelty of a beard; but their astonishment at the sight of a board, was not greater than mine, on discovering that they were destitute of an appendage, which, in the torid zone, is at once an article of luxury and utility. The people of the East invariably wear beards, not merely as a national custom, but as a matter of necessity; and, for my part, I can testify, that I found it an indispensable protection to the neck, and the lower part of the face: after a day's journey, the luxury of immerging the face in cold water, leaving the beard half dry, was most refreshing, the evaporation producing a very reviving and agreeable effect. In addition to my beard, I had the farther protection of a broad brimmed straw-hat, the crown of which was deeply wadded with cotton wool, and which completely screened me from the piercing rays of a tropical sun.

Having occasion for some castor-oil, I sent to an apothecary to procure it, which amused the people exceedingly, who declared their astonishment at our simplicity, in sending to a doctor for an article so common here, that it is generally used for lamp-oil, and to obtain which, it is only necessary to gather the beans from the plant, which grows wildly and luxuriantly in this country, and express the juice in the ordinary way.

Soon after leaving Valencia, we passed a venda, kept by another countryman of ours, but we did not stop there, being anxious to reach the town of Prëta before night. About sunset we arrived at Rio Prëta (or Black River), passing over a long wooden bridge to the town, where we waited for the authorities, to have our passports, &c. examined, which we had previously procured at Rio, from the Minister of the Interior. We had now entered the Minas Geraës, or Mine Country, the opposite bank of the river forming the boundary of the province of Rio de Janeiro. Every package was examined, and a duty demanded for each article of merchandize, &c. excepting our personal baggage; after this ceremony, we proceeded to a house, where they were accustomed to receive, I cannot say accommodate, travellers, for its appointments and arrangements, were neither elegant nor convenient; and the host, an old man with a young wife, was by no means civil: attentive he was, to the most minute point of etiquette, and somewhat more attentive than agreeable, for he watched us with a most pertinacious vigilance, in order that we might have no opportunity of conversing with our pretty hostess, whom he closely followed about with looks of angry jealousy, while she prepared our supper. It was truly pitiable to observe the misery the old dotard endured, every time his wife entered our apartment, constantly fidgetting at her elbow, and scrutinizing, suspiciously, every look that passed between her and her guests. His fears served us for a jest, however, and produced a vein of jocularity, that reconciled us to our earthen flooring, upon which some of our party were doomed to seek repose for that night.

We had made the longest journey to-day of any since we left Rio, having travelled twenty-eight miles. This is also the largest town we entered, since leaving Rio, and had once been a place of considerable importance.

CHAP. XV.

Advantages of early Travelling—Funelle—"A Traveller stopped at a
Widow's Gate"—Bright Eyes and Breakfast—Smiles and Sighs—The
Fish River—Cold Lodgings—Fowl Massacre—Bad Ways—Gigantic Ant-
hills—The Campos—Insect Warriors—Insinuating Visitors (Tick)—The
Simpleton—Bertioga—A Drunkard—Cold Shoulders—Mud Church—
Feasting and Fasting; or, the Fate of Tantalus—Method in a Slow
March—Gentlemen Hungry and Angry—No "Accommodation for Man
or Horse"—A Practical Bull—Curtomi—Hospitable Treatment at
Grandie—Horse-dealer—A "Chance" Purchase—Bivouac—Mule
Kneeling—Sagacious Animal—Quilos—A Mist—Gold-washing—Ora
Branca—Hazardous Ascent of the Serra D'Ora Banca—Topaz District—
A Colonel the Host—Capoa—Jigger-hunters—Mineralogical
Specimens—Mortality of Animals—Pasturage—Account of Ora Prëta—
Gold Essayed—Halt—Journey resumed—Arrival at Gongo Soco

Monday, August 4, 1828.—Our muleteers had no small trouble to collect their
animals in readiness for us to start at the appointed time (four in the morning);
indeed, they had been full two hours beating about the bush to get them
together. Fortunately, however, these men go to rest so early, that they think
little of getting up in the middle of the night, to collect and load their mules,
which is a common occurrence, as an early start is desirable for both man and
beast, because two hours travelling before sunrise, is not half so fatiguing as one
hour after it; the muleteers are also glad to promote any measure that will enable
them to complete their day's journey before sunset, that they may get their
supper and go to rest so soon as it is dark, which, in this tropical region, is
always at an early hour. Between nine and ten we arrived at a venda, called
Funelle, where we breakfasted on eggs and milk, standing at a counter, there
being no other apartments in this small habitation, except the bed-room of a
pretty young black-eyed widow, who was laughing and flirting with our party the
whole time we remained. Having made but a third of our intended day's journey,
we were obliged to tear ourselves away from the interesting widow's
fascinations, greatly to the annoyance of some of my companions, who would
fain have prolonged the pleasure of her agreeable trifling:—but *malgré* the Loves
and the Cupids, with the accompaniments of beauty's witcheries, we were
obliged to press forward, towards our quarters for the night, which we proposed
to take up at a house called Rosa Gomez, six leagues from Funelle, and nine
from Villa Prëta, making thirty-six miles to-day. About a mile or two before we
arrived at Rosa Gomez, we passed the Fish River.

Tuesday, August 5.—We endured a very cold and comfortless night in bad
quarters, where, had it not been for the exertions of our own people who were
obliged to knock down a few wretched straggling fowls for our use, we should
not have been able to procure any thing either for supper, or breakfast, except a
disagreeable mess of flour and water.

The thermometer at daylight this morning was so low as 45° F., which temperature we all felt keenly, especially as we had nothing but our cloaks for our night covering, on cold and comfortless cane couches. However, we did not set off till near eight o'clock, and after the sun rises, the warmth rapidly increases. We made but a short journey to-day, of two leagues and a half, for the roads were rugged and precipitous, and intersected by several abrupt and broken streams, so that we were obliged to be extremely cautious in our progress, and chary of the services of our mules. We passed some very large ant-hills to-day, from eight to twelve feet in height; the summits of which form excellent arches for the tops of ovens, while slabs cut out of the more solid parts, serve for the ends and sides.

Wednesday, 6.—We set out at daylight, leaving the woody country behind us, and entering on the Campos, or Downs, where our annoyances from the insect tribe commenced. The brushwood here being infested by Tick and other tormentors, who mercilessly attacked our whole party, mules included, insinuating themselves imperceptibly into our sleeves and pantaloons, when burying their heads in our flesh, and feasting on our blood, they made us acutely sensible of their presence, by the intolerable irritation they produced: and from which we had no means of escaping until the hour of disrobing for the night. After travelling three leagues we stopped at a village called Souza, where we took breakfast, the comfort of which meal was, however, destroyed, by the importunate absurdities of an old man, half lunatic, half simpleton.

After breakfast we proceeded to Bertioga (three leagues and a half), where we put up for the night. Soon after our arrival, several people came hastily to Captain Lyon to complain of an Englishman, who was very drunk, and had been making a great disturbance in their house. On inquiry, the offender proved to be a blacksmith on his way to Gongo Soco, he had been engaged by the agent for the Company, and sent off from Rio, thirty-six days previously, which time he had wasted in drunkenness and idleness, having only completed forty leagues of his journey; Captain Lyon consequently ordered him to return to Rio, as the specimen of ill conduct already given, shewed him to be unworthy of being received into the Company's service.

Our accommodations to night were much us usual, mud floors, and our cloaks for a covering. Total six leagues and a half to-day.

Thursday, 7.—We set off before daylight, which did not agree very well with me, the morning air being still too keen for my lungs, which, with a pain in my side, made me very unwell to-day. About noon we stopped at a farm-house in a village, called Os Ilhos. There was a church in progress here, the walls of which they were building with mud. After refreshing ourselves, and our mules, for about an hour, we resumed our journey toward a large farm, called Baroga, having made 24 miles to-day. My companions fared sumptuously, as we had brought a turkey with us from our last resting place, and with the addition of a roasting pig, it made the grandest feast imaginable, and far exceeded any thing we had met with since we left Rio de Janeiro; however, it proved a fast to me, as I was obliged to take medicine, and leave them to their enjoyment.

Our host and hostess were plain honest good farming people, and appeared desirous to do every thing they could for Captain Lyon, but for all that, they could not be roused out of their accustomed methodical manner, and the preparation of our meal was, to them, a business of serious delay and labour.

> And all entreaties were vain,
> For they'd promise and promise again,
> But still go on the same.

My friends, therefore, were compelled to take policy for their counsellor, and patience for their remedy. The most provoking part of the affair was, that they were expected to consider themselves obliged, by the condescension of their hosts, in undertaking upon any terms to minister to their necessities: consequently there was no possibility of giving utterance to any hasty feelings of impatience; no opening for those little outbreaks of anger so common to hungry gentlemen. These, might they have been indulged, would have amused, as well as comforted the sufferers, but unhappy travellers! they were compelled to

> Let *keen hunger*, like a worm in the bud,
> Feed on their *inner man*.

Here, however, our accommodations were quite superior, when compared with what we had found at other resting-places; indeed they did not profess to "*accommodate travellers*," an assurance which is I presume intended to reconcile the guest to such reception as they choose to give: but if these people are unwilling to "*profess*," they do not allow their *scruples* to limit their *expectations*; these are always directed towards a recompense, which they are just as eager to receive as those who accord more to the convenience of the stranger.

Their curiosity is also unparalleled, and when you dismount you are received with a string of questions; respecting your health. Where you have been? The news of Rio? Whom you have met on the road? Who are expected to go up? or down the country? &c. &c. Having obtained all the information your patience will grant, they at length begin to consider what provision they can make for you, and generally commence operations by slaughtering a few fowls, (or sometimes a turkey or a roasting pig;) then a large pot of water must be boiled to dip the fowls in, by way of removing the feathers in the most expeditious manner; a practical bull, for if they plucked the birds the moment they were dead, and before the body was allowed to cool, the process would be completed in less time than they could boil the water. After this preparation, they proceed with their tedious cookery, all of which is conducted in an equally awkward manner. Sometimes after arriving in the evening, tired and hungry, three or four hours elapsed, before any knives and forks were put on the table, or any other visible progress made in the arrangement of our meal: and not unfrequently my companions gave the matter up in despair, and resigned themselves to sleep, while all were completely worn out with waiting, long before the dinner appeared.

Friday, 8.—We set out at daylight, and about ten miles distance, we stopped a short time at a farm house, named Curtomi; we then proceeded ten miles further to Grandie. Just before we arrived at this place, about four miles and a half distant, the road from Rio over the Campos, and the Caminha Real, or Royal road, from Porta de Estrella meet, forming one main road from hence into the interior. We stopped at a large house, which belonged to very civil people, where we were well lodged, and very hospitably entertained.

Saturday, 9.—We had a comfortable breakfast before we set off this morning, and I felt much recruited to-day; we had also all the advantage to be derived from the warm rays of the sun, as we did not start till near eight o'clock. In the course of our journey this forenoon, we met a horse dealer with a train of horses, on his way to Rio, when Mr. Sharpe took a fancy to one, and purchased it for thirty-six milreas, in silver, something less than five pounds sterling. From being purchased in this accidental way, I suggested that the animal ought to be named "Chance," to which his master assented. In consequence of our wishing to avoid a disagreeable old fellow, who kept a venda on the road side, we proceeded a short distance beyond his domicile, and having previously provided our refreshment, we sat down near the bank of a river to partake of it, at about two o'clock in the afternoon.

On our journey afterwards, my poor mule was so thirsty, that he ran to a little stream by the road-side, to drink, but as he could not conveniently reach it standing, he very quietly went down on his knees, upon which hint, I, of course, dismounted, until he had finished his draught. This mule was the most docile, intelligent animal I ever rode, and it was a knowledge of these good qualities, that induced Captain Lyon to appropriate him to my use; I was frequently considerably in advance of the party, without feeling any apprehension about my safety, from the perfect confidence I reposed in the mule's sagacity. About five in the afternoon, we arrived at the town of Qualos, where we were well lodged, had good fare, and where the excellence of the bread was quite remarkable, being superior to any I had tasted in the Brazils. This town gives the title to a Marquess, but it is not of any importance in other respects.

Sunday, 10.—We started long before daylight, and for two or three hours rode through a mist, as cold and dense as a November one in England, but after the sun had gained sufficient power to disperse it, the day was proportionably hot. We this forenoon passed the first gold-washing place of any consideration, which has, however, long since been abandoned for others more profitable. About eleven, we arrived at the village of Ora Branca, so called from the light colour of the gold procured here, the gravel or sand of every stream, henceforward, produces a greater or lesser proportion of gold.

The owner of the house where we refreshed, had a collection of mineralogical specimens, which interested Captain Lyon very much, he being himself a collector. At about a league distance, we commenced the ascent of the Serra D'Ora Branca, which was almost impracticable even for our mules. It is so steep and difficult, that it is the universal custom to dismount, to which, I believe, I formed the only exception, an undertaking of considerable hazard to ride either up, or down, this mountain. At about a league beyond the summit, on the opposite side, we entered what is called the Topaz District, where we soon passed many washings for Topazes, and put up for the night at the celebrated one of Capoa, where we were not very well entertained, although the proprietor of this venda was a Colonel in the Brazilian militia. It is the general custom, while travelling in this country, for the inhabitants to bring you a panela, or large bowl of hot water, every night, when you are going to bed, for your feet, and it is usual to have a black man in attendance, for the purpose of examining the feet, and extracting the jiggers with a needle, at which operation they are very expert.

Monday, 11.—Although our journey on this day, was only intended to be three leagues to the imperial city of Ora Prëta (Black Gold), the Villa Rica (Rich City) of the maps, capital of the mining districts, we set off at daylight, and arrived about ten at the house that is kept for the use of the Gongo Soco Mining Company. The gold that is collected at the Gongo Soco mines, is sent from time to time to the mint at this place, where it is essayed and melted into bars, the government reserving, a tax of 25 per cent. before it is suffered to be transmitted to Rio. On leaving Capoa this morning, we visited several mud huts in the village, and neighbourhood, in search of those mineralogical specimens, which are commonly known in this country by the name of Raridadës.

During our route, but more especially before we arrived at the Campos, not a day passed without our meeting droves of oxen and pigs as well as many troops of loaded mules, with coffee, cotton, sugar, &c. all proceeding from the interior for Rio; and our olfactory nerves were not unfrequently assailed by a very offensive odour, arising from dead animals, principally oxen, among whom there is usually a great mortality on these journeys, in consequence of excessive fatigue from travelling 500 or 600 miles, as also from the bad and insufficient pasturage they find on their road. When these unfortunate animals sink down under their sufferings, they are left to die, and putrify on the spot where they happen to fall. These cattle are chiefly brought from the Sertao, which is a wild country beyond the mountains of the gold district, intervening between it and the diamond district, which is a fine pasture country, but with few habitations. The term Sertao, however, is general all over the interior of Brazil, for inland places unredeemed by culture. Ora Prëta is the most considerable town that we have yet met with, and it owes it respectability and extent to the circumstance of its being the town residence of the proprietors of gold mines, dealers in precious stones, &c; and there is an Imperial Mint, with a government essayer settled here, for the purpose of examining all the gold produced from the mines, causing it to be melted and stamped, and a duty of 25 per cent. taken from it for the Government.

This duty had, a short time previous to my visit, been reduced to 10 per cent. for Brazilian subjects, the Government, however, continued to exact 25 per cent, from Gongo Soco, or the Imperial British Brazilian Mining Company; although, in their charter from the Brazilian Government, it was understood, if not expressed, that the Company should be allowed to work their mines on the same terms with the Brazilians, however advantageous those terms might happen to be: at the time the charter was granted, the Brazilians paid 25 per cent.; but after their neglecting several mines, they petitioned the Government for a reduction of duty, on the plea, that it was too high, to allow them a profit on their expenses. The Government, upon this application, consented to receive only ten per cent. from their own subjects, but absolutely refused to accord to the British Mining Company any reduction of the original duty.

Captain Lyon found it necessary to pass a couple of days here, to transact some business; this proved a seasonable rest, particularly for our mules, who had been worked fifteen days in succession.

Tuesday, August 14.—We this morning renewed our journey for Gongo Soco, and immediately on leaving Ora Prëta, began to ascend the Ferreiria (Iron Mountain). After having rode over the top of it for about six miles, we descended by a very steep and dangerous road, the bed of a great part of which was composed of ironstone rock: very few persons ever venture to ride down it; for, in case a mule should lose its footing, both the animal and its rider would be hurled down a precipice, so gigantic, that the state of their remains could not even be ascertained. Our mules were, at times, on their haunches, actually sliding over the rocky surface of the road, and although Captain Lyon had travelled this path several times, he had never ventured to ride down it before: but not knowing any better way to manage me and my mule, than by allowing us to follow him mounted, down the hill, he most kindly braved the danger for my sake, and I resigned myself to the intelligence of my mule, who very soon assumed the entire control of his own conduct, shaking his head whenever he felt the reins tighter than convenient, and picking his way with all imaginable care: I always found, when the ground appeared uncertain, that the sagacious animal would pause, and putting out his foot, discover, by scratching, whether the ground might be trusted, before he would advance a step further.

After leaving the mountain, we arrived at the village of Antonio Ferreira, which is ten miles from Ora Prëta. At this village, the Company have some landed property, which they intended to mine, but they had not yet commenced their operations. From thence we passed on to Inficionado, where the Company have another estate, Ceta Prëta. The road from Antonio Ferreira to this place, was very hilly and circuitous, as well as very bad in particular places. We arrived about sunset, and got comparatively well lodged, by some of the Company's servants, who reside here to look after the estate: it had produced a little gold, but the quantity was not considered sufficient to induce them to prosecute their operations; and the people were consequently ordered to return to Gongo.

Friday, 15.—We breakfasted with Mr. and Mrs. Bilden (one of the clerks of the Gongo establishment); and about nine miles distant we stopped to refresh, at the village of Catas Altas; where we had tidings by an *avant courier* from Gongo, that the heads of the mining department were on their way to receive their chief (Captain Lyon), at Brunado, which is about twelve miles from the establishment; and we accordingly met them. After an exchange of civilities, we all proceeded in grand cavalcade, towards Gongo, Lieutenant Tom, of the navy (Lieutenant-Governor), and myself, leading the way. On our arrival, we were received with cheers and gratulations, from all the individuals in the establishment; and the day concluded by an entertainment to the officers, given by Captain Lyon, at the government-house.

Having arrived at this point of my journey, which brings me to a new and interesting scene, I pause to look back upon the past, and to prepare for the future. The traveller must rest in his book, as well as in his route, and, bespeaking the reader's favour for the sequel of my adventures and researches in the Gold Mines, I take my leave for the present—hoping that the perusal of my discursive journal, may prove but one-half as entertaining to others, as the consolatory resource of producing it has been pleasurable to myself.

END OF VOL. I.

Echo Library

www.echo-library.com

Echo Library uses advanced digital print-on-demand technology to build and preserve an exciting world class collection of rare and out-of-print books, making them readily available for everyone to enjoy.

Situated just yards from Teddington Lock on the River Thames, Echo Library was founded in 2005 by Tom Cherrington, a specialist dealer in rare and antiquarian books with a passion for literature.

Please visit our website for a complete catalogue of our books, which includes foreign language titles.

The Right to Read

Echo Library actively supports the Royal National Institute of the Blind's Right to Read initiative by publishing a comprehensive range of large print and clear print titles.

Large Print titles are in 16 point Tiresias font as recommended by the RNIB.

Clear Print titles are in 13 point Tiresias font and designed for those who find standard print difficult to read.

Customer Service

If there is a serious error in the text or layout please send details to feedback@echo-library.com and we will supply a corrected copy. If there is a printing fault or the book is damaged please refer to your supplier.

LaVergne, TN USA
30 November 2010
206791LV00002B/15/A